Ho
Pe

2023
with
World Peace Directory

70th Edition   ISSN 0957-0136

Published and distributed by

HOUSMANS BOOKSHOP
5 Caledonian Road, Kings Cross, London N1 9DX, UK
(tel +44-20-7837 4473; email diary@housmans.com)

ISBN 978 0 85283 286 8

Editor — Albert Beale
Cover design & month illustrations — Lois Iredale
Quotations research — Sara Davidson
Lay-out & production — Chris Booth (formandfunction.coop)

Directory from Housmans Peace Resource Project,
editor Albert Beale (www.housmans.info)

Copyright © 2022 Housmans Bookshop Ltd

Printed by Artisan Print Solutions, Oxfordshire, on FSC paper

Personal Notes

Name

Address

Telephone

_____
_____
_____
_____
_____
_____
_____
_____

EXPLANATORY NOTES

National public holidays in the UK, Republic of Ireland, Canada and the USA are noted by the abbreviation HOL, followed by abbreviations for relevant countries: ENG – England, NI – Northern Ireland, SCOT – Scotland, W – Wales; UK – United Kingdom (ie all the preceding four); IRE – Republic of Ireland; CAN – Canada; US – United States. We regret that we are not able to show holidays in other countries.

Dates of moon phases, solstices and equinoxes are for GMT; users in other time zones will find that the local date is different in some cases.

The places of historical events referred to in the Peace Diary – whether in articles or in anniversary notes – are as at the date of the event, regardless of subsequent changes in name, frontiers etc.

Similarly, the **dates** are recorded in the form that was applicable at the relevant period in that place, that is in Old Style where relevant, New Style being disregarded – hence in some cases we are noting nominal anniversaries rather than mathematically correct ones.

ORDERING INFORMATION

Copies of the Diary may be ordered from:
Housmans, 5 Caledonian Road, Kings Cross, London N1 9DX, UK
(tel +44-20-7837 4473; email orders@housmans.com)

Introduction

We're proud to say that this is the 70th edition of the *Housmans Peace Diary*; as always it's intended as both a resource and an inspiration for campaigners around the world.

This year's feature pages are mostly taken up with an article about the history of the *Peace Diary* through the decades – looking at its origin, its significant developments, and at the range of themes it's covered. But we have also taken the opportunity to tell – briefly – the story of an influential, though little-known, international peace movement action in 1973 on its 50th anniversary.

The *Diary* includes a fresh selection of weekly quotations and daily anniversaries. The latter include the centenary of the founding of the War Resisters League in the USA and of the birth of pacifist musician Donald Swann, as well as the 80th anniversary of the arrest and execution of Hans and Sophie Scholl by the Nazi regime and of the birth of British nonviolent activist Roger Moody.

We also mark the 75th anniversary of Costa Rica disbanding its army and of the assassination of Mahatma Gandhi; and the 60th anniversary of Spies for Peace revealing Britain's secret Regional Seats of Government, of the police killing of Gregory Lambrakis in Greece, and of the acquittal in London of Donald Rooum in the infamous "half-brick" case. We note the 50th anniversary of the US-backed military coup in Chile, the 40th anniversary of nonviolent guerilla actions closing an arms fair in Brussels and of the USA invading Grenada, and the 25th anniversary of the death of British pacifist composer Michael Tippett.

This publication is a non-profit service for fellow activists; we're grateful for the variety of voluntary support which makes its production possible. Help to promote the Peace Diary is always welcome – contact Housmans Diary Group, 5 Caledonian Road, London N1 9DX (e-mail diary@housmans.com).

HOUSMANS DIARY GROUP

The 70th Housmans Peace Diary

The *Housmans Peace Diary* is marking its 70th edition this year. Its style has evolved over this period, but – with its international directory of peace organisations a consistent feature since its first edition – it has become a peace movement institution, both in Britain and around the world. This feature tells some of the story of the diary's origin and development.

The *Peace Diary* owes its existence to Harry Mister. Harry had been one of the original members of the Peace Pledge Union (PPU) in 1934, one of the group which founded *Peace News* in 1936, and one of the people setting up Housmans Bookshop in 1945; in 1953 he was the general manager of both *Peace News* and Housmans. The shop had been established by the PPU as a means of publishing and promoting pacifist and other peace books and pamphlets, as well as making available publications dealing with other progressive issues. The shop initially operated from bomb-damaged premises in central London. But after a few years it switched to operating as a mail order and bookstall business, based at the *Peace News* offices in Finsbury Park, north London; in 1959 it moved – with *Peace News* – to the shop and office premises in Kings Cross, central London, where they remain today.

Harry Mister in Trafalgar Square, running a Housmans stall during a 1960s demonstration
(photo: Phil Rickard)

The origins of the Diary

In 1953, it was the height of the first phase of the Cold War, with a burgeoning British peace movement, following the first major British public demonstration against nuclear weapons in 1950 and the first anti-nuclear civil disobedience demonstration in 1952. Harry was conscious of a gap that had arisen in communications between the expanding number of peace organisations. The National Peace Council – then the co-ordinating organisation for British peace groups – had traditionally published a Year Book including a directory of organisations. In latter years this had reduced to simply the annual directory; then, for economic reasons, even this had ceased publication.

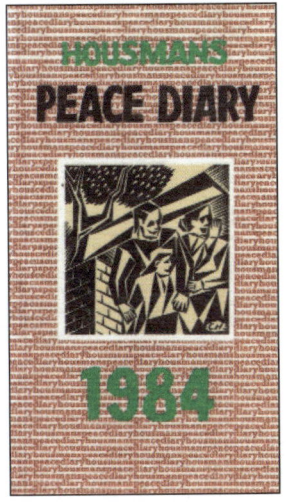

Harry conceived the idea that an annual directory could be made viable by combining it with a diary, and the *Housmans Peace Diary* was born. From the very first (1954) edition, the directory was expanded to be an international one, covering national organisations in major countries around the world, as well as international peace organisations. Initially, the main diary pages were based on an ordinary commercial product, with the publisher agreeing to print and bind the directory pages – and a small amount of related material – alongside the standard diary pages. The Diary continued in essentially this format for 30 years, though with the addition in later years of a range of peace symbols embossed on the cover.

Early development

For the 1984 edition, two members of the Housmans staff, Alexander Donaldson and Nigel Kemp, designed a new format, incorporating the peace directory in a

A range of themes

With the in-house design allowing flexibility, it was possible to adjust the pagination to include thematic material and other information alongside the directory pages, in addition to the normal week-to-an-opening diary pages themselves. The space given over to the feature material varied greatly from year to year.

1984 had an introduction by Sheila Oakes, long-time co-ordinator of the National Peace Council, discussing the interconnectedness of issues addressed by the *Peace Diary* and its directory.

1985 included material about War Resisters' International (WRI), the Campaign Against Arms Trade (and the arms trade in general), a short bibliography, and a reprint of Paul Goodman's classic "A Message to the Military-Industrial Complex".

1986 included the stories of 50 years of *Peace News*, and of 100 years of the anarchist paper *Freedom*, and a brief round-up of other peace publications. The insightful *Peace News* story – in the words of its author, Harry Mister – was "not a history ... but a personal impression of how it began and what it has done, put together by a non-journalist who has worked for it over that period".

1987 dealt with Peace Education and Education for Peace.

1988 had a lengthy article about the history, politics, structure and work of War Resisters' International (WRI).

1989 had food as its theme, including its politics and some recipes. One popular recipe, for Saturnalia Pudding, ended up being reprinted in other peace movement publications. On this occasion, the feature material was spread through the diary, rather than being together at the start.

- **1990**, similarly, had material spread through the publication, the theme being "Children's Visions of the Future".
- **1991**'s edition had articles on the theme, "The Earth – Our Common Home", dealing with both environmental and political issues from a global perspective.
- **1992** and **1993** had no significant feature material.
- **1994** included a celebration of 75 years of the International Fellowship of Reconciliation (IFOR) and its network of religious pacifist organisations around the world.
- **1995** included brief histories of 80 years of the Women's International League for Peace and Freedom (WILPF) and of 50 years of Pax Christi.
- **1996** carried short articles on the 75th birthday of WRI and the 60th birthday of *Peace News*.
- **1997**'s feature tackled multinationals – including McDonald's (then in the process of suing two members of London Greenpeace in what turned out to be the biggest corporate PR own goal imaginable), Rio Tinto Zinc (scourge of indigenous communities around the world), and COPEX (which had just failed in a libel action against *Peace News* and CAAT following their condemnation of the company's arms fairs where torture equipment was for sale).
- **1998** saw a celebration of the 50th anniversary of the Universal Declaration of Human Rights.
- **1999** was the year of the Hague Appeal for Peace (a nod to the Hague Peace Conference exactly 100 years earlier), so the *Peace Diary* that year included material about the new Hague event, as well as an article about Abolition 2000, the international network against nuclear weapons.

specially printed diary which also marked significant "peace days", such as United Nations Day and Prisoners for Peace Day, as well as noting anniversaries of significant events. As explained above, having full control over the publication also enabled other more substantial additional material to be included. This change – leaving behind the original idea of simply adding special material to an existing commercial product – was popular, and the *Peace Diary* has, ever since, been a fully individual production each year.

There was an initial experiment in producing two versions of the diary, one with the full British directory listings, and a summary list of international organisations, and another with fuller international listings for overseas sales. But it quickly turned out not to be economically viable to produce two separate versions.

From the outset, the new-style *Peace Diary* also had a few pages devoted to a region-by-region listing of significant local peace organisations in Britain, to supplement – for British users – the main list of national and international organisations.

A further addition, from the 1988 *Peace Diary*, was the inclusion of a quotation for each week's pages.

There were experiments with various shapes and sizes of diary for a few years, until – by 1990 – it settled on the format which has been more or less unchanged since. The aim was to have a publication which was, literally, pocket-sized, but which would be spacious enough to contain a useful amount of material and to allow users to jot things down day by day. One reason for settling on the particular shape was the surge in popularity in that era of Filofax ring-binder notebooks

("organisers"). Some users of the *Peace Diary* experimented with slicing off the spine, punching holes in all the pages, and inserting the whole thing into their Filofax – and so having pages the same size as standard Filofax pages made sense.

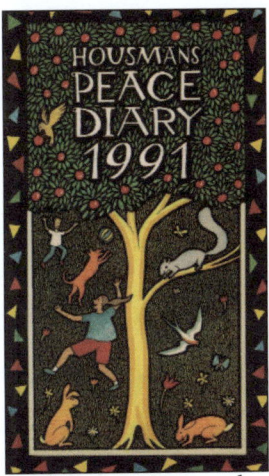

As an experiment, two versions were produced in 1991 – one loose-leaf, with holes punched ready for insertion into a Filofax, and one normal bound version. But sales were insufficient to cover the extra production costs of two versions, and – as with the earlier experiment of having separate British and international versions of the *Peace Diary* – the experiment only lasted the one year; but the size remained.

Directory developments

The compilation of the annual directory had always been a labour-intensive and time-consuming process, involving regularly sending letters to all the organisations listed, asking them to confirm or amend their details. The information was logged on a card index, with a kind of "If it's in red biro does it supersede what's in blue ink?" approach, and amendments were then typed up ready for typesetting.

In 1989 Albert Beale, a recent *Peace News* co-editor who was a Housmans volunteer helping with the *Peace Diary*, seeing how the system operated, suggested to the staff that the work of compiling, updating, and typesetting the directory pages would be more efficient if the information were in a computerised database. The staff, discovering that he'd once worked as a computer programmer, challenged him to establish such a system. Hence, from the 1990 edition onwards, the directory compilation – though still a major task – was partly automated.

The downside of having a more efficient system for the directory was that it immediately started to grow in size, with more organisations and more up-to-date information about them. This in turn meant that the cost of sending mailings to the larger number of organisations around the world would increase dramatically, and threaten the (often rather precarious) economics of the *Peace Diary*. Getting a grant to support the diary was difficult, since it was – after all – a nominally profit-making publication; nevertheless, in 1991 a one-off grant was obtained to help with the preparation of the 1992 directory.

It was then suggested that the directory work might be separated out into a distinct organisation which could more easily raise funds from charitable sources from time to time, and which might also be able to generate income from other people's use of the database information. The idea was that this separate project would still receive *some* money from Housmans Bookshop as payment for the information supplied for the *Peace Diary*, but this would be much less than it had been costing Housmans to cover the full cost of the directory updating itself.

And so the Housmans Peace Resource Project was born (with its own newfangled e-mail address), established as a small nonprofit set-up under the auspices of Peace News Trustees (parent company of both Housmans and *Peace News*). The first directory supplied for the *Peace Diary* by the new project appeared in the 1993 edition.

Co-publishing

Because of significant sales in North America, the idea arose of working with a North American publisher in order to improve the efficiency of distribution there.

So the 1999 edition was co-published with New Society Publishers in Canada; although the diary continued to be edited, and the artwork produced, in London, the copies were printed in Canada and more than half of the print-run was then shipped to Britain for distribution to everywhere outside North America.

This system was maintained for the next two years; but the cost and logistical problems of the co-publication, combined with the lack of a sufficiently major breakthrough in the North American market, led to a reversion to publication by Housmans alone from the 2002 edition.

The greater priority given to overseas sales at the time of the 1999 edition meant a reappraisal of the relevance of the inclusion of the British local directory, the region by region listing of major local peace groups. With pressure of space in the main peace directory in any case (the printed version was already unable to include all the available information), it was decided to stop publishing the local listings and use the space to include in print a larger proportion of the national and international organisations.

By this time, changes in the Housmans staff team meant that there had been no-one working in the shop whose priorities, skills, interests, and available time led them to want to play a major role in preparing the material for the *Peace Diary* each year. The work evolved into being undertaken on a voluntary basis, mostly by two then members of the Housmans company board. Albert Beale ended up looking after the main editing and co-ordinating tasks, with Bill Hetherington compiling the weekly quotations and daily anniversaries, as well as taking on a lot of the historical research which was often needed for the feature articles. The Housmans staff, of course, retained responsibility for

More themes

2000's edition of the diary included a round-up of the main international peace days, with a brief look at their origins and how they are commemorated.

2001 celebrated the start of the International Decade for a Culture of Peace and Nonviolence for the Children of the World (in 2001–2010). This was being instituted by a consortium including UNESCO, the International Fellowship of Reconciliation (IFOR), and Nobel Peace Laureates.

2002 dealt with using the World-Wide Web for peace movement activism; something which is now commonplace was then still mysterious to many.

2003's *Peace Diary* celebrated being the 50th edition with a run-down of its history.

2004's feature was entitled "Where next for the peace movement?", looking at the failure of a mass mobilisation to stop US and British attacks on Iraqis.

2005 told the story of 60 years of Housmans Bookshop.

2006 marked the 70th birthday of *Peace News*, sister publication of Housmans Bookshop (both are projects of Peace News Trustees, owners of the London building where they're based).

2007's feature explained the origin of various peace signs and symbols, including dealing with the frequently misinterpreted origin and meaning of the famous nuclear disarmament symbol.

2008 looked at the history of anti-nuclear weapons campaigning; this was sparked partly by it being the 50th anniversary of the first march from London to the Atomic Weapons Research Establishment at Aldermaston – an event organised, from the offices of *Peace News*, by the Direct

> Action Committee Against Nuclear War.
> (This was also the event for which the nuclear disarmament symbol was first designed.)
>
> **2009** marked 50 years of the *Peace News* and Housmans building in London's Kings Cross; there was also an article about the 75th anniversary of the founding of the Peace Pledge Union.
>
> **2010** had a feature called "Sixty ways to save the world...", with a collection of questions and suggestions from the jokey to the profound.
>
> **2011** celebrated the 75th birthday of *Peace News*, including a look at its evolving political role and its continuing political importance.

ensuring the promotion and sale of the diaries, and the whole project has continued to depend on a variety of other voluntary support.

Special Days

A distinctive feature of *Housmans Peace Diary* is recording, in the same way as "conventional" public holidays, a number of widely-recognised Days – and some Weeks – of special significance to campaigners who use the diary. These Days and Weeks include ones designated by official bodies such as the United Nations, as well as others declared and adopted by significant peace organisations. The nomenclature used is carefully chosen, since there's a great deal of casual – and inaccurate – application of generic terms like "World Peace Day" to several different UN-recognised dates with their own specific nomenclature and history. Indeed, the peace movement is quite capable of confusion even over its "own" Days: for example, International Conscientious Objectors' Day has, in recent years, sometimes been called International Conscientious Objection Day – giving it a political meaning quite different from that intended by its originators more than 40 years ago. (The original political purpose is still upheld by many of the activists who mark the day each year.)

At the same time, official names sometimes do need improving to fit the principles behind the diary. In 1982, the UN declared an "International Day of Innocent Children Victims of Aggression". Since it is clearly no function of a *Peace Diary* to exclude, by implication, naughty children who are victims of so-called "defence", the title of Day was modified, for inclusion in the *Peace Diary*, to the "International Day for Children as Victims of War". This amendment has had mention in the national media in Britain; the United Nations has not complained.

The Diary as a reference source

Besides many people's frequent reliance on the directory pages when trying to find peace organisations of various sorts, less obvious parts of the diary have also been used as a reliable source of information. The daily anniversary dates which appear each year – being generally fairly definitive – are often taken for use by other producers of calendars and diaries; and, naturally, the anniversaries frequently prompt celebrations or protests by readers.

The feature articles – especially when they have a historical theme – are sufficiently well respected that it's not uncommon for someone researching the topic concerned to come looking for a back copy of the *Peace Diary* for reference; this is especially the case for anyone wanting to know the history of Housmans, or *Peace News*, or the Kings Cross building. The history of War Resisters' International in 2021 was translated for use by activists abroad; and the 2010 feature was also reprinted overseas.

The choice of daily anniversaries is based on a range of factors. Round-number anniversaries are obviously popular; additionally, there are attempts to find ones which have contemporary relevance, or which link to quotes being used, or which relate to the theme of the year's feature pages. The choice of quotations can in turn be influenced by the year's theme, and by the choice of anniversaries.

Although the anniversary selection and the quotation selection are different each year, some of the anniversaries, in particular, are naturally likely to re-occur from time to time. Suggestions from readers of anniversaries and quotations are always welcomed – especially if the information sent is well-referenced!

Further changes

Although, as noted above, the number of pages allocated for the feature material varied greatly from year to year in the early days of in-house design, from the late 1990s it settled on generally being only 4–6 pages each year. But in 2012 there was a significant increase in the space allocated to thematic articles, partly by reducing the space given to the directory pages at that point. The computerised directory of peace organisations, used as the basis for the listings in the *Peace Diary* each year, had by then been used as a source for a publicly accessible on-line database; this already covered a longer list of organisations than there was room to put into print each year. So with increasing use being made of the website version of the database, it was felt reasonable to rebalance the space given to the listings and to the feature in the *Peace Diary*, with the printed directory including a reduced percentage of the full database.

It's worth noting that since the in-house originating of the *Peace Diary* started in 1984, there have been almost as many cover designers as covers, with just a few people being prevailed upon more than once. (In a handful of cases, the designers have been volunteers already involved in Housmans; generally an outside artist is commissioned, and paid for the work.) Some of the classic cover designs are illustrating this feature.

The team producing the diary have been lucky – since the late 1990s – to have Chris Booth preparing the layout for the printers each year; his background at *Peace News* and WRI brings a useful extra mind to bear on the precision and the politics of the material in the *Peace Diary*.

The latest themes

2012's theme – inspired by the 200th anniversary of the Luddite uprisings, was the politics of technology. The issues dealt with included some – like GM crops – which were already the subject of activist campaigns, and others – such as nanotechnology – where the article helped to bring the issue to more people's attention.

2013's feature – "Taking risks to resist" – looked at examples of nonviolent struggle and resistance, ranging from the White Rose group in Nazi Germany to recent Ploughshares actions in Britain and elsewhere.

2014 marked the centenary of the start of the First World War, looking at how a new era of warfare inspired a new era of war resisters and a new style of pacifist total resistance to war.

2015 covered a century of women resisting war, starting with the International Congress of Women in The Hague in 1915 which led to the founding of the Women's International League for Peace and Freedom (WILPF).

2016's article looked at a century of conscientious objection and war resistance, from the varieties of objection during the First World War, via the repression of pacifists in many countries then and since, to the way that many states continue – to this day – to try to force their citizens to train to kill other people.

2017 dealt with "indefatigable activism", looking at activists and campaigners, including the infiltration of activist groups by police and corporate spies and their unmasking by the activists themselves.

2018, continuing with themes inspired by the centenary of the First World War, discussed the need to end war, not just wars, and looked back over the last 100 years of pacifist campaigning.

2019 was a chance to look at 60 years of "5 Cally Road", the Peace News and Housmans building in London – including relating many significant political events which have taken place there, as well as legal and physical assaults it has suffered.

2020 – inspired by the 2000 edition – took a more detailed, and updated, look at Peace Days and anniversaries, and their origins and uses.

2021 covered the story of 100 years of War Resisters' International in a feature entitled "A Century of War Resistance"; it traced WRI's history from its origins in the "Never Again" era after the First World War through its development since then.

2022, partly on account of the 40th anniversary of the Falklands War, dealt with the history of ideas of alternative unarmed "defence", including the methods of nonviolent "people power" that can be used to overthrow existing tyrannies.

 And finally, this look at 70 years of the *Peace Diary* wouldn't be complete without including some thoughts from the current Housmans Bookshop staff on what this long-running annual point in the shop's calendar means to them.

It's always exciting to receive the new edition of the diary at the shop. It allows Housmans staff to interact with peace activists that we don't always get a chance to engage with throughout the rest of the year. These activists live all over the world; many have a long history of peace activism and have been buying the diary assiduously for decades. They sometimes email or call the shop, and a few continue to hand-write letters to place their orders. It is fascinating to chat to older activists in particular, who are always more than happy to share their stories and talk about their relationship with the diary and reminisce about Housmans. It reminds staff of the longevity and history of the diary, and indeed the shop. And it's a demonstration that the Peace

Directory, a key feature of every diary, has been such a crucial resource in enabling activists to connect with one another.

It is also wonderful to see younger customers and activists, who may not be aware of the history of the *Peace Diary*, or that of the building, come across it for the first time and find out about its purpose and its links to 5 Caledonian Road.

When the diary is on display in the shop, longstanding Housmans customers love to let us know their thoughts on the cover. It's fair to say that sometimes the cover can split audiences, but as with all art, you can't please everyone! It seems very apt that this 70th edition should celebrate some of these covers.

Images of the shop-front itself have featured on the cover of the diary twice, in 2009 to celebrate the 50th anniversary of *Peace News* and Housmans being at our 5 Caledonian Road address, then again a decade later for the 2019 diary cover, when the diary feature celebrated 60 years of the building. These two editions are particular favourites of the Housmans' staff, naturally, and we have continued to use those designs in publicity and social media posts. The written histories also provide a great introduction to the shop's background for new staff members and volunteers.

It is a testament to everyone involved over the decades at Housmans, *Peace News*, and the *Peace Diary*, that these interrelated projects have all broken through their respective 70th anniversary barriers, and continue to do such important work. In a world where change happens so quickly and campaign groups come and go, these projects persist steadfast in their tasks of spreading a culture of peace and fighting for social justice.

The 1973 London–Paris Walk

"At 4pm on Saturday 2 June," according to a contemporary press report, "over 30 'tourists' in Notre Dame Cathedral, central Paris, quietly took loose ends of chains from under their clothing, each passed them to the nearest person, and within a few moments three pillars were surrounded by circles of people holding banners calling for an end to French nuclear tests." The Greenpeace walkers had arrived in Paris!

After these people were secure, support actions started. At 4.05 the press were informed, leaflets were distributed outside, and the first of 100 supporters began to arrive in the church with placards, many with chains – four more pillars were surrounded.

Turn up, chain-in, sit down!

The weekend of the Notre Dame chain-in was the conclusion of a fortnight's campaigning en route from London to Paris. The event – co-ordinated by the London Greenpeace Group (the original Greenpeace in London, long predating the London branch of the international Greenpeace network), had set off with a demonstration at the French Embassy in London, and walked via Belgium

to France. People from a dozen or so countries were involved, including places in the Pacific affected by the series of French atmospheric nuclear tests at Mururoa Atoll. To avoid militarist connotations, everyone had studiously avoided calling it, in English, a "March".

London Greenpeace, which emerged in 1971 out of a lifestyle and activist group involving people from *Peace News* and War Resisters' International (then based next door to the *Peace News* building in London) had chosen the French atmospheric tests in the Pacific as their first major campaign.

The style of the London–Paris event – transnational nonviolent direct action involving people of various nationalities – was itself fairly novel (and half a century later the story is little known). In many ways this 1973 event was a precursor of the International Nonviolent Marches for Demilitarisation which took place around Europe annually from 1976 to 1986.

The CRS invade

The walkers reached southern Belgium, near the French border a couple of miles south of Mouscron, on Friday 25 May. While camped there, news came that the French authorities had declared the border closed to the activists. This led to a flurry of media interest, and interviews on Belgian radio stations. The next day, someone spotted from local maps that a kink in the border meant a street a couple hundred yards inside Belgium, but in sight of a border post, had a stretch of the pavement on one side which was technically inside France; so people squeezed onto that pavement and noisily celebrated a symbolic "victory".

The CRS – French heavy-duty riot police, who were at the border – saw what had happened, pushed the Belgian border guards aside, charged through Belgian territory and set about the walkers. Some were picked up and literally thrown across to the other side of the village road. It was all a rather good bonding experience for the walkers; and it meant the Belgian locals were suddenly very much on the activists' side. Free food and drink flowed.

The following day, walkers started crossing the border in small numbers away from the official crossings – some by driving across fields in borrowed French cars. In the following days, whenever groups of campaigners managed to link up on the way south towards Paris, a cat-and-mouse game with the French police ensued. Nevertheless, almost everyone eventually reached Paris in time for the planned (but also banned) 2 June demonstration.

While in the cathedral in Paris, campaigners were interviewed by BBC World Service journalists in several languages, and by other international news outlets. In the evening, everyone unchained themselves and left voluntarily; there had been a tacit agreement with the Archbishop that if he, in effect, allowed the campaigners sanctuary (so that they could talk to the press without the police trying to cut them free and drag them out) they would leave before a scheduled evening service.

Singing on several levels

After forming up outside the Notre Dame with French supporters, and starting to walk towards the Presidential Palace a mile or so away, 150 of them were surrounded by police and subsequently carried into police coaches and taken to the underground Opéra police station. There people were subdivided by sex, age and nationality, and locked into a series of "cages", meaning everyone could still communicate while being held.

Some extremely loud community singing got under way, to keep spirits up. The name of the police station was no coincidence – there was an opera house above – and after a while someone came down to complain to the police that the campaigners could be heard upstairs and were interfering with the entertainment of the bourgeoisie. Everyone was eventually released – without charge – once the Metro had stopped for the night.

London Greenpeace (and many others) of course continued various campaigns against nuclear weapons tests; the intense pressure led the French government to at least abandon atmospheric testing on the atolls after 1974, though it continued underground tests in the Pacific for another twenty years.

Dec-Jan

War will disappear only when men shall take no part whatever in violence and shall be ready to suffer every persecution that their abstention will bring them. It is the only way to abolish war.
Anatole France

WEEK 52 (2022)
(HOL UK/IRE/CAN)

MON
26

(HOL UK)

TUE
27

WED
28

THU
29

FRI
30

SAT
31

NEW YEAR'S DAY
WORLD DAY OF PEACE

SUN
1

1863 - Proclamation of emancipation of slaves comes into force, USA

January

Let there be peace
So frowns fly away like albatross
And skeletons foxtrot from cupboards,
So war correspondents become travel show presenters…
Lemn Sissay

WEEK 1
(HOL UK/IRE/CAN/US)

MON

2

1893 - Sybil
Morrison, pacifist
feminist, born,
Britain

(HOL SCOT)

TUE

3

1793 - Lucretia
Mott, feminist and
abolitionist, born,
USA

WED

4

1913 - Christian
Peace Society
founded, Denmark

THU

5

1963 - Military regime declares "state of siege", arrests numbers of dissidents, Peru

FRI

6

1983 - Police launch teargas bombs on Greenpeace ship protesting against arrival of Japanese nuclear waste, Cherbourg, France

SAT

7

1963 - Conference of non-aligned disarmament organisations sets up ICDP, Oxford, Britain

SUN

8

1998 - Death of Michael Tippett, pacifist composer, Britain

January

Those who love peace must learn to organise as effectively as those who love war.
Martin Luther King

WEEK 2

MON

9

1988 - Women in Black begin regular vigil against militarism of government, Israel

TUE

10

1983 - Public enquiry opens on proposed nuclear power station B, Sizewell, Britain

WED

11

1923 - Start of French and Belgian military occupation of Ruhr, Germany

THU
12
1987 - 20 judges arrested for blockading US rocket depot, Mutlangen, W Germany

FRI
13
1993 - Vigil against arrival of ship bringing plutonium for nuclear reactor, Tokai, Japan

SAT
14
1923 - Fascist squads formed into militia, Italy

MARTIN LUTHER KING DAY

SUN
15
1943 - Pentagon, originally planned as research hospital, completed, Washington DC, USA

January

All the moral instructions and the Ten Commandments and the good characteristics I can bring down to one commandment: Do not cause pain. That is all.
Amos Oz

WEEK 3

MON

16

MLK DAY OBSERVED
(HOL US)

1943 - War against Axis powers declared by Iraq

TUE

17

1983 - 30 arrested in protest against construction of hydro dam, Tasmania, Australia

WED

18

1978 - UK found guilty of inhuman & degrading treatment of prisoners in N Ireland, ECHR, Strasbourg

THU
19
1963 - Committee of 100 holds public assembly on homelessness, Newington Lodge, London, Britain

FRI
20
1993 - After 10 years, 2500 refugees return from Mexico to Guatemala

SAT
21
1963 - Death of Helen Allegranza, anti-nuclear activist, Britain

YUAN TAN
CHINESE NEW YEAR 4721

SUN
22
1963 - President De Gaulle and Chancellor Adenauer sign Elysée Treaty, first French-German bilateral pact in generations, Paris, France

January

A country is considered the more civilised the more the wisdom and efficiency of its laws hinder a weak man from becoming too weak and a powerful one too powerful.
Primo Levi

WEEK 4

MON
23
1982 - 10,000 demonstrate against nuclear power plans, Frankenberg, W Germany

TUE
24
2000 - 2000 Albanians demonstrate for release of hundreds detained by Serbs, Pristina, Kosovo, Yugoslavia

WED
25
1998 - 11 killed by Tamil Tiger suicide bombers, Kandy, Sri Lanka

THU

26

1973 - Selective draft put on stand-by, USA

INT'L HOLOCAUST MEMORIAL DAY

FRI

27

1853 - Wendell Phillips calls for nonviolent, rather than armed, resistance to slavery, Boston, USA

◐

SAT

28

1903 - Kathleen Lonsdale, pacifist scientist, born, Britain

SUN

29

1983 - Demonstrators against military aid to El Salvador blockade naval base, Port Chicago, California, USA

Jan-Feb

War is elective. It is not an inevitable state of affairs. War is not the weather.

Susan Sontag

WEEK 5

MON
30
1948 - Mahatma Gandhi assassinated, New Delhi, India

TUE
31
1903 - Donald Soper, pacifist pastor, born, Britain

WED
1
1982 - Peace camp resolves to become "women only", Greenham Common USAF base, Berkshire, Britain

THU
2
1998 - Declaration to reduce nuclear weapons signed by over 100 world leaders

FRI
3
1998 - First execution of woman in state since 1860s, Texas, USA

SAT
4
1913 - Rosa Parks, first sitter-in on segregated buses, born, USA

SUN
5
1942 - Quisling government orders all teachers to join Nazi "Teachers' Front", Norway

February

Nonviolence is hard work. It is the willingness to sacrifice. It is the patience to win.
Cesar Chavez

WEEK 6

MON

6

1998 - 9 killed by Tamil Tiger suicide bomber, Colombo, Sri Lanka

TUE

7

1993 - Women's tribunal against rape in war, Zagreb, Croatia

WED

8

1983 - Conscientious objection recognised as basic right by European Parliament

THU
9
1933 - Union debating society resolves it will in no circumstances fight for King and Country, Oxford University, Britain

FRI
10
1953 - General Mohammed Neguib voted 3-year dictatorial powers, Egypt

SAT
11
1968 - Death of Muriel Lester, Christian pacifist, Britain

SUN
12
1967 - 60 burn draft cards, New York, USA

February

Lest my way of life sounds puritanical or austere, I always emphasise that in the long run one can't satisfactorily say no to war, violence, and injustice unless one is simultaneously saying yes to life, love and laughter.

Dave Dellinger

WEEK 7

MON

13

1903 - Georges Simenon, writer and nonviolent anarchist, born, Belgium

TUE

14

1943 - Stanley Murphy & Louis Taylor begin fast over discrimination against COs, Danbury, Connecticut, USA

WED

15

2003 - Millions march worldwide against war on Iraq

THU
16
1993 - 8 Nobel Peace laureates urge release of Aung San Suu Kyi by regime in Burma

FRI
17
1958 - Meeting to found Campaign for Nuclear Disarmament (CND), London

SAT
18
1943 - Hans and Sophie Scholl distribute "White Rose" leaflets at University; arrested, Munich, Germany

SUN
19
1963 - USSR agrees withdrawal of troops from Cuba

February

You just hold your head high and keep those fists down. No matter what anybody says to you, don't you let 'em get your goat. Try fightin' with your head for a change.

Atticus Finch in *To Kill a Mockingbird* by Harper Lee

WEEK 8

MON
20

●
PRESIDENTS' DAY
(HOL US)

1783 - USA declares cease-fire in war of independence, N America

TUE
21

1973 - 104 killed as Libyan airliner crashes after interception by Israeli planes, Sinai

WED
22

ASH WEDNESDAY

1943 - Hans & Sophie Scholl, "White Rose" nonviolent resisters to Nazis, beheaded, Munich, Germany

THU
23
1933 - Japan begins occupation north of Great Wall, China

FRI
24
1883 - Swedish Peace and Arbitration Society founded, Sweden

SAT
25
1988 - USSR withdraws SS-12 missiles from E Germany & Czechoslovakia

SUN
26
2003 - 199 members vote that case for war against Iraq is not proven, Parliament, Britain

Feb-Mar

I only want to live in peace, plant potatoes and dream!
Tove Jansson

WEEK 9

MON
27
1933 - Nazis set fire to Reichstag (parliament), blaming communists, Berlin, Germany

TUE
28
1988 - 80,000 demonstrate against nuclear power, Brokdorf, W Germany

WED

NUCLEAR-FREE & INDEPENDENT PACIFIC DAY

1
1943 - Mass rally calls on government to offer sanctuary to Jewish refugees, Madison Square, New York, USA

THU
2
1992 - Rally against ethnic barricades, Sarajevo, Bosnia

FRI
3
1918 - Signing of treaty between Russia and the Central Powers, Brest-Litovsk

SAT
4
1963 - 2 airmen gaoled 4 months by court martial for proposing a Forces CND, Britain

SUN
5
1988 - Demonstrations against "nuclear mafia", Essen, Gorleben, Frankfurt & Regensburg, W Germany

March

Whatever you're meant to do, do it now. The conditions are always impossible.
Doris Lessing

WEEK 10

MON

6

1983 - Break the Nuclear Chain demonstration at uranium enrichment plant, Capenhurst, Britain

TUE

7

1873 - John Beresford, pacifist author, born, Britain

WED

INT'L WOMEN'S DAY

8

1983 - 40,000 rally against war on Lebanon, Tel Aviv, Israel

THU
9
1983 - 30 women ejected (12 later deported) from International Peace Camp, cruise missile base, Comiso, Sicily

FRI
10
1913 - Death of Harriet Tubman, organiser of slave escape route "Underground Railroad", USA

SAT
11
2007 - Police brutally break up rally calling for end to country's political and economic crisis, Harare, Zimbabwe

SUN
12
1938 - German troops enter Austria

March

Not everything that is faced can be changed, but nothing can be changed until it is faced.
James Baldwin

WEEK 11

MON
13
1938 - Anschluss: annexation of Austria by Germany

TUE
14
1978 - 50,000 march against construction of uranium enrichment plant, Almelo, Netherlands

WED
15
1973 - *Fri* leaves for French nuclear test zone from Whangarei, New Zealand

THU
16
1988 - Massacre of Kurds with mustard and nerve gases, Halabja, Iraq

ST PATRICK'S DAY
(HOL NI/IRE)

FRI
17
1813 - Friedrich Wilhelm III begins formation of Landwehr, conscript army, Prussia

SAT
18
1893 - Wilfred Owen, poet of the pity of war, born, Britain

SUN
19
1943 - Roger Moody, activist against violence of extractive industries, born, Britain

March

As an artist I come to sing, but as a citizen, I will always speak for peace, and no one can silence me in this.
Paul Robeson

WEEK 12

MON
20
EQUINOX

1948 - USSR withdraws from Allied Control Commission for Germany

TUE
21
INT'L DAY FOR ELIMINATION OF RACIAL DISCRIMINATION

1978 - Israel calls cease-fire. Lebanon

WED
22
SAKA
(INDIAN NEW YEAR 1945)

2003 - Opposing war on Iraq, thousands blockade USAF base, Fairford, Britain

THU
23
1983 - President Ronald Reagan announces "Star Wars" concept, USA

FRI
24
1993 - Rally for peace in N Ireland, held in Dublin, Republic of Ireland

SAT
25
1949 - Execution reported of John Tsourakis as conscientious objector, Greece

BST BEGINS

SUN
26
2001 - Hundreds in blockade of French nuclear waste train, Gorleben, Germany

Mar-Apr

Here's what we can do to change the world, right now ... Take all that money that we spend on weapons and defence each year and instead spend it feeding and clothing and educating the poor of the world which it would many times over – not one human being excluded ...

Bill Hicks

WEEK 13

MON

27

1988 - Mordechai Vanunu gaoled 18 years for disclosing nuclear weapons programme, Israel

TUE

28

1913 - Military conscription introduced, Belgium

WED

29

1973 - Last US troops leave South Vietnam

THU
30
1919 - Hartal - closure of shops in protest against Rowlatt Bills - begins, New Delhi, India

FRI
31
1998 - Air force permanently withdraws nuclear bombs from service, Britain

SAT
1
1983 - 14-mile human chain links nuclear arms establishments, Burghfield, Greenham Common & Aldermaston, Britain

SUN
2
1982 - Argentina occupies Falkland Islands

April

Secrets are kept from you because you may be a spy. Not for Russia, but for all people everywhere. Because you may believe you have the right to know what is being done about your future, in your name, at your expense, but without your consent.

"Danger - Official Secret!" – Spies for Peace, Good Friday, 1963

WEEK 14

MON

3

1963 - 700 in Budget Day protest against taxation for nuclear arms, House of Commons, London, Britain

TUE

4

1958 - 4000 begin first march to Aldermaston AWRE from Trafalgar Square, London, Britain

WED

5

1963 - Airman Francis Smith placed under close arrest for wearing ND badge instead of RAF insignia, Britain

THU
6
1888 - Hans Richter, Dadaist artist and anarchist, born, Berlin, Germany

GOOD FRIDAY
(HOL UK/CAN)

FRI
7
1933 - Première of *Zéro de Conduite* by anarchist film-maker Jean Vigo, Paris, France

SAT
8
1993 - Women in Black demonstrate in solidarity with their Serbian sisters, Lund, Sweden

EASTER DAY

SUN
9
1893 - Victor Gollancz, pacifist publisher, born, Britain

April

Let us wage a moral and political war against war itself, so that we can cut military spending and use that money for human needs.
Bernie Sanders

WEEK 15

MON
10

EASTER MONDAY
(HOL ENG/W/NI/IRE/CAN)

1583 - Hugo Grotius, founder of international law, born, Delft, Netherlands

TUE
11

1963 - Pope John XXIII calls for end to nuclear arms race in encyclical *Pacem in Terris*, Vatican

WED
12

1963 - Spies for Peace pamphlet reveals WW3 Regional Seats of Government, Britain

THU
13
1963 - Hundreds of Aldermaston marchers divert to Regional Seat of Government 6, Warren Row, Warminster, Britain

FRI
14
1963 - British anti-nuclear activists refused entry end 2-day sit-in, Dusseldorf airport, W Germany

SAT
15
1963 - RSG secrets announced to 80,000 at Easter March final rally, Hyde Park, London, Britain

SUN
16
1983 - Bridge blocked to stop boat loaded with guns for export, Sweden

April

I think that I still have it in my heart someday to paint a bookshop with the front yellow and pink in the evening ... like a light in the midst of the darkness.

Vincent Van Gogh

WEEK 16

MON

17

1983 - 15,000 demonstrate for public accounting for thousands of "disappeared", Buenos Aires, Argentina

TUE

18

1983 - 47 killed by suicide bomber, US Embassy, Beirut, Lebanon

WED

19

1948 - Army formally disbanded, Costa Rica

THU
20
1963 - British supporters deported for attempting to join banned Marathon peace march, Greece

FRI
21
1963 - 400 march to WW3 Regional Seat of Government, Edinburgh, Scotland

SAT
22
1993 - Bill for unilateral disarmament tabled in Senate, France

SUN
23
1993 - Death of Cesar Chavez, nonviolent activist, USA

April

Poems, regardless of any outcome, cross the battlefields, tending the wounded, listening to the wild monologues of the triumphant or the fearful. They bring a kind of peace.
John Berger

WEEK 17

MON
24
1938 - At instigation of Adolf Hitler, Konrad Henlein demands autonomy for Sudetenland, Czechoslovakia

TUE
ANZAC DAY (AUS)
25
1983 - 175 women arrested for marching to mourn the rape of women in war, Melbourne & Sydney, Australia

WED
26
1993 - Women in Black demonstrate in solidarity with their Serbian sisters, Toronto, Canada

THU
27
1963 - 200 demonstrate at WW3 Regional Seat of Government 10, Preston, Lancashire, Britain

FRI
28
1988 - Death of Fenner Brockway, peace campaigner, Britain

SAT
29
1983 - Military junta tells relatives of 20,000 "disappeared" to presume them dead, Argentina

SUN
30
1913 - Svend Haugaard, peace activist, born, Denmark

May

Theirs is a land of hope and glory
Mine is the green field and the factory floor
Theirs are the skies all dark with bombers
And mine is the peace we knew between the wars.

Billy Bragg

WEEK 18

MON

MAY DAY
(HOL UK/IRE)

1

1963 - UN hands over West New Guinea (as West Irian) to regime of Indonesia

TUE

2

1982 - British navy kills 368 in sinking of Argentinian *General Belgrano*, South Atlantic

WED

3

1963 - Water hoses used against civil rights protesters, Birmingham, Alabama, USA

THU
4
1963 - 120 march to Regional Seat of Government 12, Dover Castle, Kent, Britain

FRI
5
1993 - Dhammayietra II to Pnom Penh leaves Siem Reap, Cambodia

SAT
6
1973 - Demonstrations against Pacific nuclear tests in 14 cities, France

SUN
7
1963 - Former naval intelligence operator renounces Official Secrets Act "indoctrination", Britain

May

Though I sit behind prison walls, I still believe that I can build further on your love and devotion in the days to come. And should I have to leave this life, I will still [rest easy in] my grave, for you know that I am not here as a criminal.

Franz Jägerstätter, writing to his wife from prison before his sentence to death as a conscientious objector in 1943.

WEEK 19

MON
8
1933 - Gandhi begins 21-day fast - government releases him from gaol, India

TUE
9
1993 - Network for deserters and COs from former Yugoslavia established, Salzburg, Austria

WED
10
1933 - Nazis begin burning of books by left and Jewish authors, Germany

THU

11

1963 - 68 charged under Official Secrets Acts after double walk-on by 300, RAF Marham, Norfolk, Britain

FRI

12

1978 - Icelandic gunboat attacks British trawler, Atlantic Ocean

SAT

13

1943 - Germany and Italy surrender in North Africa

SUN

14

1948 - Unilateral declaration of the State of Israel, Tel Aviv, Palestine

May

CHRISTIAN AID WEEK 14–20 MAY
Christian Aid is the aid and development wing of the Council of Churches in Britain. The week focuses on the need for helping the self-development and achievement of justice of people affected by poverty, famine or war in many parts of the world.

Contact: Christian Aid, 35–41 Lower Marsh, London SE1 7RL, Britain; tel +44-20-7620 4444; email info@christian-aid.org; www.christianaid.org.uk.

WEEK 20

MON

15

INT'L CONSCIENTIOUS OBJECTORS' DAY

1963 - Mark Chagall window "Peace" dedicated in Meditation Room, UN HQ, New York, USA

TUE

16

1973 - Martha Tranquilli gaoled 9 months for war tax resistance, USA

WED

17

1982 - Last of 3 days of closure of uranium mine in occupation by 450, Honeymoon, S Australia

THU
18
1963 - Return walk-on reduces charges for 11 May event, RAF Marham, Norfolk, Britain

FRI
19
1934 - 10,000 in "No More War" march, New York, USA

SAT
20
1973 - Jury acquits 17 of destroying draft files after argument over illegality of Vietnam War, USA

SUN
21
1983 - Christian witness for peace, Upper Heyford USAF base, Britain

May

It's odd how those who dismiss the peace movement as utopian don't hesitate to proffer the most absurdly dreamy reasons for going to war: to stamp out terrorism, install democracy, eliminate fascism, and, most entertainingly, to "rid the world of evil-doers".

Arundhati Roy

WEEK 21

VICTORIA DAY (HOL CAN)

MON

22

1963 - Gregory Lambrakis, peaceful parliamentarian, run down by police motor cyclist, Salonika, Greece

TUE

23

1983 - Crashing plane kills pastor and family, military air display, Frankfurt, W Germany

WED

INT'L WOMEN'S DAY FOR DISARMAMENT

24

1883 - Cecil Cadoux, pacifist theologian, born, Turkey

THU
25
1993 - UN War Crimes Tribunal created for Yugoslavia

FRI
26
1973 - London Greenpeace activists physically ejected from France while opposing atmospheric nuclear tests, France/Belgium border

SAT
27
1943 - National Resistance Council of politicians, unionists & others formed, France

SUN
28
1933 - Nazis elected to power, free city of Danzig

May-Jun

There is very little you can beat into a child, but no limit to what you can hug out of it.
Astrid Lindgren

WEEK 22

MEMORIAL DAY (US)
(HOL UK/US)

MON
29
1983 - Demonstrations against conscription mark Armed Forces Week, Basque country, Spain

TUE
30
1982 - Spain joins NATO

WED
31
1983 - Activists arrested during 4-day blockade of USAF base at Upper Heyford, Oxfordshire, Britain

THU
1
1993 - Police brutally repress mass demonstrations against regime, Serbia

FRI
2
1973 - Chain-in in Notre Dame at end of London-Paris Walk opposing atmospheric nuclear tests, Paris, France

SAT
3
1981 - Farmers win 10-year campaign to keep army off their land, Larzac, France

INT'L DAY FOR CHILDREN AS VICTIMS OF WAR

SUN
4
1983 - Demonstrations against nuclear power, Cape Town, S Africa

June

We children are doing this to wake the adults up. We children are doing this for you to put your differences aside and start acting as you would in a crisis. We children are doing this because we want our hopes and dreams back.

Greta Thunberg

WEEK 23

MON
(HOL IRE)

5

2022 - Roger Moody, inspirational *Peace News* writer and campaigner, died, Britain

TUE

6

1993 - Guerillas massacre 450 in attack on refugee camp, Harbel, Liberia

WED

7

1963 - 150 visit WW3 Regional Seat of Government 7, Dartmouth, Devon, Britain

THU
8
2022 - Bruce Kent, nuclear disarmament and justice campaigner, died, Britain

FRI
9
1952 - Publication of document which led to War on Want, Britain

SAT
10
1973 - British Withdrawal from Northern Ireland Campaign launched by displaying manifesto on railings, Parliament Sq, Britain

SUN
11
1948 - UN Truce Team established, Palestine

June

The great thing about democracy is that although harsh things are sometimes said, we are not actually trying to kill each other.
Chris Mullin

WEEK 24

MON

12

1982 - 800,000 in largest ever US demonstration, UNSSD2, New York, USA

TUE

13

1993 - UN "peacekeepers" shoot 14 unarmed demonstrators, Mogadishu, Somalia

WED

14

1963 - Women Against the Bomb members leave for Moscow with letters calling for complete test ban, Britain

THU
15
1943 - Congress of Racial Equality founded, Chicago, USA

FRI
16
1963 - 50 climb over fence, War Department establishment, Inchterf, Scotland

SAT
17
1953 - USSR suppresses workers' strike for democracy, East Berlin

SUN
18
1983 - Women's Peace Camp established, nuclear submarine base, Puget Sound, Washington, USA

June

I appeal on behalf of four millions of men, women, and children who are chattels in the Southern States of America. Not because they are identical with my race and colour, though I am proud of that identity, but because they are men and women.

Sarah Parker Remond

WEEK 25

MON
(HOL US)

19

1953 - Execution of Julius and Ethel Rosenberg, USA

TUE

20

1963 - Washington-Moscow "hot-line" agreement signed, Geneva, Switzerland

WED
SOLSTICE

21

1973 - Agreement on arms limitation signed by USA and USSR

THU
22
1843 - First Universal Peace Convention opens, London, Britain

FRI
23
1983 - General strike against military regime, Chile

SAT
24
1963 - Special Branch raids Committee of 100 offices, London, Britain

SUN
25
1993 - Armed Afrikaner Volksfront members storm talks on constitutional change, World Trade Centre, Johannesburg, S Africa

Jun-Jul

War is what happens when language fails.
Margaret Atwood

WEEK 26

MON
26

1953 - Albert Lutuli calls for bonfires and candles to symbolise spark of freedom, S Africa

INT'L DAY FOR VICTIMS OF TORTURE

TUE
27

1973 - *HMNZS Otago* in protest against French nuclear tests sails to Mururoa Atoll from Auckland, New Zealand

WED
28

1973 - Convention on International Trade in Endangered Species agreed

THU
29
1963 - 53 arrested as 300 walk on to C&B Warfare research establishment, Porton Down, Wiltshire, Britain

FRI
30
1913 - Bulgaria begins Second Balkan War with attacks on Serbia and Greece

CANADA DAY
(HOL CAN)

SAT
1
1963 - 35 civil rights protesters occupy Mayor's office 24 hours, Seattle, Washington, USA

SUN
2
1983 - 8000 demonstrate against nuclear armed ships in port, Fremantle, Western Australia

July

It takes no compromise to give people their rights. It takes no money to respect the individual. It takes no survey to remove repressions.
Harvey Milk

WEEK 27

MON

3

1963 - Death of Garth Macgregor, pacifist theologian, Scotland

TUE

4

INDEPENDENCE DAY (HOL US)

1983 - Presentation of British Declaration of Independence from US Militarism to over 100 US bases, Britain

WED

5

1953 - Liberalising government takes power, Hungary

THU
6
1983 - Government confirms plans to deploy cruise missiles at Greenham and Molesworth, Britain

FRI
7
1963 - "Police State Visit" headline as government bans protests against coming visit by Greek royalty, London, Britain

SAT
8
1973 - French government declares "exclusion zone" around nuclear weapon test site, Mururoa Atoll, Pacific

DAY OF COMMEMORATION (IRE)

SUN
9
1963 - Jane Buxton warned wearing of black sash to mark visit of Greek royalty constitutes illegal uniform, London, Britain

July

Whether it be a matter of personal relations within a marriage or political initiatives within a peace process, there is no sure-fire do-it-yourself kit.

Seamus Heaney

WEEK 28

MON

10

1963 - King & Queen of Hellenes booed over oppression of Greek peace movement, London, Britain

TUE

11

1960 - Direct Action Committee begins picket of Siddeley Engines, Bristol, Britain

WED

12

BATTLE OF THE BOYNE (HOL NI)

1998 - Three young brothers killed in Loyalist arson attack on house, Ballymoney, Co Antrim, N Ireland

THU
13
1863 - Anti-conscription riots, New York, USA

FRI
14
1933 - Political parties other than Nazis suppressed, Germany

SAT
15
1983 - Women's temporary peace camp set up to oppose cruise missiles, Reckenhausen, W Germany

SUN
16
1983 - Human chain of 10,000 links US & USSR embassies, London, Britain

July

If I've made it, it's half because I was game to take a wicked amount of punishment along the way, and half because there were an awful lot of people who cared enough to help me.

Althea Gibson

WEEK 29

MON

●

17

1973 - French navy boards *Fri* as it sails for nuclear test zone, Mururoa Atoll, Pacific

TUE

MUHARRAM
(ISLAMIC NEW YEAR 1445)

18

1998 - Truce declared between Chiapas rebels and government, Mexico

WED

19

1977 - OAS Human Rights Treaty comes into force

THU
20
1963 - Christian CND begins 3-day vigil for world peace, Lambeth Palace, London, Britain

FRI
21
1983 - Martial law lifted in response to popular agitation, Poland

SAT
22
1983 - COs forbidden to consort with school pupils, Baden-Wurttemberg, W Germany

SUN
23
1983 - Protest against US testing of cruise missiles across frontier of Canada

July

If you want to avoid war, then instead of sending guns, send books. Instead of tanks, send pens. Instead of soldiers, send teachers.

Malala Yousufzai, speaking at first anniversary of the UN Global Education First initiative, 25 September 2013.

WEEK 30

MON

24

1983 - Women write graffiti on airplane, Greenham Common USAF base, Berkshire, Britain

TUE

25

1983 - 125 arrested in blockade of naval weapons base, Concord, Colorado, USA

WED

26

1963 - Committee of 100 convoy to support Greek peace movement leaves London, Britain

THU
27
1953 - War ends with armistice, Panmunjon, Korea

FRI
28
1943 - Fascist Party dissolved, Italy

SAT
29
1973 - NZ ship *Otago* enters "excluded" waters to prevent French nuclear test, Mururoa Atoll, Pacific

SUN
30
1963 - Committee of 100 London-Athens Convoy blockades autobahn on refusal of entry, Bad Reichenhalle, Austria

Jul-Aug

You can't do anything with anybody's body to make it dirty to me. Six people, eight people, one person – you can do only one thing to make it dirty: kill it. Hiroshima was dirty.

Lenny Bruce

WEEK 31

MON
31
1913 - Balkan states sign armistice, Bucharest, Romania

TUE
1
1923 - Nie Wieder Krieg demonstration, Berlin, Germany

WED
2
1793 - Joseph Sturge, peace activist, born, Britain

THU
3
1988 - 143 war resisters publicly refuse call-up, S Africa

FRI
4
1983 - Police and soldiers kill participants in bus and school boycott, Ciskei, S Africa

SAT
5
1963 - UK, USA, USSR sign treaty to ban atmospheric nuclear tests, Moscow, USSR

HIROSHIMA DAY

SUN
6
1998 - Minuteman III Plowshares activists damage ICBM silo, Colorado, USA

August

And when they bombed other people's houses, we protested but not enough, we opposed them but not enough.
Ilya Kaminsky

WEEK 32

MON
(HOL SCOT/IRE)

7

1963 - UN Security Council bans arms sales to S Africa

TUE

8

1963 - Donald Rooum, nonviolent activist, is acquitted of possessing half-brick planted by police, London

WED
NAGASAKI DAY

9

1943 - Austrian CO Franz Jägerstätter beheaded, Berlin, Germany

THU
10
1993 - 300 arrested in protest against rainforest clearance, Clayoquot Sound,

FRI
11
1943 - 21 COs strike against prison dining hall racial segregation, Danbury, Connecticut, USA

SAT
12
1953 - Its first H-bomb exploded by USSR

SUN
13
1673 - First American exemption of conscientious objectors, Rhode Island

August

The courage to put an end to war, to see the abysmal stupidity of it, is certainly no less than that needed to start one.
Claudio Magris

WEEK 33

MON
14
1964 - Picnic at Regional Seat of Government 6, Warren Row, Warminster, Britain

TUE
15
1982 - Members of 7th International Nonviolent March swim across "closed" Spanish-Gibraltar border

WED
16
1973 - United Farmworkers begin second grape boycott, California, USA

THU
17
1993 - Air Force dismantles first of 350 B-52s as part of START treaty, USA

FRI
18
1563 - Death of Etienne de la Boetie, peace philosopher

SAT
19
2003 - 20 killed in bombing of UN local HQ, Baghdad, Iraq

SUN
20
1993 - 5 make country's first joint declaration of conscientious objection, Buenos Aires, Argentina

August

Peace is not an absence of war, it is a virtue, a state of mind, a disposition for benevolence, confidence, justice.
Spinoza

WEEK 34

MON
21
1963 - Martial law imposed; Buddhists arrested, S Vietnam

TUE
22
1988 - 68 pacifist-feminists rally against Israeli-Palestinian violence, Italy

INT'L DAY FOR VICTIMS OF VIOLENCE BASED ON RELIGION OR BELIEF

WED
23
1933 - Gandhi released from gaol after week's fast, India

THU
24
1993 - Government announces immediate cessation of military conscription, S Africa

FRI
25
1993 - Women in Black demonstrate in solidarity with their Serbian sisters, London, Britain

SAT
26
1346 - English army introduces longbow and bombard to continental warfare. Crecy, France

SUN
27
1983 - Demonstration against biological warfare experiments, Allington Farm, Porton, Britain

Aug-Sept

You. Mother in Normandy, mother in the Ukraine, you, mother in San Francisco and London, you, on the Yellow River and the Mississippi River, you, mother in Naples and Hamburg and Cairo and Oslo – mothers of all continents, mothers of the world, when they tell you tomorrow to raise children to be nurses for field hospitals and to be soldiers for new battles, then there's only one choice: Say NO! Mothers, say NO!

Wolfgang Borchert, writing in the aftermath of the Second World War.

WEEK 35

MON
(HOL E/W/NI)

28
1963 - 250,000 march for civil rights, Washington DC, USA

TUE

29
1533 - Spanish conquistadores overthrow Inca empire, southern America

WED

30
1948 - Convention on Protection of Civilians in War signed, Stockholm, Sweden

THU
31
1983 - Police use teargas & watercannon on 10,000 Solidarnosc demonstrators, Nowa Huta, Poland

FRI
1
1983 - 269 killed by Soviet shooting down of S Korean airliner, Sea of Okhotsk, USSR

SAT
2
1993 - Women in Black demonstrate in solidarity with their Serbian sisters, Lancaster, Pennsylvania, USA

SUN
3
1953 - European Convention on Human Rights comes into force

September

Without facts, you can't have truth. Without truth, you can't have trust. Without trust, we have no shared reality, no democracy, and it becomes impossible to deal with our world's existential problems: climate, coronavirus, the battle for truth.

Maria Ressa

WEEK 36

MON

4

LABOUR DAY
(HOL CAN/US)

1953 - World Government of World Citizens founded by Gary Davies, USA

TUE

5

1798 - Military conscription ordained, France

WED

6

1963 - Marchers from Glasgow attempt to present dummy Polaris missile to Imperial War Museum, London, Britain

THU
7
1938 - Sudeten Germans break off relations with government of Czechoslovakia

FRI
8
1941 - Workers strike against diversion of milk to military use, Norway

SAT
9
1983 - 100 Christian women and children massacred by Druze militia, Al Bire, Lebanon

SUN
10
1983 - Thousands demonstrate for restoration of democracy, Chile

September

Es el canto universal
Cadena que hará triunfar
El derecho de vivir en paz

It is the universal song / chain that will triumph / the right to live in peace.

Víctor Jara

WEEK 37

MON

11

1973 - US-backed military coup d'état, Chile

TUE

12

1943 - German force releases Benito Mussolini from prison, Abruzzi Mountains, Italy

WED

13

1993 - Israel & PLO sign peace accord, Washington DC, USA

THU
14
1963 - First Factory for Peace, Rowen, opens, Glasgow, Scotland

●
ROSH HASHANAH
(JEWISH NEW YEAR 5784)

FRI
15
1963 - 6 Sunday schoolchildren killed in racial bombing of Baptist Church, Birmingham, Alabama, USA

SAT
16
1973 - Victor Jara, poet and songwriter, tortured and killed in Chile Stadium by Pinochet régime, Chile

SUN
17
1963 - Station for early warning of ballistic missiles comes into operation, Fylingdales, Yorkshire, Britain

September

Peace is only sustainable when we see the well-being and security of others as being as important as our own.

Conciliation Resources, International Alert, Saferworld joint statement.

WEEK 38

MON

18

1963 - UN Special Committee on apartheid calls for prohibition of arms trade with S Africa

TUE

19

1982 - Massacre by Phalangist troops of 1000 Palestinian refugees begins, Sabra & Chatila camps, Lebanon

WED

20

1933 - Death of Annie Besant, women's rights activist and supporter of Indian self-rule, India

UN INT'L DAY OF PEACE

THU
21

1963 - WRL organises first demonstration against Vietnam War, USA

◐

FRI
22

1938 - PPU leaders hand in demand for peaceful solution of Czechoslovak crisis, Downing St, London, Britain

EQUINOX

SAT
23

1993 - Parliament votes in special sitting to allow blacks first ever share in political power, Pretoria, S Africa

INT'L DAY OF PRAYER FOR PEACE

SUN
24

1993 - In response to change, other states begin lifting trade sanctions against S Africa

Sept-Oct

The greatest crimes in the world are not committed by people breaking the rules but by people following the rules. It's people who follow orders that drop bombs and massacre villages.
Banksy

WEEK 39

MON
25
1983 - World Maritime Day first observed

TUE
26
1953 - Australian Convention on Peace and War opens, Sydney, Australia

INT'L DAY FOR TOTAL ELIMINATION OF NUCLEAR WEAPONS

WED
27
1993 - Salih Askerogul arrested as conscientious objector, Lefkosa, N Cyprus

THU
28
1943 - Systematic smuggling of Jews to Sweden begins, Denmark

FRI
29
1983 - Nonviolent guerilla action by 8th International March prematurely closes arms fair, Brussels, Belgium

SAT
30
1923 - Donald Swann, pacifist musician, born, Britain

SUN
1
1923 - Black Reichswehr attempted coup d'état fails, Germany

October

I can promise you that women working together – linked, informed and educated – can bring peace and prosperity to this forsaken planet.
Isobel Allende

WEEK 40

MON

2

INT'L DAY OF NONVIOLENCE

1938 - Withdrawal from League of Nations by Japan

TUE

3

1963 - Military coup d'état, Honduras

WED

4

1973 - Fire on USSR destroyer causes crew to jettison torpedo, North Sea

THU

5

1953 - First observance of Universal Children's Day

FRI

6

1973 - In Yom Kippur War Egypt & Syria simultaneously attack Israel

SAT

7

2001 - US and British forces begin missile attacks on towns, Afghanistan

SUN

8

1998 - Remorse for past expressed in treaty between S Korea and Japan

October

Not peace at any price, but love at all costs.
Dick Sheppard

WEEK 41

MON

9

THANKSGIVING (CAN)
COLUMBUS DAY (US)
(HOL CAN/US)

1992 - Women in Black rally against war, Belgrade, Serbia

TUE

10

1983 - Gandhi Foundation set up, London, Britain

WED

11

1963 - UN General Assembly, by 106-1, condemns repression in S Africa

THU
12
1978 - UN Centre for Human Settlements set up, Nairobi, Kenya

FRI
13
1963 - Picket of military exercise, RSG 9, Kidderminster, Worcestershire, Britain

SAT
14
1933 - Withdrawal from Disarmament Conference and League of Nations by Germany

SUN
15
1963 - Fr Ernesto Balducci gaoled 9 months for writing article on conscientious objection, Italy

October

ONE WORLD WEEK 21–29 OCTOBER
Based on UN Day, One World Week is intended to encourage people to link with international issues through taking up overseas concerns in church, school, trade union etc.

Contact: One World Week, c/o 35–38 London Street, Reading, Berkshire, RG1 4PS, Britain; www.oneworldweek.org

WEEK 42

MON 16

1963 - Death of Guy Aldred, anarchist antimiltarist, Scotland

TUE 17

1993 - International Day for Eradication of Poverty first observed

WED 18

1992 - Plaque commemorating Vietnam War Resisters dedicated, Washington Sq Methodist Church, New York, USA

THU
19
1923 - War Resisters League founded, USA

FRI
20
1993 - Women in Black attacked by paramilitaries during Wednesday vigil, Belgrade, Serbia

SAT
21
1833 - Alfred Nobel, inventor of explosives and founder of peace prize, born, Sweden

SUN
22
1973 - Cease-fire agreed by Israel, Egypt and Jordan

October

INTERNATIONAL DISARMAMENT WEEK 24–30 OCTOBER
Called for in the Final Document of the Tenth UN Special Session on Disarmament in 1978, Disarmament Week is a time for pressing governments and arms manufacturers on the urgent need for disarmament of all kinds weapons.

Contact: Your nearest national UNA (see World Peace Directory)

WEEK 43

MON

23

1993 - IRA bomb kills 9 in fish shop, Shankill Road, Belfast, Northern Ireland

TUE

UNITED NATIONS DAY

24

1983 - End of week of anti-nuclear protests, involving 2 million people over western Europe

WED

25

1983 - US marines invade Grenada

THU
26
1863 - First draft convention on humanitarian rules in war agreed, Geneva, Switzerland

FRI
27
1938 - League of Nations pronounces Japan as aggressor in China

○

SAT
28
1939 - Popular demonstrations against Nazi occupation mark Independence Day, Prague, Czechoslovakia

BST ENDS

SUN
29
1923 - Proclamation of Turkish Republic

Oct-Nov

The establishment will irritate you – pull your beard, flick your face – to make you fight. Because once they've got you violent, then they know how to handle you. The only thing they don't know how to handle is non-violence and humour.

John Lennon

WEEK 44

MON
(HOL IRE)

30

1943 - Great powers agree on necessity for UN, Moscow, USSR

TUE

31

1958 - UK/USA/USSR conference on suspension of nuclear tests opens, Geneva, Switzerland

WED

1

1993 - All men liable to conscription forbidden to leave, Serbia

THU
2
1923 - Robert Bodanzky, writer, artist, and anti-militarist, died, Austria

FRI
3
1933 - Methodist Peace Fellowship launched, Britain

SAT
4
2013 - First meeting of Close Capenhurst campaign, opposing uranium enrichment plant, Liverpool, Britain

SUN
5
1949 - Peace Pledge Union sets up Nonviolence Commission, leading to direct action against nuclear weapons, Britain

November

It's not so much lest we forget, as lest we remember. Because you should realise that so far as the Cenotaph and the Last Post and all that stuff is concerned, there's no better way of forgetting something than by commemorating it.

Irwin in *The History Boys* by Alan Bennet

WEEK 45

MON
6
1913 - Gandhi leads great march against unjust taxation, from Natal to Transvaal, S Africa

TUE
7
1913 - Albert Camus, novelist of compassion, and anarchist, born, Algeria

WED
8
1992 - 350,000 protest against racist violence, Berlin, Germany

THU
9
1923 - Attempted "beer hall" putsch by Adolf Hitler fails, Munich, Germany

---

WORLD SCIENCE DAY FOR PEACE & DEVELOPMENT
VETERANS' DAY HOLIDAY (US)

FRI
10
1973 - Copies of Kurt Vonnegut's *Slaughterhouse 5* burned by school board, Drake, North Dakota, USA

VETERANS' DAY (US)

SAT
11
1983 - 111 arrested out of 800 women marching on Pine Gap US base, Northern Territory, Australia

---

REMEMBRANCE SUNDAY (UK)

SUN
12
1983 - 15,000 physicians worldwide call for complete test ban and nuclear freeze

November

This is our world. Aye, there's more than enough of darkness in it. But over everything there's all this joy, Kit. There's all this lovely, lovely light.

Grandpa in *Kit's Wilderness* by David Almond

WEEK 46

MON
13
1983 - Pope John Paul II urges scientists to refuse research on offensive weapons, Vatican

TUE
14
1983 - Cruise missiles arrive at Greenham Common airbase, Berkshire, Britain

WED
15
1983 - 141 arrested in demonstration against cruise missiles, Greenham Common, Berkshire, Britain

THU
16
1988 - Parliament votes to give itself right to veto Soviet Union laws, Estonia SSR

FRI
17
1993 - Military coup d'état, Nigeria

SAT
18
1961 - 1000 demonstrate against nuclear tests in torchlit procession to Soviet Consulate, Glasgow, Scotland

SUN
19
1980 - Titan missile accidentally started on launch, McConnell USAF base, Wichita, Kansas, USA

November

We've begun to raise daughters more like sons... but few have the courage to raise our sons more like our daughters.
Gloria Steinem

WEEK 47

MON

20

1963 - UN Declaration on Elimination of Racial Discrimination

UNIVERSAL CHILDREN'S DAY

TUE

21

1983 - Demonstrations mark Bundestag debate on stationing of missiles, Bonn, W Germany

WED

22

1913 - Benjamin Britten, pacifist composer, born, Britain

THU 23

THANKSGIVING
(HOL US)

1983 - Following deployment of US missiles in Europe, USSR leaves arms talks, Geneva, Switzerland

FRI 24

1983 - Plowshares 7 damage B-52 bomber, Griffiths airbase, New York, USA

SAT 25

INT'L DAY FOR ELIMINATION OF VIOLENCE AGAINST WOMEN

1992 - Contract for Star Wars tracking system cancelled, USA

SUN 26

1983 - First Pershing missiles arrive, Mutlangen, W Germany

Nov-Dec

There will be no future without forgiveness. Any process of peace is bound to collapse if this is missing. There is no way peace and stability can come through the gun of vengeance.

Desmond Tutu

WEEK 48

MON

27

1988 - Graffiti painted on fighter planes due for Turkey, Woensdrecht airbase, Netherlands

TUE

28

1982 - First meeting of Cat Lovers Against the Bomb, Lincoln, Nebraska, USA

WED

29

2013 - Death of Howard Clark, British nonviolent activist and writer, Spain

ST ANDREW'S DAY
HOL (SCOT)

THU
30

1993 - President Bill Clinton signs Brady bill on limited hand-gun control, USA

PRISONERS FOR PEACE DAY

FRI
1

1893 - Ernst Toller, expressionist playwright, anarchist, and pacifist, born, Germany

SAT
2

1823 - First articulation of Monroe Doctrine, USA

SUN
3

1963 - Second nuclear submarine launched, Britain

December

Peace can only last where human rights are respected, where the people are fed, and where individuals and nations are free.
Tenzin Gyatso, 14th Dalai Lama

WEEK 49

MON
4
1983 - First German Ploughshares action: Pershing missile transporter destroyed, Schwabisch Gmund, W Germany

TUE
5
1991 - Civic Resistance Movement collects 100,000 signatures against the war, Belgrade, Serbia

WED
6
1981 - 300,000 demonstrate for removal of nuclear weapons from Europe, Bucharest, Romania

THU
7
1988 - President Mikhail Gorbachev announces unilateral 500,000 reduction of armed forces by USSR, UN, New York, USA

FRI
8
1988 - 12 arrested for hammering on cruise missile bunkers, Woensdrecht, Netherlands

SAT
9
1883 - Muriel Lester, Christian pacifist, born, Britain

HUMAN RIGHTS DAY

SUN
10
2003 - Shirin Ebadi, Iranian human rights activist, awarded Nobel Peace Prize, Oslo, Norway

December

But for the use of physical punishment by, and fear of, their oppressors, animals would never be a part of a circus.
Richard Pryor

WEEK 50

MON

11

1992 - Solidarity convoy of 500 peace activists arrives, Sarajevo, Bosnia

TUE

12

1986 - Ploughshares activists disarm Pershing missile launcher, W Germany

WED

13

1993 - Post of High Commissioner for Human Rights created by UN

THU
14
1993 - Declaration on principles for peace talks on N Ireland, Downing Street, London, Britain

FRI
15
1923 - President Calvin Coolidge releases 31 conscientious objectors still in prison, USA

SAT
16
1773 - Boston Tea Party

SUN
17
1998 - British/US airstrikes renewed against Iraq

December

The great writers of aphorisms read as if they had all known each other well.
Elias Canetti

WEEK 51

MON
18
1963 - African students protest against racial discrimination, USSR

TUE
19
1965 - Demonstrations against Vietnam War, worldwide

WED
20
1943 - Death of Anita Augsburg, feminist pacifist, Germany

THU
21
1963 - Conscientious objection to military service statutorily recognised, France

SOLSTICE

FRI
22
1943 - Racial segregation ends after 4-month strike by 23 COs, Federal Penitentiary, Danbury, Connecticut, USA

SAT
23
1873 - Death of Sarah Grimke, Quaker abolitionist, S Carolina, USA

SUN
24
1914 - First air raid, by Germany, Dover, Britain

December

On Christmas Day you can't get sore.
Your fellow man you must adore.
Tom Lehrer

WEEK 52

MON

25

1963 - 10 fast for peace, Holy Loch, Scotland

CHRISTMAS DAY
(HOL UK/IRE/CAN/US)

TUE

26

1988 - Funeral of Chico Mendes, murdered for his struggle against destruction of rain forests, Brazil

ST STEPHEN'S DAY
(HOL UK/IRE/CAN)

WED

27

1993 - 12 killed in 2 days of Bosnian Serb shelling, Sarajevo, Bosnia

HOLY INNOCENTS' DAY

THU
28
1793 - Tom Paine arrested by Robespierre at height of "Revolutionary Terror", France

FRI
29
1993 - International Day for Biological Diversity first observed

SAT
30
2013 - 13 people killed in bomb attack on trolleybus, day after lethal attack at railway station, Volgograd, Russia

NEW YEAR'S EVE

SUN
31
1983 - Campaigners release firework rockets over nuclear power site, Gorleben, W Germany

Forward Planner 2024

	January		February		March	
Mon	1	1				
Tue	2					
Wed	3					
Thu	4		1			
Fri	5		2		1	
Sat	6		3		2	
Sun	7		4		3	
Mon	8	2	5	6	4	10
Tue	9		6		5	
Wed	10		7		6	
Thu	11		8		7	
Fri	12		9		8	
Sat	13		10		9	
Sun	14		11		10	
Mon	15	3	12	7	11	11
Tue	16		13		12	
Wed	17		14		13	
Thu	18		15		14	
Fri	19		16		15	
Sat	20		17		16	
Sun	21		18		17	
Mon	22	4	19		18	12
Tue	23		20	8	19	
Wed	24		21		20	
Thu	25		22		21	
Fri	26		23		22	
Sat	27		24		23	
Sun	28		25		24	
Mon	29	5	26	9	25	13
Tue	30		27		26	
Wed	31		28		27	
Thu			29		28	
Fri					29	
Sat					30	
Sun					31	Easter

Forward Planner 2024

	April		May		June	
Mon	1	14				
Tue	2					
Wed	3		1			
Thu	4		2			
Fri	5		3			
Sat	6		4		1	
Sun	7		5		2	
Mon	8	15	6	19	3	23
Tue	9		7		4	
Wed	10		8		5	
Thu	11		9		6	
Fri	12		10		7	
Sat	13		11		8	
Sun	14		12		9	
Mon	15	16	13	20	10	24
Tue	16		14		11	
Wed	17		15		12	
Thu	18		16		13	
Fri	19		17		14	
Sat	20		18		15	
Sun	21		19		16	
Mon	22	17	20	21	17	25
Tue	23		21		18	
Wed	24		22		19	
Thu	25		23		20	
Fri	26		24		21	
Sat	27		25		22	
Sun	28		26		23	
Mon	29	18	27	22	24	26
Tue	30		28		25	
Wed			29		26	
Thu			30		27	
Fri			31		28	
Sat					29	
Sun					30	

Forward Planner 2024

	July		August		September	
Mon	1	27				
Tue	2					
Wed	3					
Thu	4		1			
Fri	5		2			
Sat	6		3			
Sun	7		4		1	
Mon	8	28	5	32	2	36
Tue	9		6		3	
Wed	10		7		4	
Thu	11		8		5	
Fri	12		9		6	
Sat	13		10		7	
Sun	14		11		8	
Mon	15	29	12	33	9	37
Tue	16		13		10	
Wed	17		14		11	
Thu	18		15		12	
Fri	19		16		13	
Sat	20		17		14	
Sun	21		18		15	
Mon	22	30	19	34	16	38
Tue	23		20		17	
Wed	24		21		18	
Thu	25		22		19	
Fri	26		23		20	
Sat	27		24		21	
Sun	28		25		22	
Mon	29	31	26	35	23	39
Tue	30		27		24	
Wed	31		28		25	
Thu			29		26	
Fri			30		27	
Sat			31		28	
Sun					29	
Mon					30	40

Forward Planner 2024

	October		**November**		**December**	
Mon						
Tue	1					
Wed	2					
Thu	3					
Fri	4		1			
Sat	5		2			
Sun	6		3		1	
Mon	7	41	4	45	2	49
Tue	8		5		3	
Wed	9		6		4	
Thu	10		7		5	
Fri	11		8		6	
Sat	12		9		7	
Sun	13		10		8	
Mon	14	42	11	46	9	50
Tue	15		12		10	
Wed	16		13		11	
Thu	17		14		12	
Fri	18		15		13	
Sat	19		16		14	
Sun	20		17		15	
Mon	21	43	18	47	16	51
Tue	22		19		17	
Wed	23		20		18	
Thu	24		21		19	
Fri	25		22		20	
Sat	26		23		21	
Sun	27		24		22	
Mon	28	44	25	48	23	52
Tue	29		26		24	
Wed	30		27		25	
Thu	31		28		26	
Fri			29		27	
Sat			30		28	
Sun					29	
Mon					30	1
Tue					31	

Calendar 2022

JANUARY
- **MON** 3 10 17 24 31
- **TUE** 4 11 18 25
- **WED** 5 12 19 26
- **THU** 6 13 20 27
- **FRI** 7 14 21 28
- **SAT** 1 8 15 22 29
- **SUN** 2 9 16 23 30

FEBRUARY
- **MON** 7 14 21 28
- **TUE** 1 8 15 22
- **WED** 2 9 16 23
- **THU** 3 10 17 24
- **FRI** 4 11 18 25
- **SAT** 5 12 19 26
- **SUN** 6 13 20 27

MARCH
- **MON** 7 14 21 28
- **TUE** 1 8 15 22 29
- **WED** 2 9 16 23 30
- **THU** 3 10 17 24 31
- **FRI** 4 11 18 25
- **SAT** 5 12 19 26
- **SUN** 6 13 20 27

APRIL
- **MON** 4 11 18 25
- **TUE** 5 12 19 26
- **WED** 6 13 20 27
- **THU** 7 14 21 28
- **FRI** 1 8 15 22 29
- **SAT** 2 9 16 23 30
- **SUN** 3 10 17 24

MAY
- **MON** 2 9 16 23 30
- **TUE** 3 10 17 24 31
- **WED** 4 11 18 25
- **THU** 5 12 19 26
- **FRI** 6 13 20 27
- **SAT** 7 14 21 28
- **SUN** 1 8 15 22 29

JUNE
- **MON** 6 13 20 27
- **TUE** 7 14 21 28
- **WED** 1 8 15 22 29
- **THU** 2 9 16 23 30
- **FRI** 3 10 17 24
- **SAT** 4 11 18 25
- **SUN** 5 12 19 26

JULY
- **MON** 4 11 18 25
- **TUE** 5 12 19 26
- **WED** 6 13 20 27
- **THU** 7 14 21 28
- **FRI** 1 8 15 22 29
- **SAT** 2 9 16 23 30
- **SUN** 3 10 17 24 31

AUGUST
- **MON** 1 8 15 22 29
- **TUE** 2 9 16 23 30
- **WED** 3 10 17 24 31
- **THU** 4 11 18 25
- **FRI** 5 12 19 26
- **SAT** 6 13 20 27
- **SUN** 7 14 21 28

SEPTEMBER
- **MON** 5 12 19 26
- **TUE** 6 13 20 27
- **WED** 7 14 21 28
- **THU** 1 8 15 22 29
- **FRI** 2 9 16 23 30
- **SAT** 3 10 17 24
- **SUN** 4 11 18 25

OCTOBER
- **MON** 3 10 17 24 31
- **TUE** 4 11 18 25
- **WED** 5 12 19 26
- **THU** 6 13 20 27
- **FRI** 7 14 21 28
- **SAT** 1 8 15 22 29
- **SUN** 2 9 16 23 30

NOVEMBER
- **MON** 7 14 21 28
- **TUE** 1 8 15 22 29
- **WED** 2 9 16 23 30
- **THU** 3 10 17 24
- **FRI** 4 11 18 25
- **SAT** 5 12 19 26
- **SUN** 6 13 20 27

DECEMBER
- **MON** 5 12 19 26
- **TUE** 6 13 20 27
- **WED** 7 14 21 28
- **THU** 1 8 15 22 29
- **FRI** 2 9 16 23 30
- **SAT** 3 10 17 24 31
- **SUN** 4 11 18 25

Calendar 2023

JANUARY
MON 2 9 16 23 30
TUE 3 10 17 24 31
WED 4 11 18 25
THU 5 12 19 26
FRI 6 13 20 27
SAT 7 14 21 28
SUN 1 8 15 22 29

FEBRUARY
MON 6 13 20 27
TUE 7 14 21 28
WED 1 8 15 22
THU 2 9 16 23
FRI 3 10 17 24
SAT 4 11 18 25
SUN 5 12 19 26

MARCH
MON 6 13 20 27
TUE 7 14 21 28
WED 1 8 15 22 29
THU 2 9 16 23 30
FRI 3 10 17 24 31
SAT 4 11 18 25
SUN 5 12 19 26

APRIL
MON 3 10 17 24
TUE 4 11 18 25
WED 5 12 19 26
THU 6 13 20 27
FRI 7 14 21 28
SAT 1 8 15 22 29
SUN 2 9 16 23 30

MAY
MON 1 8 15 22 29
TUE 2 9 16 23 30
WED 3 10 17 24 31
THU 4 11 18 25
FRI 5 12 19 26
SAT 6 13 20 27
SUN 7 14 21 28

JUNE
MON 5 12 19 26
TUE 6 13 20 27
WED 7 14 21 28
THU 1 8 15 22 29
FRI 2 9 16 23 30
SAT 3 10 17 24
SUN 4 11 18 25

JULY
MON 3 10 17 24 31
TUE 4 11 18 25
WED 5 12 19 26
THU 6 13 20 27
FRI 7 14 21 28
SAT 1 8 15 22 29
SUN 2 9 16 23 30

AUGUST
MON 7 14 21 28
TUE 1 8 15 22 29
WED 2 9 16 23 30
THU 3 10 17 24 31
FRI 4 11 18 25
SAT 5 12 19 26
SUN 6 13 20 27

SEPTEMBER
MON 4 11 18 25
TUE 5 12 19 26
WED 6 13 20 27
THU 7 14 21 28
FRI 1 8 15 22 29
SAT 2 9 16 23 30
SUN 3 10 17 24

OCTOBER
MON 2 9 16 23 30
TUE 3 10 17 24 31
WED 4 11 18 25
THU 5 12 19 26
FRI 6 13 20 27
SAT 7 14 21 28
SUN 1 8 15 22 29

NOVEMBER
MON 6 13 20 27
TUE 7 14 21 28
WED 1 8 15 22 29
THU 2 9 16 23 30
FRI 3 10 17 24
SAT 4 11 18 25
SUN 5 12 19 26

DECEMBER
MON 4 11 18 25
TUE 5 12 19 26
WED 6 13 20 27
THU 7 14 21 28
FRI 1 8 15 22 29
SAT 2 9 16 23 30
SUN 3 10 17 24 31

Calendar 2024

JANUARY
- **MON** 1 8 15 22 29
- **TUE** 2 9 16 23 30
- **WED** 3 10 17 24 31
- **THU** 4 11 18 25
- **FRI** 5 12 19 26
- **SAT** 6 13 20 27
- **SUN** 7 14 21 28

FEBRUARY
- **MON** 5 12 19 26
- **TUE** 6 13 20 27
- **WED** 7 14 21 28
- **THU** 1 8 15 22 29
- **FRI** 2 9 16 23
- **SAT** 3 10 17 24
- **SUN** 4 11 18 25

MARCH
- **MON** 4 11 18 25
- **TUE** 5 12 19 26
- **WED** 6 13 20 27
- **THU** 7 14 21 28
- **FRI** 1 8 15 22 29
- **SAT** 2 9 16 23 30
- **SUN** 3 10 17 24 31

APRIL
- **MON** 1 8 15 22 29
- **TUE** 2 9 16 23 30
- **WED** 3 10 17 24
- **THU** 4 11 18 25
- **FRI** 5 12 19 26
- **SAT** 6 13 20 27
- **SUN** 7 14 21 28

MAY
- **MON** 6 13 20 27
- **TUE** 7 14 21 28
- **WED** 1 8 15 22 29
- **THU** 2 9 16 23 30
- **FRI** 3 10 17 24 31
- **SAT** 4 11 18 25
- **SUN** 5 12 19 26

JUNE
- **MON** 3 10 17 24
- **TUE** 4 11 18 25
- **WED** 5 12 19 26
- **THU** 6 13 20 27
- **FRI** 7 14 21 28
- **SAT** 1 8 15 22 29
- **SUN** 2 9 16 23 30

JULY
- **MON** 1 8 15 22 29
- **TUE** 2 9 16 23 30
- **WED** 3 10 17 24 31
- **THU** 4 11 18 25
- **FRI** 5 12 19 26
- **SAT** 6 13 20 27
- **SUN** 7 14 21 28

AUGUST
- **MON** 5 12 19 26
- **TUE** 6 13 20 27
- **WED** 7 14 21 28
- **THU** 1 8 15 22 29
- **FRI** 2 9 16 23 30
- **SAT** 3 10 17 24 31
- **SUN** 4 11 18 25

SEPTEMBER
- **MON** 2 9 16 23
- **TUE** 3 10 17 24
- **WED** 4 11 18 25
- **THU** 5 12 19 26
- **FRI** 6 13 20 27
- **SAT** 7 14 21 28
- **SUN** 1 8 15 22 29

OCTOBER
- **MON** 7 14 21 28
- **TUE** 1 8 15 22 29
- **WED** 2 9 16 23 30
- **THU** 3 10 17 24 31
- **FRI** 4 11 18 25
- **SAT** 5 12 19 26
- **SUN** 6 13 20 27

NOVEMBER
- **MON** 4 11 18 25
- **TUE** 5 12 19 26
- **WED** 6 13 20 27
- **THU** 7 14 21 28
- **FRI** 1 8 15 22 29
- **SAT** 2 9 16 23 30
- **SUN** 3 10 17 24

DECEMBER
- **MON** 2 9 16 23 30
- **TUE** 3 10 17 24 31
- **WED** 4 11 18 25
- **THU** 5 12 19 26
- **FRI** 6 13 20 27
- **SAT** 7 14 21 28
- **SUN** 1 8 15 22 29

HOUSMANS
World Peace Directory
● 2023 ●

This Directory is provided for the *Peace Diary* by the **Housmans Peace Resource Project**, and edited by Albert Beale. **To make the best use of it, please read the next two pages.**

There is a difficult balance to be struck between the usefulness, for many people, of the information in this format, and the fact that the full World Peace Database — from which this Directory is derived — is available on-line at **www.housmans.info/wpd**. Your feedback about this is encouraged.

Groups omitted from this printed version tend to be the more localised or specialised groups — and those which are least efficient at responding to communications from the database editor! The complete on-line information is searchable, and it is also possible to obtain your own copy of the full database.

To keep the database up to date, organisations are contacted from time to time by post, and also (where possible) by e-mail. But we rely on other input as well: if your group changes any of its contact details, please send the information without waiting to be asked. There is never a wrong time to send information.

This Directory is copyright © Housmans Peace Resource Project, 2022. Even where non-profit organisations are allowed to re-use sections of the Directory at nominal charge, permission must be obtained first.

Disclaimer: Organisations listed are not necessarily responsible for their inclusion, nor for the way they are described, nor for the terminology used to describe their country.

All correspondence about the Directory should be sent to: **Housmans Peace Resource Project, 5 Caledonian Road, London N1, UK** (tel +44-20-7278 4474; e-mail worldpeace@gn.apc.org). Information is preferred in writing.

Directory Introduction

This is the 70th Peace Directory to be published with the Housmans Peace Diary. It is intended to help people find contact points for issues which interest them, and also to be a day-to-day reference resource for activists.

What's in the Directory?

The 2023 Directory lists over 1400 national and international organisations, covering the breadth of the peace movement – with the emphasis on grassroots, non-governmental groups – as well as major bodies in related fields such as environmental and human rights campaigning.

This year, around one-third of the groups listed have either had their information amended since last year's Directory, or are newly included this year.

How to find things in the Directory

Check both the national and international listings if necessary. If you can't find exactly what you want, try a less specialised organisation which might include what you're looking for. (And see the previous page for the availability of further information.)

International organisations are listed alphabetically. The national listings are in alphabetical order of English-language country name; the organisations are then arranged alphabetically within each country. Organisations' names (and addresses) are generally in the language of the country concerned.

Whilst aware of political sensitivities, we use commonly accepted postal and administrative divisions of the world to decide what is or isn't a "country". This doesn't mean we support or oppose countries' divisions or mergers – we just want the Directory to be easy to use.

In the national listings we don't repeat the country name at the end of each address, so you will need to add it.

How the entries are set out

The organisation's name is in **bold print**; or, if the name is that of a magazine, in ***bold italics***. Any common abbreviation is shown [in square brackets], in **bold** or ***bold italics*** as appropriate. Most organisations then have codes (in round brackets) giving an indication of their politics and activities (**see Note 1**). The address is shown next. Then we give (in brackets) any telephone number (**see Note 2**), fax number (**see Note 3**), electronic mail address (**see Note 4**), and web site address (**see Note 4**). Magazines published by the organisation are then shown in *italics*. Where the listing is itself a publication, details of frequency etc may be given next (**see Note 5**). There may be brief additional information where necessary.

The **Notes**, including our standard abbreviations, are given opposite.

Notes

1. Codes used to explain something about the listed organisation are as follows. The codes for international bodies in the left-hand column are used to show an official link to tbe body (or to one of its national affiliates in the country concerned). If these are not sufficient, the general codes on the right are used.

   AI Amnesty International
   FE Friends of the Earth International
   FR International Fellowship of Reconciliation
   GP Greenpeace International
   IB International Peace Bureau
   IP International Physicians for the Prevention of Nuclear War
   PC Pax Christi International
   SC Service Civil International
   SE Servas International
   SF Society of Friends (Quakers)
   UN World Federation of United Nations Associations
   WL Women's International League for Peace and Freedom
   WP World Peace Council
   WR War Resisters' International

   AL Alternativist / Anarchist
   AT Arms Trade / Conversion
   CD Citizen Diplomacy / People-to-People
   CR Conflict Resolution / Mediation
   DA Disarmament / Arms Control
   EL Environmental / Ecological
   HR Equality / Minority & Human Rights
   ND Nuclear Disarmament
   PA Anti-Militarist / Pacifist
   PO Positive Action / Lifestyle
   RA Radical Action / Direct Action
   RE Research into Peace, Conflict / Peace Education
   RP Religious Peace Group
   SD Social Defence / Civilian-Based Defence
   TR War Tax Resistance / Peace Tax Campaigning
   TW Development / Liberation / Third World
   WC International Workcamps
   WF World Federalists / World Citizens

2. Telephone numbers are given in standard international format: +[country code]-[area code]-[local number]. The "+" indicates the international access code used in the country you're phoning from. The area code (if there is one) is given without any national trunk prefix digit(s) that are used in the country concerned – for calls *within* the country you must add them if they exist. Exceptionally, a few countries without area codes still require an extra digit (generally 0) at the start of their national number for internal calls; the main culprits are Belgium, France, Switzerland, South Africa and Thailand. Note that for calls between neighbouring countries there are often non-standard codes outside the normal system.

3. The telephone number of a facsimile (telefax) machine is given without repeating codes which are the same as in the preceding ordinary telephone number; "fax" alone means the fax number is identical to the phone number. Because many groups share a fax machine, always start your message by saying clearly which person and organisation it is meant for.

4. The e-mail and web site addresses are given in standard internet format. (The e-mail address is the one with the "@" in it.) The "http://" which, by definition, starts every web address is **not** repeated each time here.

5. Abbreviations used in connection with publications are:

   dly daily
   wkly weekly
   ftly fortnightly
   mthly monthly
   x yrly x per year
   annl annual
   irreg irregular
   occl occasional
   ea each
   pa per annum
   ftm free to members
   nfp no fixed price / donation

INTERNATIONAL ORGANISATIONS

Abolition 2000 International Secretariat (ND EL), c/o METO, 62 Traps Lane, New Malden KT3 4SE, Britain (secretariat@abolition2000.org) (www.abolition2000.org).
Global network to eliminate nuclear weapons.

Alliance Against Genocide (HR), c/o Genocide Watch, 1405 Cola Drive, McLean, VA 22101, USA (+1-202-643 1405) (communications@genocidewatch.org) (www.genocidewatch.com).
Formerly Alliance Against Genocide.

Alternatives to Violence Project International (CR), PO Box 164, Purchase, NY 10577, USA (avp.international).
International network of national AVP-organisations. AVP groups organise training to aid creative responses to potentially violent situations.

Amnesty International – International Secretariat [AI] (HR RE), Peter Benenson House, 1 Easton St, London WC1X 0DW, Britain (+44-20-7413 5500) (fax 7956 1157) (contactus@amnesty.org) (www.amnesty.org).
Newsletter, *Annual Report*.
East Asia office (Hong Kong) +852-3963 7100;
Southern Africa office (Johannesburg) +27-11-283 6000;
Middle East and North Africa office (Beirut) +961-1-748751.

Architects & Planners for Justice in Palestine [APJP] (HR), c/o 100 Whitchurch Lane, Edgware, Middx HA8 6QN, Britain (info@apjp.org) (apjp.org).

Association of World Citizens [AWC] (WF CD RE), 60 Traverse des Passets, 07140 Gravières, France (rene.wadlow@gmail.com) (awcunited.org).

Association pour la Prévention de la Torture / Association for the Prevention of Torture [APT] (HR), BP 137, 1211 Genève 19, Switzerland (+41-22 919 2170) (fax 22 919 2180) (apt@apt.ch) (www.apt.ch).
Works to improve legal frameworks and detention monitoring, to prevent torture and other ill-treatment.

Bellona Foundation (EL), Vulkan 11, 0178 Oslo, Norway (+47-2323 4600) (fax 2238 3862) (info@bellona.no) (bellona.no).
Other international office in Brussels. Offices also in Russia (Murmansk and St Petersburg).

Center for Global Nonkilling [CGNK] (RE PA), 3653 Tantalus Dr, Honolulu, HI 96822-5033, USA (+1-808-536 7442) (info@nonkilling.org) (nonkilling.org).
To promote change towards the measurable goal of a killing-free world.

Child Rights International Network [CRIN] (HR), Unit 4, Old Paradise Yard, 20 Carlisle Lane, London SE1 7LG, Britain (info@crin.org) (home.crin.org). Supports UN Convention on rights of children. Work includes opposing mutilation of children.

Church and Peace (SF FR PC), Mittelstr 4, 34874 Diemlstadt-Wethen, Germany (+49-5694-990 5506) (fax 1532) (IntlOffice@church-and-peace.org) (www.church-and-peace.org).
Theology and Peace / Théologie et Paix / Theologie und Frieden.
European ecumenical network.

Climate Action Network International [CAN] (EL), Khaldeh, Dakdouk Bldg – 3rd floor, Mount Lebanon, Lebanon (+961-1-447192) (fax 448649) (administration@climatenetwork.org) (www.climatenetwork.org).
Network of 1300 organisations in 120 countries.

Co-ordinating Committee for International Voluntary Service [CCIVS] (SC TW WC EL HR), UNESCO House, 1 rue Miollis, 75732 Paris Cedex 15, France (+33-14568 4936) (fax 14568 4934) (secretariat@ccivs.org) (www.ccivs.org).

Coalition for Peace in Africa / Coalition pour la Paix en Afrique [COPA] (CR RE), PO Box 61753, 00200 Nairobi, Kenya (+254-20-386 6686) (www.copafrica.org).

Discover Peace in Europe (CD RE), c/o Konfliktkultur, Breitenfeldergasse 2/14, 1080 Wien, Germany (office@discoverpeace.eu) (www.discoverpeace.eu).
Outdoor learning; Peace Trails.

Ecumenical Accompaniment Programme in Palestine and Israel [EAPPI] (RP HR CD CR SF), c/o World Council of Churches (Public Witness section), PO Box 2100, 1211 Genève 2, Switzerland (+41-22 791 6108) (fax 22 791 6122) (eappi@wcc-coe.org) (www.eappi.org).
Accompanying Palestinians and Israelis in non-violent actions; advocacy to end occupation.
Also: PO Box 741, Jerusalem 91000 (+972-2-626 2458).

European Bureau for Conscientious Objection [EBCO] (WR SC), 35 Rue Van Elewyck, 1050 Bruxelles, Belgium (+32-2 648 5220) (ebco@ebco-beoc.org) (www.ebco-beoc.org).

European Institute of Peace [EIP] (RE), Rue des deux Églises 25, 1000 Bruxelles, Belgium (+32-2 430 7360) (info@eip.org) (www.eip.org).

INTERNATIONAL ORGANISATIONS

Independent, "augmenting EU's peace agenda".
European Network Against Arms Trade [ENAAT] (AT), Anna Spenglerstr 71, 1054 NH Amsterdam, Netherlands (+31-20-616 4684) (info@stopwapenhandel.org) (www.enaat.org).
European Peacebuilding Liaison Office [EPLO] (RE), Ave de Tervueren 12, 1040 Bruxelles, Belgium (+32-2 233 3737) (office@eplo.org) (eplo.org). Network of NGOs and others involved in peacebuilding work, promoting relevant policies at EU level.
Every Casualty (RE), 86-90 Paul St, London EC2A 4NE, Britain (team@everycasualty.org) (www.everycasualty.org). Systematic documentation of conflict casualties. Aims to ensure that the full cost of conflict is known and can be understood.
Fédération Internationale de l'Action des Chrétiens pour l'Abolition de la Torture [FIACAT] (HR), 27 rue de Maubeuge, 75009 Paris, France (+33-14280 0160) (fax 14280 2089) (fiacat@fiacat.org) (www.fiacat.org).
Fédération Internationale des Ligues des Droits de l'Homme [FIDH] (HR), 17 Passage de la Main d'Or, 75011 Paris, France (+33-14355 2518) (fax 14355 1880) (contact@fidh.org) (www.fidh.org). International Federation of Human Rights Leagues. At EU: +32-2 609 4423. At UN: +1-646-395 7103. At ICC: +31-70-356 0259.
Friends of the Earth International [FoEI] (EL), PO Box 19199, 1000 GD Amsterdam, Netherlands (+31-20-622 1369) (fax 639 2181) (www.foei.org). Europe office in Brussels (+32-2 893 1000) (www.foeeurope.org).
Friends World Committee for Consultation [FWCC] (SF), 173 Euston Rd, London NW1, Britain (+44-20-7663 1199) (world@friendsworldoffice.org) (fwccworld.org). Also 4 regional offices. Africa: PO Box 41946, Nairobi, Kenya; Americas: 1506 Race St, Philadelphia, PA 19102, USA; Asia & West Pacific: PO Box 6063, O'Connor, ACT 2602, Australia; Europe & Middle East: PO Box 1157, Histon CB24 9XQ, Cambs, Britain.
Gesellschaft für Bedrohte Völker – International (HR TW), Postfach 2024, 37010 Göttingen, Germany (+49-551-499060) (fax 58028) (info@gfbv.de) (www.gfbv.de). *Pogrom*. Society for Threatened Peoples. Campaigns against genocide and ethnocide.
Global Anabaptist Peace Network (RP), c/o Mennonite World Conference, 50 Kent Ave – Suite 206, Kitchener, ON, N2G 3R1, Canada (+1-519-571 0060) (fax 226-647 4224) (Kitchener@mwc-cmm.org).
Global Campaign Against US/NATO Military Bases (ND CD), c/o Peace and Neutrality Alliance, 17 Castle St, Dalkey, Co Dublin, Ireland, Republic of (contact@noUSNATOBases.org) (nousnatobases.org). Worldwide network.
Global Campaign on Military Spending – Co-ordination Office [GCOMS] (DA AT), c/o Centre Delàs d'Estudis per la Pau, c/ Erasme de Janer 8 – entresol – despatx 9, 08001 Barcelona, Spain (+34-93-441 1947) (coordination.gcoms@ipb.org) (demilitarize.eu). Organise Global Day of Action on Military Spending. A project of the International Peace Bureau; main IPB office in Berlin (+49-30-1208 4549).
Global Ecumenical Network for the Abolition of Military Chaplaincies (RP), c/o IDK, Postfach 280312, 13443 Berlin, Germany (global-network@militaerseelsorge-abschaffen.de) (www.globnetabolishmilitarychaplaincy.webnode.com). Opposes co-option of churches by military, financial links between arms industry and churches, and churches' acceptance of warfare.
Global Initiative to End All Corporal Punishment of Children (HR), The Foundry, 17 Oval Way, London SE11, Britain (+44-20-7713 0569) (info@endcorporalpunishment.org) (www.endcorporalpunishment.org).
Global Network Against Weapons and Nuclear Power in Space (PA EL RA), PO Box 652, Brunswick, ME 04011, USA (+1-207-607 4255) (globalnet@mindspring.com) (www.space4peace.org).
Global Partnership for the Prevention of Armed Conflict [GPPAC] (RE CR), Alexanderveld 5, 2585 DB Den Haag, Netherlands (+31-70-311 0970) (info@gppac.net) (www.gppac.net).
Greenpeace International (EL), Ottho Heldringstr 5, 1066 AZ Amsterdam, Netherlands (+31-20-718 2000) (fax 718 2002) (info.int@greenpeace.org) (www.greenpeace.org/international).

For explanation of codes and abbreviations, see introduction

INTERNATIONAL ORGANISATIONS

Housmans Peace Resource Project [HPRP] (CD RE), 5 Caledonian Rd, London N1, Britain (+44-20-7278 4474) (fax 7278 0444) (worldpeace@gn.apc.org) (www.housmans.info).
Housmans World Peace Database & Directory.

Human Rights in China [HRIC] (HR), 110 Wall St, New York, NY 10005, USA (+1-212-239 4495) (hrichina@hrichina.org) (www.hrichina.org). Hong Kong Office (+852-2710 8021) (hrichk@hrichina.org).

Human Rights Watch [HRW] (HR), Empire State Building – 34th Floor, 350 5th Ave, New York, NY 10118-3299, USA (+1-212-290 4700) (fax 736 1300) (www.hrw.org).
EU liaison office in Brussels (+32-2 732 2009) (fax 2 732 0471).
Offices also in: Britain, Canada, France, Germany, Netherlands, South Africa.

Humanists International (HR PO), The Foundry, 17 Oval Way, Vauxhall, London SE11 5RR, Britain (+44-20-3923 0244) (humanists.international).
Formerly International Humanist and Ethical Union.

Institute for Economics and Peace (RE), 205 Pacific Hwy, St Leonards, Sydney, NSW 2065, Australia (+61-2-9901 8500) (info@economicsandpeace.org) (economicsandpeace.org).
Office also in (+1-646-963 2160).

International Action Network on Small Arms [IANSA] (AT DA), 777 United Nations Plaza – 3E, Nww York, NY 10017, USA (communication@iansa.org) (www.iansa.org).

International Association of Lawyers Against Nuclear Arms [IALANA] (IB ND AT DA), Marienstr 19/20, 10117 Berlin, Germany (+49-30-2065 4857) (fax 2065 3837) (office@ialana.info) (www.ialana.info).
UN office: c/o LCNP, +1-212-818 1861; Pacific office: +64-9-524 8403.

International Campaign for Boycott, Disinvestment and Sanctions Against Israel (HR RA), c/o PACBI, PO Box 1701, Ramallah, West Bank, Palestine (bdsmovement.net).

International Campaign to Abolish Nuclear Weapons [ICAN] (ND), 150 Route de Ferney, 1211 Genève 2, Switzerland (+41-22 788 2063) (info@icanw.org) (www.icanw.org).
Launched by IPPNW and others in 2007. Promotes implementation of nuclear ban treaty.
Asia Pacific office, Australia (+61-3-9023 1958).

International Coalition to Ban Uranium Weapons [ICBUW] (AT DA), Marienstr 19-20, 10117 Berlin, Germany (+49-30-2065 4857) (info@icbuw.eu) (www.icbuw.eu).

International Committee for Robot Arms Control [ICRAC] (AT DA), c/o Noel Sharkey, Department of Computer Science, University of Sheffield, Western Bank, Sheffield 10, Yorks, Britain (www.icrac.net).
For peaceful use of robotics. Campaigns for regulation of robot weapons.

International Fellowship of Reconciliation [IFOR] (RP IB), Postbus 1528, 3500 BM Utrecht, Netherlands (+31-30-303 9930) (office@ifor.org) (www.ifor.org).

International Friendship League [IFL] (CD), PO Box 217, Ross-on-Wye HR9 9FD, Britain (+44-1989-566745) (info@iflworld.org) (iflworld.org). *Courier.*

International Network of Engineers and Scientists for Global Responsibility [INES] (DA ND), Marienstr 19-20, 10117 Berlin, Germany (+49-30-3199 6686) (fax 3199 6689) (office@inesglobal.net) (www.inesglobal.net).

International Network of Museums for Peace [INMP] (IB RE), c/o Kyoto Museum for World Peace, 56-1 Toji-in Kitamachi, Kita, Kyoto 603-8577, Japan (inmpoffice@gmail.com) (tinyurl.com/INMPMuseumsForPeace).
Worldwide network of peace museums, gardens, and other peace-related sites, centres and institutions, which share the desire to build a culture of peace.

International Network on Explosive Weapons [INEW] (DA), c/o Article 36, The Coalface – Runway East, 46 Clifton Terrace, London N4, Britain (www.inew.org).
Works for prohibition of and restrictions on uses of explosive weapons in populated areas.

International Peace Bureau [IPB] (AT TW RE ND TR), Marienstr 19-20, 10117 Berlin, Germany (+49-30-1208 4549) (info@ipb-office.berlin) (www.ipb.org).
IPB News.
Main programme: disarmament for development. Work includes Global Campaign on Military Spending.
Most broadly-based international peace networking body.
Also office in Geneva; and GCOMS co-ordination office in Barcelona.

International Peace Institute [IPI] (RE DA CR), 777 United Nations Plaza, New York, NY 10017-3521, USA (+1-212-687 4300) (fax 983 8246) (ipi@ipinst.org) (www.ipinst.org).

INTERNATIONAL ORGANISATIONS

Supports multilateral disarmament negotiations. Independent think-tank – "promoting the prevention and settlement of conflict". Offices also in Austria and Bahrain.

International Peace Research Association [IPRA] (RE), c/o Risk and Conflict Network, Dept of Media & Communication Design, Northumbria University, Newcastle-upon-Tyne NE1 8ST, Britain (+44-191-227 3567) (info@iprapeace.org) (www.iprapeace.org).

International Physicians for the Prevention of Nuclear War [IPPNW] (ND RE TW), 339 Fillmore St – Third floor, Malden, MA 02148, USA (+1-617-440 1733) (ippnwbos@ippnw.org) (ippnw.org).

International Tibet Network (HR), 1310 Fillmore St – Suite 401, San Francisco, CA 94115, USA (+1-988-225 5516) (mail@tibetnetwork.org) (www.tibetnetwork.org).
Links 180 groups around the world. Local Tibet support groups also via www.tibet.org.

Interpeace (CR), 2E Chemin Eugène-Rigot, 1202 Genève, Switzerland (+41-22 404 5900) (fax 22 404 5901) (info@interpeace.org) (www.interpeace.org).
Set up by UN; now independent peacebuilding group. Supports societies to build lasting peace.
Regional offices: Nairobi, Abidjan, Guatemala City, New York, Brussels.

Mayors for Peace (CD ND DA), c/o Hiroshima Peace Culture Foundation, 1-5 Nakajima-cho, Naka-ku, Hiroshima 730-0811, Japan (+81-82-242 7821) (fax 242 7452) (mayorcon@pcf.city.hiroshima.jp) (www.mayorsforpeace.org).
Mayors for Peace Newsletter.

Middle East Treaty Organisation [METO] (ND CD), 62 Traps Lane, New Malden KT3 4SE, Britain (meto@wmd-free.me) (www.wmd-free.me). Civil society network. Seeks to rid Middle East of weapons of mass destruction.

NATO Watch (DA ND RE), The Bothy, 29 Erradale, Gairloch IV21 2DS, Britain (+44-1445 771086) (idavis@natowatch.org) (natowatch.org).
Observatory.
Collates information about NATO. Provides regular briefings.

Network for Religious and Traditional Peacemakers (RP), c/o Finn Church Aid, PO Box 210, 00131 Helsinki, Finland (www.peacemakersnetwork.org).

Network of European Peace Scientists [NEPS], c/o Arzu Kıbrıs, Rm E2.08, University of Warwick, Coventry CV4 7AL, Britain (info@europeanpeacescientists.org) (www.europeanpeacescientists.org)

No First Use Global (ND), c/o Prague Vision, Ostrovského 253/3 – Suite 4061, 15000 Praha 5, Czech Republic (info@nofirstuse.global) (www.nofirstuse.global).
Coalition for adoption of no-first-use policy by nuclear-armed states.

No to War – No to NATO / Na i Ryfel! – Na i NATO / Não à Guerra – Não à NATO (RA DA ND), c/o IALANA, Marienstr 19-20, 10117 Berlin, Germany (+41-30-2065 4857) (fax 2065 3837) (info@no-to-nato.org) (www.no-to-nato.org).
International network to delegitimise NATO. Co-ordination of groups in many NATO states; organises actions against NATO events.
Also c/o Arielle Denis, Mouvement de la Paix, in France (Arielle.Denis@mvtpaix.org).

Nonviolence International (IB PA), PO Box 39127, Friendship Station NW, Washington, DC 20016, USA (+1-202-244 0951) (info@nonviolenceinternational.net) (www.nonviolenceinternational.net).
Links resource centres promoting use of non-violent action.

Nonviolent Peaceforce [NP] (CR HR), Rue de Lausanne 82, 1202 Genève, Switzerland (+41-22-552 6610) (headoffice@nonviolentpeaceforce.org) (www.nonviolentpeaceforce.org).
Office in USA (+1-612-871 0005).

Northeast Asia Regional Peacebuilding Institute [NARPI] (RE CR), 25 Goongchon-ro, Wabu-eup, Namyangju-si, Gyeonggi-do 12269, Korea, South (+82-70-8817 8690) (fax -31-521 8695) (admin@narpi.net) (narpi.net).

Organisation for the Prohibition of Chemical Weapons [OPCW] (DA), Johan de Wittlaan 32, 2517 JR Den Haag, Netherlands (+31-70-416 3300) (fax 360 3535) (public.affairs@opcw.org) (www.opcw.org).

Orthodox Peace Fellowship [OPF] (FR), Kanisstr 5, 1811 GJ Alkmaar, Netherlands (+31-72-515 4180) (office@incommunion.org) (incommunion.org).
In Communion.

Palestinian Return Centre [PRC] (HR), 100 H Crown House, 60 North Circular Rd, London NW10 7PN, Britain (+44-20-8453 0919) (fax 8453 0994) (info@prc.org.uk) (www.prc.org.uk).

For explanation of codes and abbreviations, see introduction

INTERNATIONAL ORGANISATIONS

Parliamentarians for Nuclear Non-proliferation and Disarmament [PNND] (ND), c/o Prague Vision Institute for Sustainable Security, Lipanská 4, 13000 Praha 3, Czech Republic (+420-773 638867) (alyn@pnnd.org) (pnnd.org).
Europe office, Basel; UN office, New York. Also London office.
Provides parliamentarians with information on nuclear weapons policies; helps them become engaged in nuclear non-proliferation and disarmament.

Pax Christi International (RP IB CD RE CR), Ave de la Reine 141, 1030 Bruxelles, Belgium (+32-2 502 5550) (fax 2 502 4626) (hello@paxchristi.net) (www.paxchristi.net). Network of autonomous organisations – Catholic.

Peace Brigades International / Brigadas Internacionales de Paz / Brigades de Paix Internationales [PBI] (HR CD CR RE), Village Partenaire, Rue de Fernard Bernier 15, 1060 Bruxelles, Belgium (+32 2 543 4443) (admin@peacebrigades.org) (www.peacebrigades.org).
Projects in Colombia, Guatemala, Mexico, Honduras, Kenya, Indonesia.

Peace Research Institute Oslo / Institutt for Fredsforskning [PRIO] (RE CR), PO Box 9229, Grønland, 0134 Oslo, Norway (+47-2254 7700) (fax 2254 7701) (info@prio.no) (www.prio.no).
Journal of Peace Research; *Security Dialogue*.
Journals from: SAGE Publications, 6 Bonhill St, London EC2, Britain (+44-20-7374 0645).

Peacebuilding Support Office of the United Nations (CR RE), UN Secretariat – 30th Floor, New York, NY 10017, USA (+1-212-963 9999) (www.un.org/en/peacebuilding).
Formerly United Nations Peacebuilding Commission.

PEN International (HR), Unit A, Koops Mill Mews, 162-164 Abbey St, London SE1 2AN, Britain (+44-20-7405 0338) (info@pen-international.org) (www.pen-international.org).
Includes Writers in Prison Committee, Writers for Peace Committee.

People to People International [PTPI] (CD), 2405 Grand Blvd – Suite 500, Kansas City, MO 64108, USA (+1-816-531 4701) (fax 561 7502) (ptpi@ptpi.org) (www.ptpi.org).

Principles for Peace [P4P] (RE), c/o Interpeace, Maison de la Paix, 2E Chemin Eugène-Rigot, 1201 Genève, Switzerland (+41-22-404 5900) (fax 404 5901) (principlesforpeace.org).
Bridging gap betweeen policy and action.

Privacy International (HR), 62 Britton St, London EC1, Britain (+44-20-3422 4321) (info@privacyinternational.org) (www.privacyinternational.org).
For data protection, and control of surveillance.

Pugwash Conferences on Science and World Affairs (ND EL RE TW), 1211 Connecticut Ave NW – Suite 800, Washington, DC 20036, USA (+1-202-478 3440) (pugwashdc@aol.com) (pugwash.org).
Offices also in Rome (+39-06-687 8376), Geneva (+41-22 907 3667), London (+44-20-7405 6661).

Quaker Council for European Affairs [QCEA] (SF HR PA EL AT), Square Ambiorix 50, 1000 Brussel, Belgium (+32-2 234 3061) (office@qcea.org) (www.qcea.org).

Quaker UN Office – Geneva [QUNO] (SF HR TW EL CR), 13 Av du Mervelet, 1209 Genève, Switzerland (+41-22 748 4800) (fax 22 748 4819) (quno@quno.ch) (www.quno.org).
Geneva Reporter.

Registry of World Citizens [WCR] (WF IB WP RE), Les Nids, 49190 St Aubin de Luigné, France (abc@recim.org) (www.recim.org).

Religions for Peace (RP IB RE CR TW), 777 United Nations Plaza, New York, NY 10017, USA (+1-212-687 2163) (fax 983 0098) (info@rfp.org) (religionsforpeace.org).
Formerly World Conference of Religions for Peace.
Regional offices in Asia, Europe, Latin America, Africa.

Resist China (HR), c/o International Tibet Network, 1310 Fillmore St, San Francisco, CA 94115, USA (campaigns@tibetnetwork.com) (resistchina.org).
Links campaigns resisting authoritarian regime. Works in relation to Tibet, Hong Kong, Uyghurs, Mongolian culture, threats to Taiwan.

Schengen Peace Foundation & World Peace Forum (RE), 14 rue Mathias Hardt, 1717 Luxembourg, Luxembourg (+352-223294) (info@worldpeaceforum.org) (www.worldpeaceforum.org).

School Day of Non-Violence and Peace / Día Escolar de la No-Violencia y la Paz [DENIP] (RE), Apdo Postal 77, 11510 Puerto Real, Spain (denip.pax@gmail.com) (denip.webcindario.com).
(30 January, anniversary of Mahatma Gandhi's death).

INTERNATIONAL ORGANISATIONS

Sea Shepherd (EL RA), PO Box 8628, Alexadria, VA 22306, USA (+1-818-736 8357) (fax -360-370 5651) (info@seashepherd.org) (seashepherd.org).
Nature conservation on the high seas. Use direct action to confront those attacking the ecosystem.

Search for Common Ground – Brussels Office (RE CD CR), Rue Belliard 205 – bte 13, 1040 Bruxelles, Belgium (+32-2 736 7262) (fax 2 732 3033) (brussels@sfcg.org) (www.sfcg.org).
Conflict transformation projects in 34 countries.
Washington DC Office (+1-202-265 4300); West Africa Office, Freetown (+232-22-223479).

Sennacieca Asocio Tutmonda – Worker Esperantists [SAT] (CD PA EL HR), 67 Av Gambetta, 75020 Paris, France (+33-14797 7190) (kontakto@satesperanto.org) (www.satesperanto.org).
Sennaciulo.

Servas International [SI] (CD PO), c/o Jonny Sågänger, Reimersholmsgatan 47 – plan 2, 11740 Stockholm, Sweden (helpdesk@servas.org) (www.servas.org).
World hospitality network for peace and goodwill. Building understanding by facilitating personal contacts between people of different nationalities.

Service Civil International – International Office [SCI] (WC PA TW PO HR), Belgiëlei 37, 2018 Antwerpen, Belgium (+32-3 226 5727) (info@sciint.org) (sci.ngo).

Service International pour les Droits de l'Homme / International Service for Human Rights (HR), CP 16, 1211 Genève 20, Switzerland (+41-22 919 7100) (information@ishr.ch) (www.ishr.ch).
Runs project to protect human rights defenders.
Also New York office (+1-212-490 2199) (information.ny@ishr.ch).

Stay Grounded (EL), c/o Periskop, Neustiftgasse 36, 1070 Wien, Austria (info@stay-grounded.org) (stay-grounded.org).
Campaigns for elimination of most aviation. For transition to mobility justice.

Stockholm International Peace Research Institute [SIPRI] (RE), Signalistgatan 9, 16972 Solna, Sweden (+46-8-655 9700) (sipri@sipri.org) (www.sipri.org).
SIPRI Yearbook.

Stop the War in Ukraine (DA CR), c/o CND, 162 Holloway Rd, London N7 8DQ, Britain (www.peaceinukraine.org).
International network opposing both Russian invasion and NATO expansion. Supporting ceasefire and negotiations rather than any "victory".

Third World Network [TWN] (TW), 131 Jalan Macalister, 10400 Penang, Malaysia (+60-4-226 6728) (fax 226 4505) (twn@twnetwork.org) (www.twn.my).
Third World Resurgence; Third World Network Features.
Latin America Secretariat: ITEM, Av 18 de Julio 2095/301, Montevideo 11200, Uruguay.
Africa Secretariat: 9 Ollenu St, PO Box AN 19452, Accra-North, Ghana (fax +233-21-511188).
Also publishes *South-North Development Monitor (SUNS).*

Transnational Institute [TNI] (HR ND RE TW EL), PO Box 14656, 1001 LD Amsterdam, Netherlands (+31-20-662 6608) (fax 675 7176) (tni@tni.org) (www.tni.org).
Transnational Institute Series.
Research in support of social movements.

UN Non-Governmental Liaison Service (New York Office) [UN-NGLS] (EL HR PO TW), Room DC1-1106, United Nations, New York, NY 10017, USA (+1-212-963 3125) (fax 963 8712) (info@un-ngls.org) (www.un-ngls.org).

UN Research Institute for Social Development [UNRISD] (HR TW EL), Palais des Nations, 1211 Genève 10, Switzerland (+41-22 917 3020) (fax 22 917 0650) (info.unrisd@un.org) (www.unrisd.org).
UNRISD News.
Research on social dimensions of problems affecting development.
Research programmes include: Social Policy and Development; Sustainable Development; Gender and Development.

Unfold Zero (ND), c/o Basel Peace Office, University of Basel, Petersgraben 27, 4051 Basel, Switzerland (info@unfoldzero.org) (www.unfoldzero.org).
Network for nuclear weapons abolition. Focus on action through UN system. Joint project of various disarmament campaigns.

UNICEF, 3 United Nations Plaza, New York, NY 10017, USA (+1-212-326 7000) (fax 887 7465) (aaltamirano@unicef.org) (www.unicef.org).

United Nations Department for Disarmament Affairs (AT CR ND DA), UN Headquarters Bldg (Rm DN25-12), New York, NY 10017, USA (+1-212-963 1570) (fax 963 4066) (www.un.org/disarmament).

For explanation of codes and abbreviations, see introduction

INTERNATIONAL ORGANISATIONS

United Nations Institute for Disarmament Research [UNIDIR] (RE), Palais des Nations, 1211 Genève 10, Switzerland (+41-22 917 1141) (fax 22 917 0176) (unidir@unog.ch) (www.unidir.org).

Universala Esperanto-Asocio [UEA] (HR CD PO), Nieuwe Binnenweg 176, 3015 BJ Rotterdam, Netherlands (+31-10-436 1044) (fax 436 1751) (uea@co.uea.org) (www.uea.org).
Esperanto; *Kontakto*.

Unrepresented Nations and Peoples Organization [UNPO] (HR CR EL), Rue du Pépin 54, Bruxelles 1000, Belgium (+32-2 513 1459) (unpo@unpo.org) (unpo.org).

War Resisters' International [WRI] (PA RA HR TR CR), 5 Caledonian Rd, London N1 9DX, Britain (+44-20-7278 4040) (fax 7278 0444) (info@wri-irg.org) (wri-irg.org).
The Broken Rifle; *CO Update*; *War Profiteers News*.
Network of organisations of nonviolent activists, pacifists, conscientious objectors, etc. Also, tel +44-20-3355 2364.

Women's International League for Peace and Freedom [WILPF] (PA HR AT ND), CP 28, 1 rue de Varembé, 1211 Genève 20, Switzerland (+41-22 919 7080) (fax 22 919 7081) (secretariat@wilpf.ch) (www.wilpf.org). WILPF UN Office: 777 UN Plaza – 6th Floor, New York, NY 10017, USA (+1-212-682 1265) (fax 286 8211).
Projects of UN office include (www.peacewomen.org) and (www.reachingcriticalwill.org).

World Congress of Faiths (RP), 21 Maple St, London W1T 4BE, Britain (+44-1935-864055) (enquiries@worldfaiths.org) (www.worldfaiths.org).

World Federalist Movement – Institute for Global Polivy [WFM-IGP] (WF HR RE TW), 708 3rd Ave – Suite 1715, New York, NY 10017, USA (+1-212-599 1320) (fax 599 1332) (info@wfm-igp.org) (www.wfm-igp.org). Also: Bezuidenhoutseweg 99A, 2594 AC Den Haag, Netherlands (+31-70-363 4484).

World Federation of United Nations Associations / Fédération Mondiale des Associations pour les NU [WFUNA/FMANU] (TW HR), 1 United Nations Plaza – Room 0240, New York, NY 10017, USA (+1-212-963 5610) (info@wfuna.org) (wfuna.org).

World Future Council Foundation (WF EL), Dorotheenstr 15, 22301 Hamburg, Germany (+49-40-3070 91420) (fax 3070 91414) (info@worldfuturecouncil.org) (www.worldfuturecouncil.org).
Promotes sustainable future.
Other offices: UN (Geneva) (+41-22 555 0950); UK (+44-20-3356 2771) (info.uk@worldfuturecouncil.org); China (+86-10-6500 8172) (info.china@worldfuturecouncil.org).

World Goodwill (RP PO), Suite 54, 3 Whitehall Court, London SW1A 2EF, Britain (+44-20-7839 4512) (fax 7839 5575) (worldgoodwill.uk@lucistrust.org) (www.worldgoodwill.org).
Newsletter. Also: Lucis Trust, Rue du Stand 40, 1204 Genève, Switzerland (geneva@lucistrust.org); 866 UN Plaza – Suite 482, New York, NY 10017, USA (worldgoodwill.us@lucistrust.org).

World Information Service on Energy [WISE] (EL ND RA), Postbus 59636, 1040 LC Amsterdam, Netherlands (+31-20-612 6368) (info@wiseinternational.org) (www.wiseinternational.org). *WISE/NIRS Nuclear Monitor*. Grassroots-oriented antinuclear information. Works with NIRS in USA.

World Orchestra for Peace [WOP] (CD UN PO), c/o Charles Kaye, 26 Lyndale Ave, London NW2 2QA, Britain (+44-20-7317 8433) (ckconsult19@gmail.com) (www.worldorchestraforpeace.com). Also tel +44-7967-108974. Established 1995. Designated UNESCO Artist for Peace in 2010.

World Peace Council / Consejo Mondial de la Paz [WPC] (ND TW), Othonos St 10, 10557 Athinai, Greece (+30-210 3316 326) (fax 210 3251 576) (wpc@otenet.gr) (www.wpc-in.org).

World Rainforest Movement (EL HR), Avenida General María Paz 1615 – Of 3, 11400 Montevideo, Uruguay (+598-2-605 6943) (fax) (wrm@wrm.org.uy) (wrm.org.uy).

World Service Authority [WSA] (WF HR PA CD), 5 Thomas Circle NW – Suite 300, Washington, DC 20005, USA (+1-202-638 2662) (fax 638 0638) (info@worldservice.org) (www.worldservice.org). *World Citizen News*.

World Student Christian Federation – Inter-Regional Office [WSCF] (TW RP HR), Ecumenical Centre, BP 2251, 1211 Genève 2, Switzerland (+41-22 791 6358) (fax 22 791 6221) (wscf@wscf.ch) (www.wscfglobal.org). *Federation News*; *Student World*.

Youth for Exchange and Understanding [YEU] (CD), Ave du Suffrage Universel 49, 1030 Bruxelles, Belgium (+32-2 649 2048) (fax) (info@yeu-international.org) (www.yeu-international.org).
Also Portugal office (+351-289-813074).

NATIONAL ORGANISATIONS

AFGHANISTAN
Revolutionary Association of the Women of Afghanistan [RAWA] (HR), see under Pakistan (www.rawa.org).

ALBANIA
Albanian Human Rights Group [AHRG] (HR), St Ibrahim Rugova - 2/39, Green Park, Tiranë (+355-42-225060) (el.ballauri@gmail.com) (www.ahrg-al.org).

Fondacioni Shqiptar Zgjidhja e Konflikteve dhe Pajtimi i Mosmarrëveshjeve [AFCR] (RE CR), Rr "Him Kolli" - Pall PF Trade - Nr 5, Tiranë (+355-4-226 4681) (fax 226 4837) (mediationalb@abcom.al) (www.mediationalb.org). *Pajtimi.*

ANDORRA
Partit Verds d'Andorra (EL), Apartat de Correus 2136, Andorra la Vella AD500 (+376-363797) (andorraverds@gmail.com) (www.verds.ad).
Green Party.

ARGENTINA
Fundación Servicio Paz y Justicia [SERPAJ] (FR IB HR), Piedras 730, 1070 Buenos Aires (+54-11-4361 5745) (secinstitucional@serpaj.org.ar) (serpaj.org.ar).

Greenpeace Argentina (GP), Zabala 3873, 1427 Buenos Aires (activismo@infogreenpeace.org.ar) (www.greenpeace.org/argentina).

ARMENIA
Civil Society Institute [CSI] (HR), 43 Aygestan 11th St, Yerevan 0025 (+374-10-574317) (csi@csi.am) (www.csi.am).

United Nations Association of Armenia (UN), 17 Nalbandyan Str - 7/1, Yerevan 0010 (+374-10-565595) (info@auna.am) (www.auna.am).

AUSTRALIA
Act for Peace [AFP] (RP RE TW DA), c/o National Council of Churches in Australia, Locked Bag Q199, Sydney, NSW 1230 (+61-2-8259 0800) (www.actforpeace.org.au).

Amnesty International Australia (AI), Locked Bag 23, Broadway, NSW 2007 (+61-2-8396 7600) (fax 9217 7663) (supporter@amnesty.org.au) (www.amnesty.org.au).

Anabaptist Association of Australia and New Zealand (RP), 190 Magpie Hollow Rd, South Bowenfels, NSW 2790 (+61-2-6351 2896) (aaanz.info@gmail.com) (www.anabaptist.asn.au).

Anglican Pacifist Fellowship - Australia [APF] (RP), c/o Philip Huggins, 5 Docker St, Richmond, Vic 2121 (phuggins@melbourne.anglican.com.au).

Anti-Nuclear Alliance of Western Australia [ANAWA] (ND EL), 5 King William St, Bayswater, WA 6053 (+61-8-9272 4252) (admin@anawa.org.au) (www.anawa.org.au).

Australia East Timor Friendship Assocaiation - South Australia [AEFTA-SA] (HR), PO Box 240, Goodwood, SA 5034 (+61-8-8344 3511) (www.aetfa.org.au).

Australia West Papua Association (HR), PO Box 105, Bunbury, WA 6231 (ash@freewestpapua.org) (www.freewestpapuaperth.org).

Australian Anti-Bases Campaign Coalition [AABCC] (IB WP AT ND RA), PO Box A899, Sydney South, NSW 1235 (+61-4-1829 0663) (denis@anti-bases.org) (www.anti-bases.org).

Centre for Peace Studies (RE EL SD), University of New England, Armidale, NSW 2351 (+61-2-6773 2442) (fax 6773 3350) (hware@une.edu.au) (www.une.edu.au/study/peace-studies). Organise annual Nonviolence Film Festival.

Christian Peacemaker Teams Australasia [CPTA] (RP RA CR), PO Box 738, Mona Vale, NSW 1660 (+61-2-9997 4632) (doug.hynd@netspeed.com.au). An initiative of various church groups.

Coalition for Justice & Peace in Palestine [CJPP] (HR), PO Box 144, Glebe, NSW 2037 (cjpp@coalitionforpalestine.org) (www.coalitionforpalestine.org).

Conflict Resolution Network [CRN] (CR UN RE), PO Box 1016, Chatswood, NSW 2057 (+61-2-9419 8500) (crn@crnhq.org) (www.crnhq.org).

Ecumenical Accompaniment Programme in Palestine and Israel - Australia (RP HR), c/o National Council of Churches in Australia, Locked Bag Q199, Sydney, NSW 1230 (+61-2-8259 0800) (www.ncca.org.au/eappi).

Footprints for Peace (ND EL), PO Box 632, Fremantle South, WA 6162 (marcus@footprintsforpeace.org) (www.footprintsforpeace.net).

Friends of the Earth (FE RA PO), PO Box 222, Fitzroy, Vic 3065 (+61-3-9419 8700) (fax 9416 2081) (foe@foe.org.au) (www.foe.org.au).

Greenpeace Australia Pacific (GP), GPO Box 2622, Sydney, NSW 2001 (support.au@greenpeace.org) (www.greenpeace.org.au).

AUSTRALIA

Independent and Peaceful Australia Network [IPAN] (PA DA), PO Box 573, Coorparoo, Qld 4151 (+61-431-597256) (ipan.australia@gmail.com) (ipan.org.au). Opposes overseas military bases.

Institute for Social Ecology (EL AL RA), PO Box 5208, West End, Brisbane, Qld 4101 (+61-4-2179 4776).

International Volunteers for Peace [IVP] (SC), 103A Goldsmith St, Goulburn, NSW 2580 (+61-2-4821 3350) (admin@ivp.org.au) (www.ivp.org.au).

Just Peace, PO Box 573, Coorparoo, QLD 4151 (+61-4-3159 7256) (JustPeaceQld@gmail.com).

Medical Association for Prevention of War [MAPW] (IP), PO Box 1379, Carlton, Vic 3053 (+61-3-9023 1958) (mapw@mapw.org.au) (www.mapw.org.au).

Nonlethal Security for Peace Campaign (DA RE WF), PO Box 724, Avalon Beach, NSW 2107 (info@tamingwar.com) (tamingwar.com). Formerly the Non-Lethal Weapons for Peace Campaign.

Pax Christi (PC IB), PO Box 31, Carlton South, Vic 3053 (+61-3-9893 4946) (mscjust@smartchat.net.au) (www.paxchristi.org.au). *Disarming Times.* Also NSW (+61-2-9550 3845).

People for Nuclear Disarmament (NSW) [PND] (ND RE), 499 Elizabeth St, Surry Hills, Sydney, NSW 2010 (+61-2-9319 4296) (johnhallam2001@yahoo.com.au). *Peace Action.*

People for Nuclear Disarmament - Western Australia [PND] (IB ND), 5 King William St, Bayswater, WA 6053 (+61-8-9272 4252) (jovall@iinet.net.au).

People's Charter to Create a Nonviolent World (PA TW EL), PO Box 68, Daylesford, Vic 3460 (flametree@riseup.net) (thepeoplesnonviolencecharter.wordpress.com).

Quaker Service Australia (SF TW), Unit 14, 43-53 Bridge Rd, Stanmore, NSW 2048 (+61-2-8054 0400) (administration@qsa.org.au) (www.qsa.org.au). *QSA Newsletter.*

Religions for Peace Australia (RP), 71 Wellington St, Flemington, Vic 3031 (+61-4-3999 5761) (wcrpaust@iinet.net.au) (religionsforpeaceaustralia.org)

Reprieve Australia (HR), PO Box 4296, Melbourne, VIC 3001 (+61-3-9670 4108) (contact@reprieve.org.au) (www.reprieve.org.au). Campaigns against death penalty.

SafeGround (DA), PO Box 2143, Morphettville, SA 5043 (info@safeground.org.au) (safeground.org.au). *SafeGround Memorandum.* Work to reduce impact of explosive remnants of war.

Schweik Action Wollongong (SD), PO Box U129, Wollongong, NSW 2500 (+61-2-4228 7860) (fax 4221 5341) (brian_martin@uow.edu.au) (www.bmartin.cc/others/SAW.html).

Servas Australia (SE), c/o Pam Webster, 2 Warili Rd, Frenchs Forest, 2076 (+61-2-9451 9669) (secretary@servas.org.au) (www.servas.org.au).

Society of Friends (SF), PO Box 556, Kenmore, Qld 4069 (ymsecretary@quakers.org.au) (www.quakers.org.au).

Tasmanian Peace Trust (RE), PO Box 451, Hobart, TAS 7002.

Tasmanian Quaker Peace & Justice Committee [TQPJC] (SF PA), PO Box 388, North Hobart, Tas 7002 (+61-400-925385).

United Nations Association of Australia (UN), Suite 206, Griffin Centre, 20 Genge St, Canberra City, ACT 2601 (admin@unaa.org.au) (www.unaa.org.au).

Universal Peace Federation - Australia [UPF] (RP), PO Box 642, Burwood, NSW 1805 (oceaniahq@gmail.com) (www.upf.org).

Vision of Humanity (RE), PO Box 42, St Leonards, NSW 1590 (+61-2-9901 8500) (info@visionofhumanity.org) (www.visionofhumanity.org).

War Resisters' League [WRL] (WR AL HR), PO Box 451, North Hobart, Tas 7002 (+61-3-6278 2380) (pdpjones@mpx.com.au).

Women's International League for Peace and Freedom [WILPF] (WL ND), PO Box 934, Dickson, ACT 2602 (wilpf.australia@wilpf.org.au) (wilpf.org.au). *Peace & Freedom.*

World Citizens Association (Australia) [WCAA] (WF), PO Box 6318, University of New South Wales, Sydney, NSW 1466 (C.Hamer@unsw.edu.au) (www.worldcitizens.org.au).

AUSTRIA

Amnesty International Österreich (AI), Möringgasse 10, 1150 Wien (+43-1-78008) (fax 780 0844) (office@amnesty.at) (www.amnesty.at).

Arbeitsgemeinschaft für Wehrdienstverweigerung und Gewaltfreiheit [ARGE WDV] (WR), Schottteng 3A/1/4/59, 1010 Wien (+43-1-535 9109) (fax 532 7416) (argewdv@verweigert.at) (www.verweigert.at).

Bürgermeister für den Frieden in Deutschland und Österreich (CD ND DA), see under Germany.

Begegnungszentrum für Aktive Gewaltlosigkeit / Centre for Encounter and Active Nonviolence [BFAG] (WR TW EL), Wolfgangerstr 26, 4820 Bad Ischl (+43-6132-24590) (info@begegnungszentrum.at) (www.begegnungszentrum.at). *Rundbrief.*

Franz Jägerstätter House (PC), St Radegund 31, 5121 Ostermiething (+43-6278-8219) (pfarre.stradegund@dioezese-linz.at).

Global 2000 (FE), Neustiftgasse 36, 1070 Wien (+43-1-812 5730) (fax 812 5728) (office@global2000.at) (www.global2000.at).

Greenpeace Austria (GP), Wiedner Hauptstr 120-124, 1050 Wien (+43-1-545 4580) (fax 5454 58098) (office@greenpeace.at) (www.greenpeace.at).

Internationaler Versöhnungsbund [IVB] (FR), Lederergasse 23/III/27, 1080 Wien (+43-1-408 5332) (fax) (office@versoehnungsbund.at) (www.versoehnungsbund.at).

Österreichische Gesellschaft für Aussenpolitik und die Vereinten Nationen [OEGAVN] (UN), Reitschulgasse 2/2, Hofburg/Stallburg, 1010 Wien (+43-1-535 4627) (office@oegavn.org) (www.una-austria.org).

Österreichisches Netzwerk für Frieden und Gewaltfreiheit (RE), c/o IVB, Lederergasse 23/III/27, 1080 Wien (www.friedensnetzwerk.at).

Österreichisches Studienzentrum für Frieden und Konfliktlösung [ÖSFK/ASPR] (HR PA RE CR), Rochusplatz 1, 7461 Stadtschlaining, Burg (+43-3355-2498) (fax 2662) (aspr@aspr.ac.at) (www.aspr.ac.at). Study Centre for Peace and Conflict Resolution.

Pax Christi Österreich [PXÖ] (PC), Kapuzinerstr 84, 4020 Linz (+43-732-7610 3254) (office@paxchristi.at) (www.paxchristi.at). *Pax.*

Peace Museum Vienna (RE), Blutgasse 3/1, 1010 Wien (office@peacemuseumvienna.com) (www.peacemuseumvienna.com). Includes Windows for Peace project in city streets.

AZERBAIJAN

Azerbaijan Institute for Democracy and Human Rights (HR), Nakhchivani Street 4B - flat 64, 1130 Baku (office@aidhr.org) (www.aidhr.org).

Azerbaijan Peace and Development Alliance (IB), 3/6 S Rustanov St - kv 65, Baku 370001 (+994-12-492 7920) (elmira@awdc.baku.az).

Azerbaycan Insan Huquqlarini Mudafie Merkezi / Human Rights Centre of Azerbaijan [AIHMM/HRCA] (HR), PO Box 31, Baku 1000 (+994-12-492 1369) (fax) (eldar.hrca@gmail.com) (penitentiary.ucoz.ru). *Human Rights in Azerbaijan.*

BANGLADESH

Bangladesh Interreligious Council for Peace and Justice [BICPAJ] (FR IB PC CR EL), 14/20 Iqbal Rd, Mohammadpur, Dhaka 1207 (+880-2-914 1410) (fax 812 2010) (bicpaj@bijoy.net) (www.bicpaj.org).

Bangladesh Peace Council [BDC] (WP), Flat 3A1 - House No 8, Road No 6 - Block C, Banani, Dhaka 1213 (+88-2-882 7007) (dr.maguassem@gmail.com) (www.bd-pc.org).

Peace For All (IB CR HR), GPO Box 3448, Dhaka 1000 (+880-2-956 5907) (peaceforallbd@yahoo.com).

Service Civil International [SCI] (SC), 57/15 East Razabazar, Panthapath West, Dhaka 1215 (+880-2-935 3993) (scibangladesh@gmail.com) (scibangladesh.org).

BARBADOS

Barbados Inter-Religious Organisation [BIRO] (RP), c/o Roman Catholic Diocese of Bridgetown, PO Box 1223, Bridgetown (vincentblackett@hotmail.com). Affiliated to Religions for Peace International.

BELGIUM

ACAT - Belgique Francophone (HR), Quai aux Foins 53, 1000 Bruxelles (+32-2 223 0159) (fax) (a.cat.belgique@gmail.com) (www.acat-belgique-francophone.be). *ACAT-info.*

ACAT België-Vlaanderen (HR), Zevenkerken 4, 8200 Sint-Andries (+32-50 406132) (info@acat-belgie-vlaanderen.be) (www.acat-belgie-vlaanderen.be).

Agir pour la Paix (WR), 35 rue van Elewyck, Ixelles, 1050 Bruxelles (+32-2 648 5220) (info@agirpourlapaix.be) (agirpourlapaix.be).

Amis de la Terre / Friends of the Earth Belgium (Wallonia and Brussels) [AT] (FE PO), Rue Nanon 98, 5000 Namur (+32-81 390639) (fax 81 390638) (contact@amisdelaterre.be) (www.amisdelaterre.be).

Amnesty International Belgique Francophone [AIBF] (AI), Rue Berckmans 9, 1060 Bruxelles (+32-2 538 8177) (fax 2 537 3729) (aibf@aibf.be) (www.amnesty.be). *Libertés!.*

BELGIUM

Amnesty International Vlaanderen (AI), Kerkstr 156, 2060 Antwerpen (+32-3 271 1616) (fax 3 235 7812) (amnesty@aivl.be) (www.aivl.be).
Artsen Voor Vrede [AVV] (IP), Karel Van de Woesti St 18, 9300 Aalst. *Gezondheidszorg en Vredesvraagstukken.*
Association Médicale pour la Prévention de la Guerre Nucléaire [AMPGN] (IP), 51 Ave Wolvendael, 1180 Bruxelles (de.salle.philippe@skynet.be) (ampgn-belgium.be).
BePax (PC HR), Chaussée Saint-Pierre 208, 1040 Bruxelles (+32-2 896 9500) (info@bepax.org) (www.bepax.org).
Brigades de Paix Internationales [BPI/PBI] (HR CR CD RE), 23 rue Lt F Wampach, 1200 Bruxelles (+32-473 878136) (info@pbi-belgium.org) (pbi-belgium.org).
Climaxi - Friends of the Earth (Flanders & Brussels) (FE ND HR), Groenlaan 39, 9550 Herzele (info@climaxi.org) (www.climaxi.org).
Commission Justice et Paix - Belgique francophone (RP), Rue Maurice Liétart 31/6, 1150 Bruxelles (+32-2 738 0801) (fax 2 738 0800) (info@justicepaix.be) (www.justicepaix.be).
Flemish War and Peace Museum (RE), IJzertoren, IJzerdijk 49, 8600 Diksmuide (+32-51 500286) (info@aandeijzer.be) (www.museumaandeijzer.be).
Greenpeace (GP), Haachtsesteenweg 159, 1030 Brussel (+32-2 274 0200) (fax 2 274 0230) (info.be@greenpeace.org) (www.greenpeace.org/belgium).
Groupe Interconfessionnel de la Réconciliation / Kinshasa [GIR] (FR), Route de Longchamp 26, 1348 Louvain-la-Neuve (buangajos@hotmail.com).
I Stop the Arms Trade (AT RA PA), c/o Vredesactie, Patriottenstr 27, 2600 Berchem (+32-3 281 6839) (ikstopwapenhandel@vredesactie.be) (istopthearmstrade.eu). Non-violent direct action against EU arms trade.
Intal Globalize Solidarity (WP TW), 53 Chausée de Haecht, 1210 Bruxelles (+32-2 209 2350) (fax 2 209 2351) (info@intal.be) (www.intal.be).
Pax Christi Vlaanderen [PCV] (PC RE CD ND CR), Italiëlei 98A, 2000 Antwerpen (+32-3 225 1000) (paxchristi@paxchristi.be) (www.paxchristi.be). *Koerier.*
Pax Christi Wallonie-Bruxelles [PCWB] (PC), Rue Maurice Liétart 31/1, 1150 Bruxelles (+32-2 738 0804) (fax 2 738 0800) (info@paxchristiwb.be) (www.paxchristiwb.be). *Signes des Temps.*
Register van Wereldburgers / Registry of World Citizens [RW] (WF PA TW), Vredestr 65, 2540 Hove (+32-3 455 7763) (verstraeten.jean@belgacom.net) (www.recim.org/cdm).
Religions for Peace - Belgium (RP), Av de la Reine 7, 1030 Bruxelles (frndali@wcrp.be).
Say No (PA), A Beernaerstr 28a, 1170 Brussel (+32-497 934716) (info@desertie.be) (www.sayno.be). Anti-militarist choral project.
Servas - Belgium & Luxembourg (SE), c/o Rita Dessauvage, Kloosterweg 30, 1652 Beersel-Alsemberg (belgium@servas.org). (belgium.servas.org).
Sortir de la Violence [SDV] (FR CR RE), Blvd du Souverain 199, 1160 Bruxelles (+32-2 679 0644) (info@sortirdelaviolence.org) (www.sortirdelaviolence.org).
VIA (SC WC), Belgiëlei 37, 2018 Antwerpen (+32-3 707 1614) (via@viavzw.be) (www.viavzw.be).
Vlaams Vredesinstituut / Flemish Peace Institute (RE), Leuvenseweg 86, 1000 Brussel (+32-2 552 4591) (fax 2 552 4408) (vredesinstituut@vlaamsparlement.be) (www.vlaamsvredesinstituut.eu). Also www.flemishpeaceinstitute.eu.
Vredesactie (WR AT ND), Breughelstr 31, 2018 Antwerpen (+32-3 281 6839) (contact@vredesactie.be) (www.vredesactie.be). *Vredesactie.*
Vrouwen in 't Zwart / Femmes en Noir / Women in Black [WiB] (PA DA HR), c/o Ria Convents, Vismarkt 8, 3000 Leuven (+32-16 291314) (marianne.vandegoorberg@telnet.be) (snellings.telenet.be/womeninblackleuven).

BERMUDA

Amnesty International Bermuda (AI), PO Box HM 2136, Hamilton HM JX (+1441-296 3249) (fax) (director@amnestybermuda.org).

BHUTAN

People's Forum for Human Rights (HR), see under Nepal.

BOSNIA-HERZEGOVINA

Centar za Zivotnu Sredinu / Centre for the Environment [CZZS] (FE), Miša Stupara 5, 78000 Banja Luka (+387-5143 3140) (fax 5143 3141) (info@czzs.org) (czzs.org).
Centar za Nenasilnu Akciju / Centre for Nonviolent Action [CNA] (CD CR PA RE), Kranjceviceva 33, 71000 Sarajevo (+387-3326 0876) (fax 3326 0875) (cna.sarajevo@nenasilje.org) (www.nenasilje.org). See also in Serbia.
Fondacia Mirovna Akademija (RE), Porodice Ribar 8, 71000 Sarajevo (+387-3395 0902) (fax) (info@mirovna-akademija.org) (www.mirovna-akademija.org).
Mreza za Izgradnju Mira / Network for Building Peace (CD CR), Marka Marulica 2, 71000 Sarajevo (+387-3374 1080)

(fax 3374 1081) (info@mreza-mira.net) (www.mreza-mira.net). Network of peace and human rights organisations.
Nansen Dialogue Centre Sarajevo [NDC Sarajevo] (CR), Hakije Kulenovica 10, 71000 Sarajevo (+387-33-556846) (fax 556845) (ndcsarajevo@nansen-dialogue.net) (www.ndcsarajevo.org).
WhyNjet / Why Not (WR), Dzemala Bijedica 309, 71000 Sarajevo (+387-33-618461) (info@zastone.ba) (www.zastone.ba). Supports conscientious objection.

BOTSWANA

Society of Friends (Quakers) (SF), c/o Shelagh Willet, Box 20166, Gaborone (+267-394 7147) (willet.shelagh@botsnet.bw).

BRAZIL

ACAT Brasil (HR), Praça Clovis Bevilaqua 351 - sala 701, 01018-001 São Paulo - SP (+55-11-3101 6084) (fax) (acatbrasil.internacional@gmail.com). Affiliated to FIACAT.
Amigos da Terra - Brasil (FE), Rua Olavo Bilac 192 - Azenha, 90040-310 Porto Alegre - RS (+55-51-3332 8884) (www.amigosdaterrabrasil.org.br).
Associação das Nações Unidas - Brasil [ANUBRA] (UN), Av Brigadeiro Faria Lima 1485 - North Tower - 19th Floor, 01452-002 São Paulo - SP (+55-11-3094 7984) (fax) (unab@unab.org.br) (www.unab.org.br).
Centro Brasileiro de Solidariedade aos Povos e Luta pela Paz [CEBRAPAZ] (WP CD SD ND), Rua Marconi 34 - Conj 51, República, 01047-000 São Paulo - SP (+55-11-3223 3469) (cebrapaz@cebrapaz.org.br) (cebrapaz.org.br).
Commissão Pastoral da Terra [CPT] (PC), Edifício Dom Abel - 1º andar, Rua 19 - Nº 35, 74030-090 Centro Goiânia, Goiás (+55-62-4008 6466) (fax 4008 6405) (cpt@cptnacional.org.br) (www.cptnacional.org.br).
Instituto Brasileiro do Não Matar / Brazilian Institute for Nonkilling (PA), Rua Uruguai 472 - Ed J Philipps - Apto 1002, Centro - Itajaí, Santa Catarina 88302-202 (+55-47-3349 6601) (info@naomatar.org).

BRITAIN

38 Degrees (EL HR TW), First Floor, 10 Queen Street Place, London EC4 (+44-20-7970 6023) (emailtheteam@38degrees.org.uk) (www.38degrees.org.uk). Organises internet lobbying on progressive issues.
Abolition 2000 UK (ND), 162 Holloway Rd, London N7 8DQ (mail@abolition2000uk.org) (www.abolition2000uk.org).
Acronym Institute for Disarmament Diplomacy (RE), Werks Central, 15-17 Middle St, Brighton BN1, Sussex (+44-1273 737219) (info@acronym.org.uk) (acronym.org.uk).

Action on Armed Violence (AT DA TW HR), 405 Mile End Rd, Bow, London E3 (info@aoav.org.uk) (aoav.org.uk).
Afghanistan Peace Project [APP] (PA CR), 31 Carisbrooke Rd, St Leonards-on-Sea TN38 0JN, Sussex (web@afghanistanpeaceproject.co.uk) (www.vcnv.org.uk). Formerly Voices for Creative Non-Violence UK.
Ahmadiyya Muslim Community (RP HR), c/o Baitul Futuh Mosque, 181 London Rd, Morden, Surrey SM4 (+44-333-240 0490) (enquiries@ahmadiyya.org.uk) (Ahmadiyya.org.uk). Anti-violence and pro freedom of thought group.
Aldermaston Women's Peace Camp(aign) [AWPC] (WR ND RA), c/o 8 Millar House, Merchants Rd, Bristol BS8 4HA (info@aldermaston.net) (www.aldermaston.net). Monthly Aldermaston peace camps; and other actions.
Alternatives to Violence Project - Britain [AVP Britain] (CR PO), 28 Charles Sq, London N1 6HT (+44-20-7324 4755) (info@avpbritain.org.uk) (www.avpbritain.org.uk).
Amnesty International - UK Section [AIUK] (AI), Human Rights Action Centre, 17-25 New Inn Yard, London EC2A 3EA (+44-20-7033 1500) (fax 7033 1503) (sct@amnesty.org.uk) (www.amnesty.org.uk).
Anglican Pacifist Fellowship [APF] (WR IB RP), Peace House, 19 Paradise St, Oxford OX1 1LD (tilly@apf.org.uk) (www.anglicanpeacemaker.org.uk). *The Anglican Peacemaker*.
Archbishop Desmond Tutu Centre for War and Peace Studies (RE CR), Liverpool Hope University - Hope Park Campus, Liverpool L16 9JD (tutu@hope.ac.uk) (tutu.hope.ac.uk).
Article 36 (DA), The Coalface / Runway East, 46 Clifton Terrace, London N4 3JP (info@article36.org) (www.article36.org). Working to change law relating to weapons.
At Ease (HR), Bunhill Fields Meeting House, Quaker Court, Banner St, London EC1Y 8QQ (+44-20-7490 5223) (info@atease.org.uk) (www.atease.org.uk). Advice, counselling for military personnel.
Baby Milk Action (TW PO EL), 4 Brooklands Ave, Cambridge CB2 8BB (+44-1223-464420) (info@babymilkaction.org) (www.babymilkaction.org). *BMA Update*.
Balkans Peace Park Project - UK Committee [B3P] (CD EL), c/o Rylstone Lodge, Rylstone, Skipton BD23 6LH, N Yorks (+44-1756-730231) (A.T.I.Young@bradford.ac.uk) (www.balkanspeacepark.org).
Baptist Peace Fellowship [BPF] (FR), c/o 21 Kingshill, Cirencester GL7 1DE, Gloucestershire (bobgardiner@yahoo.co.uk) (www.baptist-peace.org.uk). *BPF Newsletter*.

BRITAIN

Before You Sign Up, 11 Manor Rd, Stratford-upon-Avon, Warwickshire CV37 (info@beforeyousignup.info) (www.beforeyousignup.info).
For people thinking of joining the armed forces.

Bertrand Russell Peace Foundation [BRPF] (RE PA ND), Unit 5, Churchill Business Park - Private Road No 2, Colwick, Nottingham NG4 2HF (+44-115-970 8318) (fax 942 0433) (elfeuro@compuserve.com) (www.russfound.com).
The Spokesman.

Bloomsbury Ad Hoc Committee [BADHOC] (EL HR PA), c/o 26 Museum Chambers, Little Russell St, London WC1A 3PD (badhoc@activist.com).

Boycott Israel Network [BIN] (HR TW), c/o PSC, Box PM PSA, London WC1N 3XX (info@boycottisraelnetwork.net) (www.boycottisraelnetwork.net).

Bradford University Department of Peace Studies (RE CR TW), Bradford BD7 1DP, West Yorks (+44-1274-235235) (fax 235240) (www.brad.ac.uk/acad/peace/).

Brighton Peace & Environment Centre [BPEC] (RE EL), 39-41 Surrey St, Brighton BN1, Sussex (+44-1273-766610) (info@bpec.org) (www.bpec.org).

British American Security Information Council [BASIC] (RE AT ND), The Founndry, 17 Oval Way, Vauxhall, London SE11 (+44-20-3488 6974) (basicuk@basicint.org) (basicint.org).

Building Bridges for Peace (CR), c/o 2 Crossways, Cott Lane, Dartington, Totnes TQ9 6HE, Devon (joberry@buildingbridgesforpeace.org) (buildingbridgesforpeace.org).
Conflict transformation through empathy.

Burma Campaign UK (HR EL TW), Unit 110, The Bon Marche Centre, 241-251 Ferndale Rd, London SW9 (info@burmacampaign.org.uk) (www.burmacampaign.org.uk).

Campaign Against Arms Trade [CAAT] (WR AT IB RA), Unit 1.9, The Green House, 244-254 Cambridge Heath Rd, London E2 9DA (+44-20-7281 0297) (enquiries@caat.org.uk) (www.caat.org.uk).
CAAT News.

Campaign against Climate Change [CCC] (EL RA), Top Floor, 5 Caledonian Rd, London N1 9DX (+44-20-7833 9311) (info@campaigncc.org) (www.campaigncc.org).

Campaign Against Criminalising Communities [CAMPACC] (HR), c/o 44 Ainger Rd, London NW3 (+44-20-7586 5892) (estella24@tiscali.co.uk) (www.campacc.org.uk).

Campaign for Better Transport [CBT] (EL), 70 Cowcross St, London EC1M 6EJ (+44-20-3746 2225) (info@bettertransport.org.uk) (www.bettertransport.org.uk).

Campaign for Earth Federation / World Federalist Party (WF), c/o Ian Hackett, 1 Kenilworth Rd, London W5 5PB (worldfederalistparty@gmail.com) (www.federalunion.com).

Campaign for Freedom of Information [CFI] (HR), Free Word Centre, 60 Farringdon Rd, London EC1 (+44-20-7324 2519) (admin@cfoi.org.uk) (www.cfoi.org.uk).

Campaign for Homosexual Equality [CHE] (HR), c/o London Friend, 86 Caledonian Rd, London N1 9DN (+44-7941-914340) (info@c-h-e.org.uk) (www.c-h-e.org.uk).

Campaign for Human Rights in the Philippines [CHRP UK] (HR), c/o Bahay Housing Association, Hackney CVS, The Adiaha Antigha Centre, 24-30 Dalston Lane, London E8 (info@chrp.org.uk) (www.chrp.org.uk).

Campaign for Nuclear Disarmament [CND] (IB ND RA RE), 162 Holloway Rd, London N7 8DQ (+44-20-7700 2393) (enquiries@cnduk.org) (www.cnduk.org).
Campaign!.

Campaign for Nuclear Disarmament Cymru / Yr Ymgyrch dros Ddiarfogi Niwclear [CND Cymru] (ND RA AT DA), c/o 72 Heol Gwyn, Yr Alltwen, Pontardawe SA8 3AN (+44-1792-830330) (heddwch@cndcymru.org) (www.cndcymru.org). *Heddwch.*

Campaign for Press and Broadcasting Freedom [CPBF] (HR), 2nd floor, 23 Orford Rd, Walthamstow, London E17 9NL (freepress@cpbf.org.uk) (www.cpbf.org.uk).
Free Press.

Campaign Opposing Police Surveillance [COPS] (HR), 5 Caledonian Rd, London N1 9DX (info@campaignopposingpolicesurveillance.com) (campaignopposingpolicesurveillance.com).

Campaign to Protect Rural England [CPRE] (EL PO), 5-11 Lavington St, London SE1 0NZ (+44-20-7981 2800) (fax 7981 2899) (info@cpre.org.uk) (www.cpre.org.uk).
Campaigns include opposing fracking.

Ceasefire Centre for Civilian Rights (DA), 54 Commercial St, London E1 6LT (contact@ceasefire.org) (www.ceasefire.org).
Civilian-led monitoring of rights violations.

Centre for Alternative Technology / Canolfan y Dechnoleg Amgen [CAT] (EL PO AL), Machynlleth, Powys SY20 9AZ (+44-1654-705950) (fax 702782) (info@cat.org.uk) (www.cat.org.uk).
Clean Slate.

Centre for Good Relations (CR RE), 96 Pendle Gardens, Culcheth, Warrington WA3

4LU (info@centreforgoodrelations.com) (centreforgoodrelations.com). Training, workshops, "civic diplomacy".
Centre for International Peacebuilding (CR RE TW EL), The White House, 46 High St, Buntingford, Herts SG9 9AH (+44-1763-272662) (eirwenharbottle@gmail.com).
Centre for Trust, Peace and Social Relations [CTPSR] (RE), 5 Innovation Village, Coventry University Technology Park, Cheetah Rd, Coventry CV1 2TT (+44-24-7765 1182) (info.ctpsr@coventry.ac.uk) (www.coventry.ac.uk).
Centre of Religion, Reconciliation and Peace (RE RP), University of Winchester, Sparkford Rd, Winchester SO22, Hampshire (+44-1962-841515) (fax 842280) (www.winchester.ac.uk).
Chernobyl Children's Project (UK) (PO EL CD), Kinder House, Fitzalan St, Glossop SK13, Derbyshire (+44-1457-863534) (ccprojectuk@gmail.com) (www.chernobyl-children.org.uk).
Children of Peace (CR HR), 1st Floor, The Roller Mill, Mill Lane, Uckfield TN22 5AA, Sussex (+44-1825-768074) (info@childrenofpeace.org.uk) (www.childrenofpeace.org.uk). Charity working in Israel, Palestine, Jordan.
Christian Aid (TW), 35-41 Lower Marsh, London SE1 (+44-20-7620 4444) (fax 7620 0719) (info@christian-aid.org) (www.christianaid.org.uk).
Christian Campaign for Nuclear Disarmament [CCND] (ND RP), 162 Holloway Rd, London N7 8DQ (+44-20-7700 4200) (christians@cnduk.org) (www.christiancnd.org.uk). *Ploughshare*.
Christian International Peace Service [CHIPS] (RP CR PO WC), Unit 7, Warwick House, Overton Rd, London SW9 7JP (+44-20-7078 7439) (info@chipspeace.org) (chipspeace.org).
Church & Peace (RP CR RE), 39 Postwood Green, Hertford Heath SG13 7QJ (+44-1992-416442) (IntlOffice@church-and-peace.org) (www.church-and-peace.org).
City to Sea (EL PO), Unit D, Albion Dockside Studios, Hanover Place, Bristol BS1 6UT (info@citytosea.org.uk) (www.citytosea.org.uk). Campaign to stop plastic pollution at source.
Climate Outreach (EL), The Old Music Hall, 106-108 Cowley Rd, Oxford OX4 1JE (+44-1865-403334) (info@climateoutreach.org) (climateoutreach.org). Formerly Climate Outreach and Information Network.
Close Capenhurst Campaign (EL), c/o News From Nowhere, 96 Bold St, Liverpool L1 (closecapenhurst@gmail.com) (close-capenhurst.org.uk). Opposes uranium enrichment plant in Cheshire.

Co-operation Ireland (GB) (CD), Windy Ridge, Courtlands Hill, Pangbourne RG8, Berkshire (+44-118-976 7790) (fax) (murphy992@btinternet.com) (www.cooperationireland.org).
Commonweal Collection (RE AL PA EL), c/o J B Priestley Library, Bradford University, Bradford BD7 1DP, Yorks (+44-1274-233404) (commonweal@riseup.net) (bradford.ac.uk/library/libraries-and-collections/). Peace library.
Community for Reconciliation [CfR] (RP), Barnes Close, Chadwich, Malthouse Lane, Bromsgrove, Worcs B61 0RA (+44-1562-710231) (fax 710278) (cfrenquiry@aol.com) (www.cfrbarnesclose.co.uk). *Newslink*.
Conciliation Resources (CR), Burghley Yard, 106 Burghley Rd, London NW5 1AL (+44-20-7359 7728) (fax 7359 4081) (cr@c-r.org) (www.c-r.org).
Concord Media (PA EL TW), 22 Hines Rd, Ipswich IP3 9BG, Suffolk (+44-1473-726012) (sales@concordmedia.org.uk) (www.concordmedia.org.uk).
Conflict and Environment Observatory [CEOBS] (DA EL RE), The Chapel, Scout Rd, Mytholmroyd, Hebden Bridge HX7 5HZ, West Yorks (+44-300-302 1130) (ceobs.org).
Conflict Research Society [CRS] (RE), Giles Lane, Canterbury CT2 7NZ, Kent (conflictresearchsociety@kent.ac.uk) (www.conflictresearchsociety.org).
Conscience - Taxes for Peace not War (TR WR HR), c/o PPU, 1 Peace Passage, London N7 0BT (info@conscienceonline.org.uk) (www.conscienceonline.org.uk).
Conway Hall Ethical Society (HR RE) Conway Hall, Red Lion Sq, London WC1 4RL (+44-20-7405 1818) (admin@conwayhall.org.uk) (www.conwayhall.org.uk). *Ethical Record*. Formerly South Place Ethical Society.
Cord (TW CR), Floor 9, Eaton House, 1 Eaton Rd, Coventry CV2 2FJ (+44-24-7708 7777) (info@cord.org.uk) (www.cord.org.uk). International peacebuilding charity.
Corporate Occupation (HR RA TW), c/o Corporate Watch, 84b Whitechapel High St, London E1 7QX (tom@shoalcollective.org) (www.corporateoccupation.org). Opposes occupation of Palestine.
Corporate Watch (EL RA AL), c/o Freedom Press, Angel Alley, 84b Whitechapel High St, London E1 7QX (+44-20-7426 0005) (contact@corporatewatch.org) (www.corporatewatch.org). *News Update*.
Cuba Solidarity Campaign (TW WC), c/o UNITE, 33-37 Moreland St, London EC1V 8BB (+44-20-7490 5715) (office@cuba-solidarity.org.uk) (www.cuba-solidarity.org.uk). *Cuba Si*.

BRITAIN

Cumbrians Opposed to a Radioactive Environment [CORE] (EL), Dry Hall, Broughton Mills, Broughton-in-Furness, Cumbria LA20 (+44-1229-716523) (fax) (martin@corecumbria.co.uk) (www.corecumbria.co.uk).

Cymdeithas y Cymod / FoR Wales (FR PA CR), c/o 42 St Patrick's Drive, Pen-y-Bont ar Ogwr / Bridgend, CF31 1RP (cymdeithasycymod@gmail.com) (www.cymdeithasycymod.org.uk).

Cymru dros Heddwch / Wales for Peace (RE DA), c/o Welsh Centre for International Affairs, Temple of Peace, Cathays Park, Cardiff CF10 (+44-29-2082 1051) (janeharries@wcia.org.uk) (www.walesforpeace.org).

Cynghrair Wrth-Niwclear Cymru / Welsh Anti-Nuclear Alliance [CWNC/WANA] (EL), PO Box 90, Llandrindod Wells, Powys LD1 9BP (info@wana.wales) (www.wana.wales).

Darvell Bruderhof (RP PA PO), Brightling Rd, Robertsbridge, Sussex TN32 5DR (+44-1580-883330) (darvell@bruderhof.com) (www.bruderhof.com). Anabaptist community.

Defend the Right to Protest [DTRTP] (HR), BM DTRTP, London WC1N 3XX (info@defendtherighttoprotest.org) (www.defendtherighttoprotest.org).

Demilitarise Education [dED] (RE DA), Partisan Collective, 19 Cheetham Hill Rd, Manchester M4 4FY (hiya@ded1.co) (www.ded1.co).

Don't Bank on the Bomb Scotland (ND), c/o Scottish CND, PO Box 3620, Glasgow G73 9FQ (nukedivestmentscotland@gmail.com) (nukedivestmentscotland.org). Network campaignng against "nuclear investments".

Drone Campaign Network (DA), c/o Peace House, 19 Paradise St, Oxford OX1 (DroneCampaignNetwork@riseup.net) (www.dronecampaignnetwork.org.uk). Network of organisations and academics.

Drone Wars UK (DA HR RE), Peace House, 19 Paradise St, Oxford OX1 1LD (office@dronewars.net) (www.dronewars.net). Opposes growing British use of armed drones.

Economic Issues Programme of the Society of Friends (SF HR EL), QPSW, Friends House, 175 Euston Rd, London NW1 2BJ (+44-20-7663 1000) (suzannei@quaker.org.uk) (www.quaker.org.uk/economic-jutice). *Earth & Economy* newsletter.

Ecumenical Accompaniment Programme in Palestine and Israel - British and Irish Group [EAPPI] (RP HR SF SD), c/o QPSW, Friends House, 173 Euston Rd, London NW1 2BJ (+44-20-7663 1144) (eappi@quaker.org.uk) (www.quaker.org.uk/eappi).

Edinburgh Peace and Justice Centre (CR ND PA RE HR), 25 Nicolson Sq, Edinburgh EH8 9BX (+44-131-629 1058) (contact@peaceandjustice.org.uk) (peaceandjustice.org.uk). Promotes nonviolence, conflict resolution.

Egypt Solidarity Initiative (HR), c/o MENA Solidarity Network, Unit 193, 15-17 Caledonian Rd, London N1 (campaign@egyptsolidarityinitiative.net) (egyptsolidarityinitiative.org).

Ekklesia (RP RE), 235 Shaftesbury Ave, London WC2 (+44-20-7836 3930) (info@ekklesia.co.uk) (www.ekklesia.co.uk).

End Violence Against Women Coalition (HR), 17-25 New Inn Yard, London EC2 (+44-20-7033 1559) (admin@evaw.org.uk) (www.endviolenceagainstwomen.org.uk).

English PEN (HR), 51 East Rd, London N1 6AH (enquiries@englishpen.org) (www.englishpen.org). Defend writers at risk; work for freedom of speech.

Environmental Investigation Agency [EIA] (EL), 62/63 Upper St, London N1 (+44-20-7354 7960) (ukinfo@eia-international.org) (www.eia-international.org). Also operates in USA.

Environmental Network for Central America [ENCA] (EL HR), c/o Janet Bye, 5 St Edmund's Place, Ipswich IP1 (+44-20-8769 0492) (enca.info@gmail.com) (www.enca.org.uk). *ENCA*. Works with affected communities.

Esperanto-Asocio de Britio [EAB] (PO HR), Esperanto House, Station Rd, Barlaston, Stoke-on-Trent, Staffs ST12 9DE (+44-1782-372141) (eab@esperanto.org.uk) (www.esperanto.org.uk). *EAB Update*; *La Brita Esperantisto*.

Ethical Consumer Research Association (EL PO AL), Unit 21, 41 Old Birley St, Manchester M15 (+44-161-226 2929) (fax 226 6277) (enquiries@ethicalconsumer.org) (www.ethicalconsumer.org). *Ethical Consumer*.

EuroPal Forum (HR), 21 Chalton St, London NW1 1JD (+44-20-3289 6057) (admin@europalforum.org.uk) (europalforum.org.uk). Mobilises in support of Palestinian rights.

Every Casualty Counts (RE), 86-90 Paul St, London EC2A 4NE (network@everycasualty.org) (www.everycasualty.org). Formerly Every Casualty Project.

Exeter Area CND (ND), The Peace Shop, 31 New Bridge St, Exeter EX4 3AH, Devon (+44-1392-431447) (info@exetercnd.org) (www.exetercnd.org). Formerly South West Region CND.

Extinction Rebellion (EL RA PO), The Exchange, Brick Row, Stroud GL5 1DF, Glos (extinctionrebellion@risingup.org.uk) (www.ExtinctionRebellion.uk). Actions for climate and economic justice.

Faith & Resistance Network (RP RA), c/o QPSW, Friends House, 175 Euston Rd, London NW1 (faithandresistanceblog.wordpress.com).

Faslane Peace Camp (ND RA AL), Shandon, Helensburgh, Dunbartonshire, G84 8NT (+44-1436-820901) (faslane30@gmail.com) (faslanepeacecamp.wordpress.com).

Fellowship of Reconciliation [FoR] (FR WR), Peace House, 19 Paradise St, Oxford OX1 1LD (+44-1865-250781) (office@for.org.uk) (www.for.org.uk). *Peacelinks*. Covers England and Scotland.

Filia (HR), c/o Drystone Chambers, 35 Bedford Row, London WC1 (info@filia.org.uk) (filia.org.uk). Supporting women's human rights.

Fitnah - Movement for Women's Liberation (HR), BM Box 1919, London WC1N 3XX (fitnah.movement@gmail.com) (www.fitnah.org). *Fitnah*. Opposes misogynist cultural and religious customs.

Fly Kites Not Drones (CD HR PA PO), c/o VCNV-UK, 31 Carisbrooke Rd, St Leonards-on-Sea TN38, Sussex (kitesnotdrones@gmail.com) (www.flykitesnotdrones.org). Non-violence project for young people.

Football for Peace [FFP] (CD), c/o 90 Long Acre, Covent Garden, London WC2E 9DA (44-20-7632 1225) (info@ffpglobal.org) (footballforpeaceglobal.org).

ForcesWatch (PA HR RE), 5 Caledonian Rd, London N1 (+44-20-7837 2822) (office@forceswatch.net) (www.forceswatch.net).

Free Tibet Campaign (HR TW EL), ER82, The Link, Effra Rd, London SW2 1BZ (+44-20-7324 4612) (mail@freetibet.org) (freetibet.org).

Freedom Declared Foundation [FDF] (HR), Office 3, Cathedral House, 63-68 St Thomas's Rd, Portsmouth PO1 2HA (freedomdeclaredfoundation.org). Champions universal freedom of conscience.

Freedom from Torture (HR), 111 Isledon Rd, London N7 (+44-20-7697 7777) (fax 7697 7799) (www.freedomfromtorture.org). *Survivor*. Supports survivors of torture.

Friends of the Earth - England, Wales and Northern Ireland [FOE] (FE PO), The Printworks, 1st Floor, 139 Clapham Rd, London SW9 0HP (+44-20-7490 1555) (fax 7490 0881) (info@foe.co.uk) (friendsoftheearth.uk).

Friends of the Earth Cymru / Cyfeillion y Ddaear Cymru (FE), 33 The Balcony, Castle Arcade, Cardiff CF10 1BY (+44-29-2022 9577) (cymru@foe.co.uk) (www.foecymru.co.uk).

Friends of the Earth Scotland (FE), Thorn House, 5 Rose St, Edinburgh EH2 2PR (+44-131-243 2700) (fax 243 2725) (info@foe.scot) (www.foe.scot).

Gandhi Foundation (HR RE PO), Kingsley Hall, Powis Rd, Bromley-by-Bow, London E3 3HJ (contact@gandhifoundation.org) (www.gandhifoundation.org). *The Gandhi Way*.

Gender Action for Peace and Security UK [GAPS] (HR RE AT CR), c/o Women for Women International UK, 32-36 Loman St, London SE1 0EH (+44-20-7922 7836) (info@gaps-uk.org) (gaps-uk.org). Network of organisations and individual experts.

GeneWatch UK (EL HR), 86 Dedworth Rd, Windsor SL4 5A, Berks (+44-3300-010507) (mail@genewatch.org) (www.genewatch.org). Monitors genetic engineering.

Global Campaign on Military Spending - UK [GCOMS-UK] (DA AT TW), c/o CND, 162 Holloway Rd, London N7 8DQ (contact@demilitarize.org.uk) (demilitarize.org.uk). Organise UK end of annual international action day.

Global Justice Now (TW HR), 66 Offley Rd, London SW9 0LS (+44-20-7820 4900) (offleyroad@globaljustice.org.uk) (www.globaljustice.org.uk). *Ninety Nine*. Formerly World Development Movement.

Global Witness (EL HR TW CR), Lloyds Chambers, 1 Portsoken St, London E1 (+44-20-7492 5820) (fax 7492 5821) (mail@globalwitness.org) (www.globalwitness.org). Also in USA.

GM Watch (EL), c/o 26 Pottergate, Norwich NR2 1DX, Norfolk (+44-1603-624021) (fax 766552) (ngin@gmwatch.org) (www.gmwatch.org). Analyses and counters GM industry propaganda.

GM-Free Cymru (EL), c/o Dyffryn Dwarch, Abermawr, nr Mathry, Pembrokeshire SA62 (gm@caerhys.co.uk) (www.gmfreecymru.org).

GM-free Scotland (EL), c/o 35 Hamilton Drive, Glasgow G12 (gmfreescotland@yahoo.co.uk) (gmfreescotland.blogspot.co.uk).

Greater Manchester & District CND [GM&DCND] (ND), Bridge 5 Mill, 22a Beswick St, Ancoats, Manchester M4 7HR (+44-161-273 8283) (gmdcnd@gn.apc.org) (gmdcnd.com). *Nuclear Alert*.

Green Alliance (EL), 40 Broadway, London SW1H 0BU (+44-20-7233 7433) (ga@green-alliance.org.uk) (www.green-alliance.org.uk). Environmental thinktank.

Green Christian [GC] (EL PO), 97 Plumpton Ave, Hornchurch RM12 6BB, Essex (info@greenchristian.org.uk) (www.greenchristian.org.uk). *Green Christian*.

Green CND (ND), c/o CND, 162 Holloway Rd, London N7 (+44-20-7700 2393).

Green Party of England and Wales (EL ND HR RA), The Biscuit Factory - A Block (201), 100 Clements Rd, London SE16 4DG (+44-20-3691 9400) (office@greenparty.org.uk) (www.greenparty.org.uk). *Green World*.

BRITAIN

Greener UK (EL), c/o Green Alliance, 40 Broadway, London SW1H 0BU (amount@green-alliance.org.uk) (greeneruk.org). Tracking environmental implications of BREXIT.

GreenNet (TW HR PO), Oxford House, Derbyshire St, London E2 6HG (+44-330-335 4011) (info@gn.apc.org) (www.gn.apc.org). Internet services for campaigners.

Greenpeace UK (GP), Canonbury Villas, London N1 2PN (+44-20-7865 8100) (info.uk@greenpeace.org) (www.greenpeace.uk). *Connect.*

Growing Against Violence (CR PO), 18 Stoneleigh Broadway, Epsom, Surrey KT17 2HU (operations@growingagainstviolence.org.uk) (www.growingagainstviolence.org.uk). Against peer-to-peer violence and exploitation.

Gun Control Network (AT RE PO EL), PO Box 11495, London N3 2FE (gcn-uk@btconnect.com) (www.gun-control-network.org).

Housmans Bookshop (WR EL AL HR), 5 Caledonian Rd, Kings Cross, London N1 9DX (+44-20-7837 4473) (fax 7278 0444) (shop@housmans.com) (www.housmans.com). *Peace Diary & World Peace Directory.* Peace/political books, magazines, cards, etc.

Human Rights Watch - London Office (HR), First Floor, Audrey House, 16-20 Ely Place, London EC1 (+44-20-7618 4700) (londonoutreach@hrw.org) (www.hrw.org/london).

Humanists UK (HR PO), 39 Moreland St, London EC1V 8BB (+44-20-7324 3060) (fax 7324 3061) (info@humanists.uk) (humanism.org.uk). Formerly British Humanist Association.

Humanity United for Universal Demilitarisation [HUFUD] (PA PO DA), 14a Lakeside Rd, London W14 0DU (info.hufud@gmail.com) (www.hufud.org). For universal abolition of militarism and weapons.

Index on Censorship (HR RA TW), 1 Rivington Place, London EC2A 3BA (+44-20-7963 7262) (david@indexoncensorship.org) (www.indexoncensorship.org). *Index on Censorship.*

International Alert Training and Learning (CR RE), 346 Clapham Rd, London SW9 (+44-20-7627 6811) (fax 7627 6900) (vmatovic@international-alert.org) (www.internationalalert.org).

International Association for Religious Freedom - British Chapter (HR), c/o Essex Hall, 1 Essex St, London WC2R 3HY (Pejman_Khojasteh@btinternet.com) (www.iarf.net). *IARF World.*

International Campaign to Abolish Nuclear Weapons - UK [ICAN-UK] (ND), c/o MEDACT, 28 Charles Sq, London N1 6HT (infouk@icanw.org) (www.icanw.org/unitedkingdom).

International Centre of Justice for Palestinians [ICJP] (HR), Office 4, 219 Kensington High St, London W8 6ED (info@icjpalestine.com) (www.icjpalestine.com).

International Friendship League - UK (CD), PO Box 578, Northampton NN5 4WY (www.ifl.org.uk).

International Service [UNAIS] (TW UN), Second Floor, Rougier House, 5 Rougier St, York YO1 6HZ (+44-1904-647799) (fax 652353) (contact@internationalservice.org.uk) (www.internationalservice.org.uk).

International Voluntary Service [IVS] (SC), Thorn House, 5 Rose St, Edinburgh EH2 2PR (+44-131-243 2745) (fax 243 2747) (info@ivsgb.org) (ivsgb.org). *Interactions.*

Iona Community (FR PA HR), Suite 9, Fairfield, 1048 Govan Rd, Glasgow G51 4XS (+44-141-429 7281) (admin@iona.org.uk) (iona.org.uk). (On Iona: +44-1681-700404).

Israeli Committee Against House Demolitions UK [ICAHD UK] (HR RA), BM ICAHD UK, London WC1N 3XX (+44-20-3740 2208) (info@icahduk.org) (www.icahduk.org). Opposes Israeli occupation of Palestinian land.

JD Bernal Peace Library (RE), c/o Marx Memorial Library, 37a Clerkenwell Green, London EC1R 0DU (+44-20-7253 1485) (archives@mml.xyz) (www.marx-memorial-library.org). *Theory and Struggle.*

Jews for Justice for Palestinians [JJP] (HR), 20-22 Wenlock Rd, London N1 7GU (jfjfpexecutive@gmail.com) (jfjfp.com).

Jubilee Debt Campaign (TW), The Grayston Centre, 28 Charles Sq, London N1 6HT (+44-20-7324 4722) (info@jubileedebt.org.uk) (jubileedebt.org.uk). *Drop It!.*

Jubilee Scotland (TW), 41 George IV Bridge, Edinburgh EH1 1EL (+44-131-225 4321) (mail@jubileescotland.org.uk) (www.jubileescotland.org.uk). Successor to Jubilee 2000 Scottish Coalition.

Justice & Peace Scotland / Ceartas agus Sìth (RP), 65 Bath St, Glasgow G2 2BX (+44-141-333 0238) (office@justiceandpeacescotland.org.uk) (justiceandpeacescotland.org.uk).

Justice, Peace and Integrity of Creation project of the Columban Fathers [JPIC] (RP), St Joseph's, Waford Way, Hendon, London NW4 4TY (+44-20-8202 2555) (fax 8202 5775) (jpicssc@btconnect.com) (www.columbans.co.uk). *Vocation for Justice.*

Khulisa - Breaking the cycle of violence
(CD CR PO), Wells House (Unit 7), 5-7 Wells Terrace, London N4 (+44-20-7561 3727) (info@khulisa.co.uk) (www.khulisa.co.uk) Modelled on programmes in South Africa.

Kick Nuclear (EL RA), c/o CND, 162 Holloway Rd, London N7 8DQ (+44-20-7700 2393) (kicknuclearlondon@gmail.com) (kicknuclear.com). Opposes UK's addiction to nuclear power.

Kindness UK (PO), Turpin's Yard, Oaklands Rd, London NW2 6LL (+44-20-8452 8518) (kindnessuk.com).

Labour CND (ND), 162 Holloway Rd, London N7 8DQ (+44-1425-279307) (labourcnd@gmail.com) (www.labourcnd.org.uk).

Land Justice Network (HR EL RA), c/o The Land Magazine, Monkton Wyld Court, Charmouth, Bridport, Dorset DT6 (landjusticeuk@gmail.com) (www.landjustice.uk). Network challenging use and ownership of land.

Lawyers for Palestinian Human Rights (HR TW), c/o Bates Wells & Braithwaite, 10 Queen Street Place, London EC4R 1BE (contact@lphr.org.uk) (lphr.org.uk).

Liberation (HR TW DA CR), 77 St John St, Clerkenwell, London EC1M 4NN (+44-20-7324 2498) (info@liberationorg.co.uk) (www.liberationorg.co.uk). *Liberation*.

Liberty - The National Council for Civil Liberties (HR), Liberty House, 26-30 Strutton Ground, London SW1P 2HR (+44-20-7403 3888) (fax 7799 5306) (www.libertyhumanrights.org.uk).

Living Streets (EL HR PO), 4th Floor, Universal House, 88-94 Wentworth St, London E1 7SA (+44-20-7377 4900) (info@livingstreets.org.uk) (www.livingstreets.org.uk).

Local Futures / ISEC [ISEC-UK] (EL), PO Box 239, Totnes TQ9 9DP (+44-1392-581175) (info@localfutures.org) (www.localfutures.org).

London Catholic Worker [LCW] (RP RA PA AL), 49 Mattison Rd, London N4 (+44-20-8348 8212) (londoncatholicworker@yahoo.co.uk) (www.londoncatholicworker.org). *London Catholic Worker*.

London Mining Network [LMN] (HR EL), Finfrute, 225-229 Seven Sisters Rd, London N4 (contact@londonminingnetwork.org) (www.londonminingnetwork.org).

London Region CND [LRCND] (ND), Mordechai Vanunu House, 162 Holloway Rd, London N7 8DQ (+44-20-7607 2302) (info@londoncnd.org) (www.londoncnd.org).

Low-Impact Living Initiative [LILI] (PO EL), Redfield Community, Winslow MK18, Bucks (+44-1296-714184) (fax) (lili@lowimpact.org) (www.lowimpact.org).

Low-Level Radiation Campaign [LLRC] (EL), Times Building, South Crescent, Llandrindod Wells, Powys LD1 5DH (+44-1597-824771) (lowradcampaign@gmail.com) (www.llrc.org).

MEDACT (IP IB EL), The Grayston Centre, 28 Charles Sq, London N1 6HT (+44-20-7324 4739) (fax 7324 4734) (office@medact.org) (www.medact.org). *Communiqué*.

Medical Aid for Palestinians [MAP] (HR), 33a Islington Park St, London N1 1QB (+44-20-7226 4114) (fax 7226 0880) (info@map.org.uk) (www.map.org.uk). *Witness*.

Merseyside CND (ND), 151 Dale St, Liverpool L2 2AH (+44-151-229 5282) (mcnd@care4free.net) (www.mcnd.org.uk).

Methodist Peace Fellowship [MPF] (FR), c/o 133 Manchester Rd, Hapton, nr Burnley BB11 5RF (bea_foster@hotmail.com) (www.mpf.org.uk).

Milton Keynes Peace & Justice Network (ND HR DA), 300 Saxon Gate West, Central Milton Keynes, Bucks MK9 2ES (office@mkpeaceandjustice.org.uk) (www.mkpeaceandjustice.org.uk). *MK Network News*.

Mines Advisory Group [MAG] (DA TW PO), Suite 3A, South Central, 11 Peter St, Manchester M2 5QR (+44-161-236 4311) (fax 236 6244) (info@maginternational.org) (www.maginternational.org).

Movement for Compassionate Living [MCL] (PO EL), 105 Cyfyng Rd, Ystalyfera, Swansea SA9 2BT (+44-1639-841223) (mcl.ystalyfera@googlemail.com) (www.MCLveganway.org.uk).

Movement for the Abolition of War [MAW] (IB), c/o 11 Venetia Rd, London N4 1EJ (+44-20-3397 3019) (info@abolishwar.org.uk) (www.abolishwar.org.uk). *Abolish War*.

Musicians for Peace and Disarmament [MPD] (IB ND DA), 37 Bolton Gdns, Teddington TW11 9AX (info.mpdconcerts@gmail.com) (www.mpdconcerts.org).

National Federation of Atheist, Humanist and Secularist Student Societies [AHS] (HR), 39 Moreland St, London EC1 (communications@ahsstudents.org.uk) (ahsstudents.org.uk).

National Justice & Peace Network [NJPN] (RP), 39 Eccleston Sq, London SW1V 1BX (+44-20-7901 4864) (fax 7901 4821) (admin@justice-and-peace.org.uk) (www.justice-and-peace.org.uk). *Justice and Peace*.

National Secular Society [NSS] (HR), Dutch House, 307-308 High Holborn, London WC1V 7LL (+44-20-7404 3126) (enquiries@secularism.org.uk) (www.secularism.org.uk).

BRITAIN

Network for Peace [NfP] (DA ND PA), 5 Caledonian Rd, London N1 9DX (mail@networkforpeace.org.uk) (www.networkforpeace.org.uk)

Network of Christian Peace Organisations [NCPO] (RP), c/o FOR, Peace House, 19 Paradise St, Oxford OX1 1LD (+44-1865-250781) (enquiries@ncpo.org.uk) (ncpo.org.uk).

New Economics Foundation [NEF] (EL CD PO), 10 Salamanca Place, London SE1 7HB (+44-20-7820 6300) (info@neweconomics.org) (www.neweconomics.org).

New Economy Organisers Network [NEON] (EL HR PO), 10 Salamanca Place, London SE1 7HB (hello@neweconomyorganisers.org) (neweconomyorganisers.org). Network of organisers.

New Israel Fund UK (HR), Unit 2, Bedford Mews, London N2 9DF (+44-20-7724 2266) (fax 7724 2299) (info@uknif.org) (uknif.org). Supports progressive civil society in Israel.

Nicaragua Solidarity Campaign [NSC] (HR TW WC), 86 Durham Rd, London N7 7DT (+44-20-7561 4836) (nsc@nicaraguasc.org.uk) (www.nicaraguasc.org.uk). *Nicaragua Now*.

Nipponzan Myohoji (RP), Peace Pagoda, Willen, Milton Keynes MK15 0BA, Bucks (+44-1908-663652) (fax). Also in London: +44-20-7228 9620.

No 2 Nuclear Power (EL), c/o Pete Roche, Friends of the Earth Scotland, Thorn House, 5 Rose Street, Edinburgh EH2 (rochepete8@aol.com) (www.no2nuclearpower.org.uk). Provides key website and nuclear information.

No Sweat (HR RA TW), 5 Caledonian Rd, London N1 (admin@nosweat.org.uk) (www.nosweat.org.uk). Against sweatshops; for workers' and TU rights.

NO2ID (HR RA TW), Box 412, 19-21 Crawford St, London W1H 1PJ (+44-20-7340 6077) (office@no2id.net) (www.no2id.net). *NO2ID Newsletter*. Opposes ID cards and the database state.

Non-Violent Resistance Network [NVRN] (RA ND PA), c/o David Polden, CND, 162 Holloway Rd, London N7 8DQ (+44-20-7700 2393) (davidtrpolden1@gmail.com). *Newsletter*.

Northern Friends Peace Board [NFPB] (SF), Victoria Hall, Knowsley St, Bolton BL1 2AS (+44-1204-382330) (nfpb@gn.apc.org) (nfpb.org.uk). *NFPB Update*.

Norwich Environment Resource Centre (EL PO), The Greenhouse, 42-46 Bethel St, Norwich NR2 1NR (+44-1603-631007) (www.GreenhouseTrust.co.uk).

Nuclear Awareness Group [NAG] (EL), 16 Back St, Winchester SO23 9SB, Hants (+44-1962-890160) (fax) (nuclearawarenessgroup.org.uk). *Newsletter*.

Nuclear Information Service [NIS] (RE ND), 35-39 London St, Reading RG1 4PS (+44-118-327 4935) (fax) (office@nuclearinfo.org) (nuclearinfo.org).

Nuclear Morality Flowchart Project (ND), c/o Martin Birdseye, 88 Fern Lane, Hounslow TW5 0HJ, Middlesex (+44-20-8571 1691) (info@nuclearmorality.com) (nuclearmorality.com). Helps people to think about ethical accountability.

Nuclear Trains Action Group [NTAG] (ND RA), c/o Mordechai Vanunu House, 162 Holloway Rd, London N7 8DR (+44-20-7700 2393) (davidtrpolden1@gmail.com) (www.nonucleartrains.org.uk). *Newletter*. Working Group of London Region CND.

Nuclear Weapons Financing Research Group (RE ND RP), c/o Christian CND, 162 Holloway Rd, London N7 8DQ (investinginchange.enquiries@gmail.com) (investinginchange.org). Network of religious peace organisations.

Nuclear-Free Local Authorities Secretariat [NFLA] (ND EL), c/o Manchester City Council, Town Hall, Manchester M60 3NY (+44-161-234 3244) (fax 274 7379) (s.morris4@manchester.gov.uk) (www.nuclearpolicy.info).

Nukewatch UK (ND RA RE), c/o Edinburgh Peace & Justice Centre, 25 Nicholson Sq, Edinburgh EH8 9BX (+44-345 458 8365) (spotters@nukewatch.org.uk) (www.nukewatch.org.uk).

Oasis of Peace UK (CD CR HR), 192B Station Rd, Edgware HA8 7AR, Middx (+44-20-8952 4717) (office@oasisofpeace.org.uk) (www.oasisofpeaceuk.org). Formerly British Friends of NSWaS.

One World Trust [OWT] (WF), Coombe Head, Tresham, Wotton under Edge, Glos GL12 7RW (info@oneworldtrust.org) (www.oneworldtrust.org).

One World Week (HR TW EL), 35-39 London St, Reading RG1 4PS, Berks (+44-118-939 4933) (oww@oneworldweek.org) (www.oneworldweek.org).

OneVoice Movement - Europe (CD CR), Unit 4, Benwell Studios, 11-13 Benwell Rd, London N7 7BL (+44-20-8004 6431) (europe@OneVoiceMovement.org.uk) (www.onevoicemovement.org). See also under Israel, Palestine, and USA.

Orthodox Peace Fellowship UK [OPF] (RP), c/o Seraphim Honeywell, "Birchenhoe", Crowfield, nr Brackley NN13 5TW, Northants (oxpeacefp@aol.com) (www.incommunion.org). *In Communion*.

Oxford Network of Peace Studies [OxPeace] (RE), c/o Dept of Politics and International Relations, Manor Road Building, Manor Rd, Oxford OX1 3UQ (+44-1865-278700) (liz.carmichael@sjc.ox.ac.uk). Promotes study of peacemaking and peace-building.

Oxford Research Group (RE CR DA), The Green House, 244-254 Cambridge Heath Rd, London E2 9DA (+44-20-3559 6745) (org@oxfordresearchgroup.org.uk) (www.oxfordresearchgroup.org.uk).

Palestine Solidarity Campaign [PSC] (TW CR), Box BM PSA, London WC1N 3XX (+44-20-7700 6192) (fax 7700 5747) (info@palestinecampaign.org) (www.palestinecampaign.org).

Pax Christi (PC PA RE), Christian Peace Education Centre, St Joseph's, Watford Way, Hendon, London NW4 4TY (+44-20-8203 4884) (fax 8203 5234) (admin@paxchristi.org.uk) (www.paxchristi.org.uk). *Justpeace.*

Pax Christi Scotland (PC), c/o Xaverian Missionaries, Calder Ave, Coatbridge ML5 4JS (admin@paxchristiscotland.org) (www.paxchristiscotland.org).

Peace Brigades International UK [PBI UK] (PA RE HR CD), 29c Oakfield Rd, London N4 4NP (admin@peacebrigades.org.uk) (peacebrigades.org.uk).

Peace Direct (CR RE), Second Floor, 72-74 Mare St, London E8 4RT (+44-20-3422 5549) (info@peacedirect.org) (www.peacedirect.org).

Peace Education Network (RE), c/o Pax Christi, St Joseph's, Watford Way, London NW4 4TY (+44-20-8203 4884) (education@paxchristi.org.uk) (www.peace-education.org.uk).

Peace Hub - Quaker Peace and Justice Centre (SF PO CD), 41 Bull St, Birmingham B4 6AF (+44-121-238 2869) (office@peacehub.org.uk) (peacehub.org.uk).

Peace in Kurdistan (HR), 44 Ainger Rd, London NW3 3AT (+44-20-7586 5892) (estella24@tiscali.co.uk) (www.peaceinkurdistancampaign.com).

Peace Museum UK (RE PA CR), 10 Piece Hall Yard, off Hustlergate, Bradford BD1 1PJ (+44-1274-780241) (info@peacemuseum.org.uk) (www.peacemuseum.org.uk).

Peace News - for nonviolent revolution [PN] (WR HR AL RA ND), 5 Caledonian Rd, London N1 9DY (+44-20-7278 3344) (fax 7278 0444) (editorial@peacenews.info) (www.peacenews.info).

Peace One Day (CR PO RE), St George's House, 15 St George's Rd, Richmond, Surrey TW9 (+44-20-8334 9900) (fax 8948 0545) (info@peaceoneday.org) (www.peaceoneday.org).

Peace Party - Non-violence, Justice, Environment (PA HR EL), c/o John Morris, 39 Sheepfold Rd, Guildford GU2 9TT, Surrey (+44-1483-576400) (info@peaceparty.org.uk) (www.peaceparty.org.uk). *Peace.* Secular pacifist electoral movement.

Peace Pledge Union [PPU] (WR RE), 1 Peace Passage, Brecknock Rd, London N7 0BT (+44-20-7424 9444) (mail@ppu.org.uk) (www.ppu.org.uk). *Peace Matters.*

Peace Tax Seven (TR), c/o Woodlands, Ledge Hill, Market Lavington, Wilts SN10 (info@peacetaxseven.com) (www.peacetaxseven.com).

Peaceful Schools UK (RP), Witch Hazel Cottage, Linden Rd, Headley Down GU35 8EN, Hants (+44-1428-717090) (anna@peacefulschools.org.uk) (peacefulschools.org.uk). Formerly Peaceful Schools Movement.

People & Planet (TW HR EL), The Old Music Hall, 106-108 Cowley Rd, Oxford OX4 1JE (+44-1865-403225) (people@peopleandplanet.org) (peopleandplanet.org). National student network.

People Against Rio Tinto and its Subsidiaries [PARTiZANS] (HR EL TW), 41A Thornhill Sq, London N1 1BE (+44-20-7700 6189) (fax) (partizans@gn.apc.org) (www.minesandcommunities.org).

Police Spies Out of Lives [PSOOL] (HR), c/o 84b Whitechapel High St, London E1 7QX (contact@policespiesoutoflives.org.uk) (policespiesoutoflives.org.uk). Supports women abused by undercover police.

Possible (EL), 8 Delancey Passage, Camden Town, London NW1 7NN (+44-20-7388 6688) (hello@wearepossible.org) (www.wearepossible.org). Formery 10:10 Climate Action.

Practical Action (PO TW), Schumacher Centre for Technology and Development, Bourton Hall, Bourton-on-Dunsmore, Rugby, Warwickshire CV23 9QZ (+44-1926-634400) (fax 634401) (enquiries@practicalaction.org.uk) (www.practicalaction.org.uk).

Public Interest Case Against Trident [PICAT] (ND), 6 Church St, Knighton, Powys LD7 1AG (+44-1547-520929) (reforest@gn.apc.org) (picat.online).

Pugwash Conferences on Science and World Affairs (DA EL RE TW CR), Ground Floor Flat, 63A Great Russell St, London WC1B 3BJ (+44-20-7405 6661) (office@britishpugwash.org) (britishpugwash.org). *Pugwash Newsletter.* Part of international Pugwash network.

Quaker Concern for the Abolition of Torture [Q-CAT] (SF HR), c/o 38 The Mount, Heswall CH60 4RA, Wirral (+44-151-342 4425) (chasraws@onetel.com) (q-cat.org.uk).

BRITAIN

Quaker Peace & Social Witness [QPSW]
(SF DA PA), Friends House, 175 Euston Rd, London NW1 2BJ (+44-20-7663 1000) (qpsw@quaker.org.uk) (www.quaker.org.uk/qpsw).

Quaker Sustainability and Peace Programme (SF EL RE DA PA), QPSW, Friends House, 175 Euston Rd, London NW1 2BJ (+44-20-7663 1067) (fax 7663 1001) (survival@quaker.org.uk) (www.quaker.org.uk). Previously Peace and Disarmament Programme.

Radical Routes (AL PO), c/o Cornerstone Resource Centre, 16 Sholebroke Ave, Leeds LS7 3HB (+44-1603-776445) (enquiries@radicalroutes.org.uk) (www.radicalroutes.org.uk). Network of radical housing, worker & other co-ops.

Redress (HR), 87 Vauxhall Walk, London SE11 (+44-20-7793 1777) (fax 7793 1719) (info@redress.org) (www.redress.org). Seeks justice for torture survivors.

Religions for Peace UK [WCRP-UK] (RP RE), c/o 18 Little Acres, Ware SG12 9JW, Hertfordshire (+44-1920-465714) (fax) (secretary@religionsforpeace.org.uk) (www.religionsforpeace.org.uk).

Religious Society of Friends in Britain (Quakers) (SF), Friends House, Euston Rd, London NW1 2BJ (+44-20-7663 1000) (fax 7663 1001) (www.quaker.org.uk). *Quaker News*; *The Friend*; *Quaker Voices*.

Reprieve (HR), PO Box 72054, London EC3P 3BZ (+44-20-7553 8140) (info@reprieve.org.uk) (www.reprieve.org.uk).

Rethinking Security (RE DA EL), c/o Saferworld, The Grayston Centre, 28 Charles Sq, London N1 (celia@rethinkingsecurity.org.uk) (rethinkingsecurity.org.uk). Network of academics, activists, organisations.

Rising Tide UK [RTUK] (EL RA AL), c/o London Action Resource Centre, 62 Fieldgate St, Whitechapel, London E1 1ES (info@risingtide.org.uk) (www.risingtide.org.uk). Direct action for climate justice.

RoadPeace (EL RE HR), Shakespeare Business Centre, 245a Coldharbour Lane, London SW9 8RR (+44-20-7733 1603) (info@roadpeace.org) (roadpeace.org). Supports road traffic victims and families.

Saferworld (RE AT), The Grayston Centre, 28 Charles Sq, London N1 (+44-20-7324 4646) (fax 7324 4647) (general@saferworld.org.uk) (www.saferworld.org.uk). Helping people turn away from armed violence.

Scientists for Global Responsibility [SGR] (RE ND EL AT DA), Unit 2.8, Halton Mill, Mill Lane, Halton, Lancaster LA2 6ND, Lancashire (+44-1524-812073) (info@sgr.org.uk) (www.sgr.org.uk). *SGR Newsletter*.

Scotland's for Peace (ND RE AT), c/o 77 Southpark Ave, Glasgow G12 (+44-141-357 1529) (info@scotland4peace.org) (www.scotland4peace.org). Umbrella body.

Scottish Campaign for Nuclear Disarmament [SCND] (ND), PO Box 3620, Glasgow G73 9FQ (+44-141-357 1529) (scnd@banthebomb.org) (www.banthebomb.org). *Nuclear Free Scotland*.

Scottish Friends of Palestine (HR TW), 31 Tinto Rd, Glasgow G43 2AL (+44-141-637 8046) (info@scottish-friends-of-palestine.org) (www.scottishfriendsofpalestine.org).

Scrap Trident Coalition (ND PA RA), c/o Edinburgh Peace and Justice Centre, 5 Upper Bow, Edinburgh EH1 2JN (+44-131-629 1058) (scraptrident@gmail.com) (scraptrident.org). Network in Scotland.

SCRAP Weapons (DA), Centre for Int'l Studies and Diplomacy, SOAS, University of London, 10 Thornhaugh St, Russell Sq, London WC1H 0XG (+44-20-7898 4322) (scrap.weapons@soas.ac.uk) (www.scrapweapons.com).

Sea Shepherd UK (EL RA), 27 Old Gloucester St, London WC1N 3AX (+44-300-111 0501) (admin@seashepherd-uk.org) (www.seashepherd.org.uk). Conserving nature on the high seas.

Seeds of Peace (CD CR PO), Suite 1, 3rd Floor, 11-12 St James's Square, London SW1Y 4LB (london@seedsofpeace.org) (www.seedsofpeace.org). Trains people for conflict transformation.

Servas Britain (SE), c/o 1 Wrekin Course, Wellington, Telford TF6 5AJ (www.servas.org.uk).

Soil Association (EL PO TW), South Plaza, Marlborough St, Bristol BS1 (+44-117-314 5000) (fax 314 5001) (memb@soilassociation.org) (www.soilassociation.org). Scotland office: +44-131-666 2474.

Solidarity with People of Turkey [SPOT] (HR), 22 Moorefield Rd, London N17 6PY (spot@daymer.org) (spotturkey.co.uk).

South Cheshire & North Staffs CND [SCANS CND] (ND), Groundwork Enterprise Centre, Albany Works, Moorland Rd, Burslem, Stoke-on-Trent ST6 1EB, Staffs (+44-1782-829913) (scanscnd@ymail.com) (www.scanscnd.org.uk). *Banner*.

Southdowns Peace Group (DA), c/o Vida, 22 Beaufort Rd, Bedhampton, Havant PO9 3HU (+44-23-9234 6696) (vida.henning@ntlworld.com).

Southern Region CND (ND), 3 Harpsichord Place, Oxford OX4 1BY (+44-1865-248357) (oxfordcnd@phonecoop.coop).

Stop Climate Chaos Scotland [SCCS] (EL), 2nd Floor, Thorn House, 5 Rose St, Edinburgh EH2 2PR (+44-131-243 2701) (info@stopclimatechaosscotland.org) (www.stopclimatechaos.org/scotland). Development, environment, etc, groups' coalition.

Stop Hinkley (EL), 8 The Bartons, Yeabridge, South Petherton TA13 5LW, Somerset (+44-1749-860767) (admin@stophinkley.org) (www.stophinkley.org). Against nuclear power in south-west England.

Stop the War Coalition [STWC], 86 Durham Rd, London N7 (+44-20-7561 4830) (office@stopwar.org.uk) (www.stopwar.org.uk).

Student Christian Movement [SCM] (RP), Grays Court, 3 Nursery Rd, Edgbaston, Birmingham B15 3JX (+44-121-426 4918) (scm@movement.org.uk) (www.movement.org.uk).

Surfers Against Sewage [SAS] (EL), Unit 2, Wheal Kitty Workshops, St Agnes TR5 0RD, Cornwall (+44-1872-553001) (fax 552615) (info@sas.org.uk) (www.sas.org.uk). *Pipeline News.*

Syria Peace & Justice Group (CR CD AT DA), c/o LARC, 62 Fieldgate St, London E1 (syriapeaceandjustice@gmail.com) (syriapeaceandjustice.wordpress.com). Anti-militarist human rights campaign.

Syrian Human Rights Committee [SHRC] (HR), PO Box 123, Edgware HA8 0XF, Middlesex (fax +44-870-1377678) (walid@shrc.org) (www.shrc.org). Syrian human rights group in exile.

Tapol (HR AT TW RE), Durham Resource Centre, 86 Durham Rd, London N7 (+44-20-7561 7485) (info@tapol.org) (www.tapol.org).

The Brotherhood Church (WR AL EL), Stapleton, nr Pontefract, Yorkshire WF8 3DF (+44-1977-620381).

The Climate Coalition (EL), Romero House, 55 Westminster Bridge Rd, London SE1 7JB (+44-20-7870 2213) (admin@theclimatecoalition.org) (www.theclimatecoalition.org).

The Corner House (HR TW EL), Station Rd, Sturminster Newton, Dorset DT10 1BB (+44-1258-473795) (fax) (enquiries@thecornerhouse.org.uk) (www.thecornerhouse.org.uk). *Briefing Papers.*

The Forgiveness Project (CR PO), 10 Buckingham Palace Rd, London SW1W 0QP (+44-20-7821 0035) (fax) (info@theforgivenessproject.com) (www.theforgivenessproject.com).

Tibet Foundation (HR), Hamilton House, Mabledon Place, London WC1H 9BB (+44-20-7930 6001) (info@tibet-foundation.org) (www.tibet-foundation.org).

Tibet Society (HR TW CR), 2 Baltic Place, London N1 5AQ (+44-20-7923 0021) (info@tibetsociety.com) (www.tibetsociety.com). Campaigns for Tibetan self-determination.

Together Against Sizewell C [TASC] (EL), Wood Farm, Westward Ho, Leiston IP16 4HT, Suffolk (info@tasizewellc.org.uk) (tasizewellc.org.uk). Opposing proposed new nuclear power station.

Town and Country Planning Association [TCPA] (EL), 17 Carlton House Terr, London SW1Y 5AS (+44-20-7930 8903) (fax 7930 3280) (tcpa@tcpa.org.uk) (www.tcpa.org.uk). *Town & Country Planning.*

Trade Justice Movement (TW HR EL), 66 Offley Rd, London SW9 0LS (mail@tjm.org.uk) (www.tjm.org.uk).

Trident Ploughshares (WR ND RA), c/o Edinburgh Peace & Justice Centre, 25 Nicolson Sq, Edinburgh EH8 9BX (+44-345 458 8361) (tp2000@gn.apc.org) (tridentploughshares.org).

Turning the Tide (SF PO RA), Friends House, Euston Rd, London NW1 2BJ (+44-20-7663 1064) (fax 7663 1049) (stevew@quaker.org.uk) (www.turning-the-tide.org). *Making Waves.* Offers workshops, nonviolence training, etc.

Tyne & Wear CND (ND), 1 Rectory Ave, Gosforth, Newcastle-upon-Tyne NE3 1XS (+44-191-285 1290) (rhpg@btinternet.com).

UK Committee for UNICEF [UNICEF UK] (TW HR), UNICEF House, 30a Great Sutton St, London EC1 (+44-20-7490 2388) (fax 7250 1733) (www.unicef.org.uk).

UNA Exchange (UN WC PO), Temple of Peace, Cathays Park, Cardiff CF10 3AP (+44-29-2022 3088) (fax 2022 2540) (info@unaexchange.org) (www.unaexchange.org). *Opinions.*

UNA-UK Members for Civil Society Link with UN General Assembly [UNGA-Link UK] (UN), 11 Wilberforce House, 119 Worple Rd, London SW20 8ET (+44-20-8944 0574) (fax) (info@ungalink.org.uk) (www.ungalink.org.uk).

Unitarian and Free Christian Peace Fellowship [UPF] (RP), c/o Sue Woolley, 5 Martins Rd, Piddinston, Northampton NN7 2DN (+44-1604-870746) (www.unitariansocieties.org.uk/peace).

United Nations Association - UK [UNA-UK] (UN HR RE TW), 3 Whitehall Court, London SW1A 2EL (+44-20-7766 3454) (fax 7000 1381) (info@una.org.uk) (www.una.org.uk). *UNA-UK.*

Uniting for Peace [UfP] (DA ND CD AT RE), 14 Cavell St, London E1 2HP (+44-20-7791 1717) (info@unitingforpeace.com) (unitingforpeace.com). *Uniting for Peace.* Also in Edinburgh (+44-131-446 9545).

BRITAIN

Vegan Society (EL TW PO HR), Donald Watson House, 34-35 Ludgate Hill, Birmingham B3 1EH (+44-121-523 1730) (info@vegansociety.com) (www.vegansociety.com). *The Vegan.*

Vegetarian Society of the UK (EL TW PO), Parkdale, Dunham Rd, Altrincham, Cheshire (+44-161-925 2000) (fax 926 9182) (info@vegsoc.org) (www.vegsoc.org). *The Vegetarian.*

Veggies (PO EL), c/o Sumac Centre, 245 Gladstone St, Nottingham NG7 (+44-115-960 8254) (info@veggies.org.uk) (www.veggies.org.uk).

Violence Research Centre (RE), c/o Institute of Criminology, Sidgwick Ave, Cambridge CB3 9DA (+44-1223-335360) (fax 335356) (vrc@crim.cam.ac.uk) (www.vrc.crim.cam.ac.uk). Studies interpersonal violence.

Voluntary Service Overseas [VSO] (TW), 100 London Rd, Kingston-upon-Thames KT2, Surrey (+44-20-8780 7500) (enquiry@vsoint.org) (www.vsointernational.org).

Volunteer Action for Peace [VAP UK] (WC HR EL), 16 Overhill Rd, East Dulwich, London SE22 0PH (action@vap.org.uk) (www.vap.org.uk). Within UK, tel 0844-209 0927.

Volunteering Matters (PO CD), The Levy Centre, 18-24 Lower Clapton Rd, London E5 (+44-20-3780 5870) (information@volunteeringmatters.org.uk) (volunteeringmatters.org.uk). Formerly Community Service Volunteers.

War Child (RE PA PO), Studio 320, Highgate Studios, 53-79 Highgate Rd, London NW5 1TL (+44-20-7112 2555) (info@warchild.org.uk) (www.warchild.org.uk). Aid organisation for children in war zones.

War On Want [WOW] (TW), 44-48 Shepherdess Walk, London N1 7JP (+44-20-7324 5040) (fax 7324 5041) (support@waronwant.org) (www.waronwant.org).

Week of Prayer for World Peace (RP), c/o 126 Manor Green Rd, Epsom KT19 8LN, Surrey (+44-1628-530309) (j.jackson215@btinternet.com) (www.weekofprayerforworldpeace.com).

West Midlands CND [WMCND] (ND), 54 Allison St, Digbeth, Birmingham B5 5TH (+44-121-643 4617) (wmcndall@gmail.com) (www.wmcnd.org.uk).

West Midlands Quaker Peace Education Project [WMQPEP] (SF RE CR), 41 Bull St, Birmingham B4 6AF (+44-121-236 4796) (office@peacemakers.org.uk) (www.peacemakers.org.uk).

Western Sahara Campaign UK (HR TW), Manora, Cwmystwyth, Aberystwyth SY23 4AF (+44-1974-282214) (coordinator@wsahara.org.uk) (www.wsahara.org.uk).

White Ribbon Campaign (PO), White Ribbon House, 1 New Rd, Mytholmroyd, Hebden Bridge HX7 5DZ (+44-1422-886545) (info@whiteribboncampaign.co.uk) (www.whiteribboncampaign.co.uk).

Women's International League for Peace and Freedom [UK WILPF] (WL), 52-54 Featherstone St, London EC1Y 8RT (+44-20-7250 1968) (ukwilpf.peace@gmail.com) (www.wilpf.org.uk). Also Scottish office (scottishwilpf@yahoo.co.uk).

Woodcraft Folk (PA EL PO RE TW), Units 9/10, 83 Crampton St, London SE17 (+44-20-7703 4173) (fax 7358 6370) (info@woodcraft.org.uk) (www.woodcraft.org.uk). *The Courier.* Co-operative children's and youth organisation.

World Future Council - UK Office (WF EL DA ND), 4th Floor, Rex House, 4-12 Regent St, London SW1Y 4PE (info.uk@worldfuturecouncil.org) (www.worldfuturecouncil.org). Promotes sustainable future.

World Harmony Orchestra (CD PO), 12d Princess Crescent, London N4 2HJ (www.worldharmonyorchestra.com). Raises funds for humanitarian causes.

World Peace Campaign, Hill House, Cookley, Kidderminster DY10 3UW, Worcs (+44-1562-851101) (fax 851824) (office@worldpeacecampaign.co.uk) (www.worldpeacecampaign.co.uk).

World Peace Prayer Society [WPPS] (RP PO EL RE), Allanton Sanctuary, Auldgirth, Dumfries DG2 0RY (+44-1387-740642) (allanton@worldpeace-uk.org) (www.worldpeace-uk.org). Promote the message "May peace prevail on earth".

XR Peace (EL RA), via Trident Ploughshares, c/o Edinburgh Peace & Justice Centre, Central Methodist Church, 25 Nicolson Sq, Edinburgh EH8 9BX (+44-1547-520929) (xrpeace@gn.apc.org) (xrpeace.org). Peace activists supporting Extinction Rebellion.

Yorkshire CND (ND), The Deaf Centre, 25 Hallfield Rd, Bradford BD1 3RP, W Yorks (+44-1274-730795) (info@yorkshirecnd.org.uk) (www.yorkshirecnd.org.uk). *Action for Peace.*

Youth and Student CND [YSCND] (ND RA), 162 Holloway Rd, London N7 8DQ (+44-20-7700 2393) (yscnd@riseup.net) (www.yscnd.org).

BURMA

Peace Way Foundation (HR), see under Thailand.

CANADA

Amnesty International Canadian Section - English Speaking (AI), 312 Laurier Ave E, Ottawa, ON, K1N 1H9 (+1-613-744 7667) (fax 746 2411) (members@amnesty.ca) (www.amnesty.ca). *The Activist.*

Amnistie Internationale - Section Canadienne Francophone (AI), 50 rue Ste-Catherine Ouest - bureau 500, Montréal, QC, H2X 3V4 (+1-514-766 9766) (fax 766 2088) (www.amnistie.ca). *Agir.*

Artistes pour la Paix (PA ND AT), CP 867 - Succursale C, Montréal, QC, H2L 4L6 (artistespourlapaix.org).

Baptist Peace Fellowship of North America - Bautistas por la Paz (RP), see under USA.

Boundary Peace Initiative (FR), Box 2572, Grand Forks, BC, V0H 1H0 (+1-250-442 0434) (l4peace@telus.net) (boundarypeaceinitiative.org).

Canadian Centres for Teaching Peace (RE PO), 230 Belle Isle St, Shediac, NB, E4P 1G8 (+1-403-461 2469) (fax 309-407 6576) (stewartr@peace.ca) (www.peace.ca).

Canadian Coalition for Nuclear Responsibility / Regroupement pour la Surveillance du Nucléaire [CCNR] (ND DI CD), 53 Dufferin Rd, Hampstead, QC, H3X 2X8 (+1-514-489 5118) (ccnr@web.ca) (www.ccnr.org).

Canadian Peace Congress (WP), PO Box 73593, Wychwood Post Office, Toronto, ON, M6C 4A7 (info@CanadianPeaceCongress.ca) (www.canadianpeacecongress.ca).

Canadian School of Peacebuilding (RE CR), Canadian Mennonite University, 500 Shaftesbury Blvd, Winnipeg, Manitoba, R3P 2N2 (+1-204-487 3300) (fax 837 7415) (csop@cmu.ca) csop.cmu.ca).

Canadian Secular Alliance [CSA] (HR), 802 - 195 St Patrick St, Toronto, ON, M5T 2Y8 (+1-416-402 8856) (info@secularalliance.ca) (secularalliance.ca).

Centre de Ressources sur la Non-violence [CRNV] (WR EL), 1945 rue Mullins - bureau 160, Montréal, QC, H3K 1N9 (+1-514-504 5012) (crnv@nonviolence.ca) (nonviolence.ca).

Christian Peacemaker Teams [CPT Canada] (RP PA RA), 103 Bellevue Ave, Torontoo, ON, M5T 2N8 (+1-647-339 0991) (canada@cpt.org) (cpt.org). Also based in USA.

Civilian Peace Service Canada (CD PO), 2106-1025 Richmond Rd, Ottowa, ON, K2B 8G8 (+1-613-721 9829) (gbreedyk@civilianpeaceservice.org) (civilianpeaceservice.org).

Coalition for Gun Control, PO Box 90062, 1488 Queen St West, Toronto, ON, M6K 3K3 (+1-416-604 0209) (coalitionforguncontrol@gmail.com) (guncontrol.ca). Also in Montreal (+1-514-528 2360).

Coalition to Oppose the Arms Trade [COAT] (AT), 191 James St, Ottawa, ON, K1R 5M6 (+1-613-231 3076) (overcoat@rogers.com) (coat.ncf.ca).

Collectif Échec À la Guerre (PA RE DA), c/o AQOCI, 1001 Rue Sherbrooke Est - Bur 540, Montréal, QC, H2L 1L3 (+1-514-919 7249) (info@echecalaguerre.org) (echecalaguerre.org).

Conscience Canada (TR), 515 Langs Dr - Unit J, Cambridge, ON, N3H 5E4 (+1-250-537 5251) (info@consciencecanada.ca) (www.consciencecanada.ca).

Edmonton Peace Council (WP), 392 Meadowview Drive, Fort Saskatchewan, Alberta T8L 0N9 (+1-587-873 9739) (canadianpeace@gmail.com). *Alberta Peace News.*

Friends of the Earth / Les Ami(e)s de la Terre [FoE] (FE), 150 - 18 Louisa St, Ottawa, ON, K1R 6Y6 (+1-613-241 0085) (foe@foecanada.org) (www.foecanada.org).

Greenpeace Canada (GP), 33 Cecil St, Toronto, ON, M5T 1N1 (+1-416-597 8408) (fax 597 8422) (supporter.ca@greenpeace.org) (www.greenpeace.ca).

IPPNW Canada (IP IB), 30 Cleary Ave, Ottawa, ON, K2A 4A1 (+1-613-233 1982) (info@ippnwcanada.org) (www.ippnwcanada.ca).

Mennonite Central Committee Canada (RP HR EL), 134 Plaza Dr, Winnipeg, MB, R3T 5K9 (+1-204-261 6381) (fax 269 9875) (canada@mcccanada.ca) (www.mcccanada.ca).

Pace e Bene Canada (PA RP), 4058 Rivard, Montreal, Quebec, H2L 4H9 (veronow@sympatico.ca).

Peace Brigades International - Canada [PBI-Canada] (CR RE SD), 211 Bronson Ave - Suite 220, Ottawa, ON, K1R 6H5 (+1-613-237 6968) (direction@pbicanada.org) (pbicanada.org).

Peace Magazine (PA AT CR), Box 248, Toronto P, Toronto, ON, M5S 2S7 (+1-416-789 2294) (office@peacemagazine.org) - (www.peacemagazine.org). 4 yrly, Can$20 (Can$24 US, Can$35 elsewhere).

Peace Studies Program (RE), McMaster University, Togo Salmon Hall 721, 1280 Main St West, Hamilton, Ontario L8S 4M2 (+1-905-525 9140) (peacestudies.humanities.mcmaster.ca). Formerly Centre for Peace Studies.

PeaceWorks, c/o MSCU Centre for Peace Advancement, CGUC, University of Waterloo, 140 Westmount Road North, Waterloo, ON, N2L 3G6 (+1-519-591 1365) (mail@peaceworks.tv) (peaceworks.tv). Youth movement.

Project Ploughshares (RE AT ND RP DA), 140 Westmount Rd North, Waterloo, ON, N2L 3G6 (+1-519-888 6541) (fax 888 0018) (plough@ploughshares.ca) (www.ploughshares.ca).

CANADA

Project Save the World, c/o Box 248, Toronto P, Toronto, ON, M5S 2S7 (+1-416-789 2294) (project@peacemagazine.org) (peacemagazine.org).
A project of Peace Magazine.
Religions for Peace - Canada / Religions pour la Paix - Canada (RP RE PA), 3333 Queen Mary Rd 490-1, Montréal, QC, H3Z 1A2 (pascale.fremond@videotron.ca).
Servas Canada (SE), c/o Christine Fernie, PO Box 147, Rimbey, AB, T0C 2J0 (canada@servas.org) (www.canadaservas.org).
Trudeau Centre for Peace, Conflict and Justice (RE), Monk School of Global Affairs, University of Toronto, 1 Devonshire Place, Toronto, ON, M5S 3K7 (+1-416-946 0326) (pcj.programme@utoronto.ca) (www.munkschool.utoronto.ca/trudeaucentre).
United Nations Association in Canada / Association canadienne pour les Nations-Unies [UNAC/ACNU] (UN EL RE HR CD), 400 - 30 Metcalfe St, Ottawa, ON, K1P 5L4 (+1-613-232 5751) (fax 563 2455) (info@unac.org) (unac.org).
USCC Doukhobors (RP CD PA), Box 760, Grand Forks, BC, V0H 1H0 (+1-250-442 8252) (fax 442 3433) (info@uscc-doukhobors.org) (www.usccdoukhobors.org). *Iskra*.
Union of Spiritual Communities of Christ.
Voice of Women for Peace / La Voix des Femmes pour la Paix [VOW] (IB UN PA), 25 Cecil St - Suite 310, Toronto, ON, M5T 1N1 (+1-416-603 7915) (info@vowpeace.org) (www.vowpeace.org).
Women's International League for Peace and Freedom [WILPF] (WL), PO Box 365, 916 West Broadway, Vancouver, BC, V5Z 1K7 (+1-604-224 1517) (judydavis@telus.net).
World Federalist Movement - Canada / Mouvement Fédéraliste Mondial (Canada) (WF), Suite 207, 110 - 323 Chapel St, Ottowa, ON, K1N 7Z2 (+1-613-230 0647) (wfcnat@web.ca) (www.worldfederalistscanada.org). *Mondial*.

CHAD

Tchad Non-Violence [TNV] (WR FR), BP 1266, N'Djamena (astnv@yahoo.fr).

CHILE

Greenpeace Chile (GP), Argomedo 50, Santiago (+56-2-2634 2120) (fax 2634 8580) (info-chile@greenpeace.org) (www.greenpeace.org/chile).
Grupo de Objeción de Conciencia "Ni Casco Ni Uniforme" (WR), Bremen 585, Ñuñoa, Santiago (+56-2-556 6066) (objetores@yahoo.com) (nicasconiuniforme.wordpress.com).
Grupo de Objeción de Conciencia - Rompiendo Filas (WR), Prat 289 - Oficina 2-A, Temuco (rompiendofilas@entodaspartes.org).
Servicio Paz y Justicia - Chile [SERPAJ] (FR), Orella Nº 1015, Valparaíso (+56-32-215 8239) (serpaj@serpajchile.cl) (serpajchile.cl).

CHINA

China Committee on Religion and Peace [CCRP] (RP), 23 Taipingqiao St, Xichen District, Beijing 100811 (+86-10-6619 1655) (fax 6619 1645) (ccrp1994@hotmail.com) (www.cppcc.gov.cn/ccrp).
Friends of Nature [FON] (EL), Rm 406, Building C, Huazhan Guoji Gongyu, 12 Yumin Road, Chaoyang District, Beijing 100029 (+86-10-6523 2040) (office@fonchina.org) (www.fon.org.cn).

COLOMBIA

Acción Colectiva de Objetores y Objetoras de Conciencia [ACOOC] (WR), Cr 19 - No 33A - 26/1, Bogotá (+57-1-560 5058) (objecion@objetoresbogota.org) (objetoresbogota.org).

CONGO, DEMOCRATIC REPUBLIC OF

Association pour les Nations Unies de la RDC [ANU-RDC] (UN), BP 2214, Kinshasa 1 (www.unadrcongo.org).
Cercle des Jeunes Leaders pour la Paix / Circle of Young Leaders for Peace (RP), Av Kwango - No 7, Kintambo Magasin, Ngaliema, Dist Lukunga, Kinshasa (+243-81-514 0938) (jcsaki2000@yahoo.fr).
Congo Peace Network (DA CR), 42 Ave Bunagana, Q Katindo, Commune de Goma (+243-85-222 4225) (info@congopeacenetwork.org) (cpn.congopeacenetwork.org).
Groupe Interconfessionnel de la Réconciliation / Kinshasa [GIR] (FR), see under Belgium.
Life & Peace Institute (CR RP), Bukavu (for postal address see under Rwanda) (pieter.vanholder@life-peace.org).
Peace & Conflict Resolution Project (CR), for postal address see under Rwanda (+243-993-463279) (peacecrp@yahoo.com) (www.peaceconflictresolutionproject.webs.com). Based in Bukavu.

COSTA RICA

Centro de Estudios Para la Paz [CEPPA] (RE), Apdo 8-4820, 1000 San José (+506-2234 0524) (fax) (info@ceppacr.org) (www.ceppacr.org).
Liga Internacional de Mujeres pro Paz y Libertad [LIMPAL] (WL), Avenida sexta Bis No 1336 - por Calle 15, Costado Oeste de los Tribunales San José (limpalcr@yahoo.es).

Monteverde Friends Meeting (SF), Monteverde 5655, Puntarenas (+506-2645 5530) (fax 2645 5302) (MonteverdeQuakers@gmail.com) (MonteverdeQuakers.org).

CROATIA
Centar za Zene Zrtve Rata / Centre for Women War Victims - ROSA [CZZR] (CR HR), Kralja Drzislava 2, 10000 Zagreb (+385-1-455 1142) (fax 455 1128) (cenzena@zamir.net) (www.czzzr.hr). Feminist, anti-militarist.
Centar za Mirovne Studije [CMS] (WR CR RE HR), Selska cesta 112a, 10000 Zagreb (+385-1-482 0094) (fax) (cms@cms.hr) (www.cms.hr).

CUBA
Movimiento Cubano por la Paz y la Soberanía de los Pueblos (WP), Calle C No 670, e/ 27 y 29, Vedado, Habana (+53-7-831 9429) (secretariat@movpaz.cu) (www.movpaz.cu).

CYPRUS
Hands Across the Divide - Women Building Bridges in Cyprus (HR CD CR DA), Ellispontos 10, Dasoupolis 2015, Nicosia (handsacrossthedivide@gmail.com) (www.handsacrossthedivide.org). Supports feminist values and demilitaristion.
Oikologiki Kinisi Kyprou / Ecological Movement of Cyprus (EL), TK 28948, Nicosia 2084 (+357-2251 8787) (fax 2251 2710) (ecological_movement@cytanet.com.cy) (www.ecologicalmovement.org.cy). *Ecologiki Enimerosi.*
Philoi tes Ges (Kypros) / Friends of the Earth (Cyprus) [FOE] (FE), 361 Saint Andrews St, Lemesos 3035 (+357-2534 7042) (office@foecyprus.org) (www.foecyprus.org).
United Nations Association of Cyprus [UNAC] (UN), TK 21508, 1510 Nicosia (+357-2465 6318) (c.a.theodoulou@cytanet.com.cy).

CYPRUS (NORTHERN)
Hands Across the Divide - Women Building Bridges in Cyprus (HR CD CR DA), see under Cyprus (www.handsacrossthedivide.org). Supports feminist values and demilitaristion.

CZECH REPUBLIC
České Mírové Hnutí / Czech Peace Movement (WP), Josefa Houdka 123, 15531 Praha (mirovehnuti@email.cz) (www.mirovehnuti.cz).
Hnutí DUHA (FE RA), Údolní 33, 60200 Brno (+420-5 4521 4431) (fax 5 4521 4429) (info@hnutiduha.cz) (hnutiduha.cz). *Evergreen.*
Lékari za Bezpečný Zivot na Zemi / Physicians for Global Security (IP), c/o Vaclav Stukavec, Jizní 22, 46801 Jablonec nad Nisou 8 (+420-603 364224) (stukav@volny.cz).
Nezávislé SociálneEkologické Hnutí / Independent Socio-Ecological Movement [NESEHNUTÍ] (WR EL HR AT), Krizová 463/15, 60300 Brno (+420-5 4324 5342) (brno@nesehnuti.cz) (nesehnuti.cz). Social Ecological Movement.
Památník Mohyla Miru / Cairn of Peace Memorial (RE), K Mohyle Míru 200, 66458 Peace (+420-54 424 4724) (www.muzeumbrnenska.cz).

DENMARK
Aldrig Mere Krig / No More War [AMK] (WR AT IB), Nørremarksvej 4, 6880 Tarm (+45-9737 3163) (info@aldrigmerekrig.dk) (aldrigmerekrig.dk). *Ikkevold.*
Amnesty International (AI), Gammeltorv 8 - 5 sal, 1457 København K (+45-3345 6565) (amnesty@amnesty.dk) (www.amnesty.dk).
Center for Konfliktløsning / Danish Centre for Conflict Resolution (CR RE), Dronning Olgas Vej 30, 2000 Frederiksberg (+45-3520 0550) (center@konfliktloesning.dk) (www.konfliktloesning.dk).
Danske Laeger Mod Kernevåben [DLMK] (IP), Langdalsvej 40, 8220 Brabrand, Aarhus (+45-8626 4717) (povl.revsbech@gmail.com) (www.danskelaegermodkernevaaben.dk). *Läkare mot Kärnvapen.*
FN-Forbundet (UN WF), Tordenskjoldsgade 25 st th, 1055 København K (+45-3346 4690) (fnforbundet@fnforbundet.dk) (www.fnforbundet.dk).
Klimabevaegelsen i Danmark / Climate Movement Denmark (EL), c/o Thomas Meinart Larsen, JC Christensens Gade 2A - 3TV, 2300 København S (sek@klimabevaegelsen.dk) (www.klimabevaegelsen.dk).
Kvindernes Internationale Liga for Fred og Frihed [KILFF] (WL RE), Vesterbrogade 10 - 2, 1620 København V (wilpfdk@gmail.com) (kvindefredsliga.dk).
NOAH / Friends of the Earth Denmark (FE), Nørrebrogade 39 - 1, 2200 København N (+45-3536 1212) (fax 3536 1217) (noah@noah.dk) (www.noah.dk).
Plums Fond for Fred, Økologi og Baeredygtighed / Plums Foundation for Peace, Ecology and Sustainability (DA HR EL), Dronningensgade 14, 1420 København K (+45-3295 4417) (plumsfond@plumsfond.dk). Previously Danish Peace Foundation / Fredsfonden.
Servas Danmark (SE), c/o Jan Degrauwe, Højbakkevej 32, 9440 Aabybro (+45-2048 5087) (info@servas.dk) (www.servas.dk).

EAST TIMOR

EAST TIMOR
Haburas Foundation / Friends of the Earth Timor Leste [FE], PO Box 390, Dili (+670-331 0103) (haburaslorosae@yahoo.com) (www.haburasfoundation.org).

ECUADOR
Servicio Paz y Justicia del Ecuador [SERPAJ] (WR RP), Casilla 17-03-1567, Quito (+593-22-257 1521) (fax) (serpaj@ecuanex.net.ec) (www.serpaj.org.ec).

EGYPT
Arab Organisation for Human Rights [AOHR] (HR), 91 Merghani St, Heliopolis, Cairo 11341 (+20-2-2418 1396) (fax 2418 5346) (alaa.shalaby@aohr.net) (www.aohr.net).
No to Compulsory Military Service Movement (WR), [post should be sent via the WRI office in London] (+49-1763-141 5934) (NoMilService@gmail.com) (www.nomilservice.com).

FINLAND
Ålands Fredsinstitut / Åland Islands Peace Institute (RE HR CR), PB 85, 22101 Mariehamn, Åland (+358-18-15570) (peace@peace.ax) (www.peace.ax).
Greenpeace Finland (GP), Iso Roobertinkatu 20-22 A (5 frs), 00120 Helsinki (+358-9-6229 2200) (fax 6229 2222) (info.finland@greenpeace.org) (www.greenpeace.fi).
Kansainvälinen Vapaaehtoistyö [KVT] (SC), Rauhanasema, Veturitori 3, 00520 Helsinki (kvt@kvtfinland.org) (www.kvtfinland.org).
Laajan Turvallisuuden Verkosto / Wider Security Network [WISE] (CR DA), Siltasaarenkatu 4 - 7th floor, 00530 Helsinki (+358-44-972 4669) (info@widersecurity.fi) (www.widersecurity.fi). Formerly Civil Society Conflict Prevention Network.
Maan Ystävät / Friends of the Earth (FE), Mechelininkatu 36 B 1, 00260 Helsinki (+358-45-886 3958) (fax -2-237 1670) (toimisto@maanystavat.fi) (www.maanystavat.fi).
Peace Union of Finland / Suomen Rauhanliitto / Finlands Fredsförbundet (IB FR ND AT RE), Peace Station, Veturitori, 00520 Helsinki (+358-9-7568 2828) (fax 147297) (rauhanliitto@rauhanliitto.fi).
Physicians for Social Responsibility / Lääkärin Sosiaalinen Vastuu / Läkarens Sociala Ansvar [PSR/LSV] (IP HR PA EL), Caloniuksenkatu 9 D 40, 00100 Helsinki (+358-45-350 8516) (lsv@lsv.fi) (www.lsv.fi).
Sadankomitea / Committee of 100 (WR IB ND AT), Rauhanasema, Veturitori 3, 00520 Helsinki (sadankomitea@sadankomitea.fi) (www.sadankomitea.fi).
SaferGlobe (RE AT CR), Siltasaarenkatu 4 - 7th floor, 00530 Helsinki (+358-40-778 8523) (toimisto@saferglobe.fi) (www.saferglobe.fi). Peace and security think-tank.
Sitoutumaton Vasemmisto / Independent Left (WR HR ER), Mannerheimintie 5B 7krs, 00100 Helsinki (sitvas-hallitus@helsinki.fi) (sitvasfi.wordpress.com).
Siviilipalveluskeskus / Civiltjänstcentralen (PA), Latokartanontie 97, 07810 Ingermaninkylä (+358-295-029500) (etunimi.sukunimi@ely-keskus.fi) (www.siviilipalveluskeskus.fi). Centre for Non-Military Service.
Suomen Luonnonsuojeluliitto / Finnish Association for Nature Conservation [FANC] (EL), Itälahdenkatu 22-b A, 00210 Helsinki (+358-9-2280 8224) (toimisto@sll.fi) (www.sll.fi).
Suomen Rauhanpuolustajat / Finnish Peace Committee (IB WP TW), Hämeentie 48, 00500 Helsinki (+358-50-358 1441) (pulut@rauhanpuolustajat.fi) (www.rauhanpuolustajat.org). *Rauhan Puolesta.*
Taiteilijat rauhan puolesta / Artister för Fred / Performers and Artists for Nuclear Disarmament [PAND] (ND), Pengerkatu 22, 00750 Helsinki (+358-50-522 2748) (pandtalo@hotmail.fi).
Union of Conscientious Objectors / Aseistakieltäytyjäliitto [AKL] (WR), Rauhanasema, Veturitori 3, 00520 Helsinki (+358-40-836 2786) (toimisto@akl-web.fi) (www.akl-web.fi).
Women's International League for Peace and Freedom - Finnish Section [WILPF] (WL), PL 1174, 00101 Helsinki (wilpf@wilpf.fi) (wilpf.fi).

FRANCE
Abolition des Armes Nucléaires - Maison de Vigilance (ND), 21 ter rue Voltaire, 75011 Paris (abolitiondesarmesnucleaires@orange.fr) (abolitiondesarmesnucleaires.org). Formerly Maison de Vigilance.
Action des Chrétiens pour l'Abolition de la Torture [ACAT] (HR), 7 rue Georges Lardennois, 75019 Paris (+33-14040 4243) (fax 14040 4244) (acat@acatfrance.fr) (www.acatfrance.fr).
Action des Citoyens pour le Désarmement Nucléaire [ACDN] (ND), 31 Rue du Cormier, 17100 Saintes (+33-673 507661) (contact@acdn.net) (www.acdn.net). Opposes both military and civilian nukes.
Alternatives Non-Violentes [ANV] (PA RE CR), Centre 308, 82 rue Jeanne d'Arc, 76000 Rouen (+33-235 752344) (contact@alternatives-non-violentes.org) (alternatives-non-violentes.org).

Amis de la Terre - France (FE), Mundo M, 47 ave Pasteur, 93100 Montreuil (+33-14851 3222) (fax 14851 9512) (france@amisdelaterre.org) (www.amisdelaterre.org).

Association des Médecins Français pour la Prévention de la Guerre Nucléaire [AMF-PGN] (IP), 5 Rue Las Cases, 75007 Paris (+33-14336 7781) (revue@amfpgn.org) (amfpgn.org). *Médecine et Guerre Nucléaire.*

Association française pour les Nations Unies (UN), 26 Av Charles Floquet, 75007 Paris (+17716 2454) (contact@afnu.fr) (afnu.fr).

Brigades de Paix Internationales [PBI-France] (HR PO RE CD), 21 ter, rue Voltaire, 75011 Paris (+33-14373 4960) (pbi.france@free.fr) (pbi-france.org). *Presence Internationale.*

Centre de Ressources sur la Non-violence de Midi-Pyrénées (RE CR), 2 Allée du Limousin, 31770 Colomiers (+33-561 786680) (crnv.midi-pyrenees@wanadoo.fr) (www.non-violence-mp.org).

Centre mondial de la Paix, des Libertés et des Droits de l'Homme (RE), Place Monseigneur, BP 10183, 55100 Verdun (+33-329 865500) (contact@cmpaix.eu) (www.cmpaix.eu).

Cesser d'Alimenter la Guerre / Stop Fuelling War [SFW] (PC), c/o Centre Quaker de Paris, 114 rue de Vaugirard, 75006 Paris (stopfuellingwar@gmail.com) (stopfuellingwar.org). Countering the normalisation of the trade in arms.

Coordination pour l'Éducation à la Non-violence et à la Paix (RE), 148 rue du Faubourg Saint-Denis, 75010 Paris (+33-14633 4156) (education-nvp.org).

Greenpeace (GP), 13 rue d'Enghien, 75010 Paris (+33-18096 9696) (fax) (contact.fr@greenpeace.org) (www.greenpeace.org/france).

Groupe Non-Violent Louis Lecoin (DA PA), Maison de l'Environnement, 106 Ave du Casino, 59240 Dunkerque (+33-328 591233) (groupnonviolentlouislecoin@laposte.net).

Groupement pour les Droits des Minorités [GDM] (HR), 212 rue St-Martin, 75003 Paris (+33-14575 0137) (fax 14579 8046) (yplasseraud@wanadoo.fr). *La Lettre du GDM.*

Institut de Recherche sur la Résolution Non-violente des Conflits [IRNC] (RE SD CR PA), 14 rue des Meuniers, 93100 Montreuil-sous-Bois (+33-14287 9469) (fax) (irnc@irnc.org) (www.irnc.org). *Alternatives Non-violentes.*

Ligue d'Amitié Internationale (CD), Les Champs Fleuris - Nº 4, 14 rue Maurice Boyau, 91220 Bretigny-sur-Orge (+33-160 853407) (www.ifl-france.org). Affiliate of the International Friendship League.

Mémorial de Caen Museum - Cité de l'Histoire pour la Paix / Centre for History and Peace (PO RE), Esplanade Eisenhower, BP 55026, 14050 Caen Cedex 4 (+33-231 060644) (fax 231 060670) (contact@memorial-caen.fr) (www.memorial-caen.fr).

Mouvement de la Paix (IB WP ND PA AT), 9 Rue Dulcie September, 93400 Saint-Ouen (+33-14012 0912) (national@mvtpaix.org) (www.mvtpaix.org). *Planète Paix; La Paix en Mouvement.*

Mouvement International de la Réconciliation [MIR] (FR WR), 68 rue de Babylone, 75007 Paris (+33-14753 8405) (mirfr@club-internet.fr) (www.mirfrance.org). *Cahiers de la Réconciliation.*

Mouvement pour une Alternative Non-violente [MAN] (WR SD CR AT RA), 47 ave Pasteur, 93100 Montreuil (+33-14544 4825) (man@nonviolence.fr) (www.nonviolence.fr).

Non-Violence Actualité **[NVA]** (CR HR RE), Centre de Ressources sur la Gestion non-violente des Relations et des Conflits, BP 241, 45202 Montargis cedex (+33-238 936722) (fax 975 385985) (Nonviolence.Actualite@wanadoo.fr) (www.nonviolence-actualite.org). 6 yrly, Eu43 pa.

Non-Violence XXI (PA RE), 47 Ave Pasteur, 93100 Montreuil (+33-14548 3762) (fax 14544 4825) (coordination@nonviolence21.org) (www.nonviolence21.com).

Pax Christi France (PC), 5 rue Morère, 75014 Paris (+33-14449 0636) (accueil@paxchristi.cef.fr) (www.paxchristi.cef.fr). *Journal de la Paix.*

Réseau "Sortir du Nucléaire" / Network for a Nuclear Phase-Out (EL RA PO), 9 rue Dumenge, 69317 Lyon cedex 04 (+33-47828 2922) (fax 47207 7004) (contact@sortirdunucleaire.org) (www.sortirdunucleaire.org). Network of groups in France against nuclear energy.

Religions pour la Paix (RP), 8 bis Rue Jean Bart, 75006 Paris (Religionspourlapaix@yahoo.fr) (religionspourlapaix.org).

Service Civil International [SCI-F] (SC), 75 rue du Chevalier Français, 59800 Lille (+33-320 552258) (sci@sci-france.org) (www.sci-france.org).

Société Religieuse des Amis (SF), Centre Quaker International, 114 Rue de Vaugirard, 75006 Paris (+33-14548 7423) (assembleedefrance@gmail.com) (www.QuakersEnFrance.org). *Lettre des Amis.*

Sortir de la Violence - France (FR CR RE), 11 rue de la Chaise, 75007 Paris (sdv-France@sortirdelaviolence.org) (www.sortirdelaviolence.org).

FRANCE

Stop Fuelling War (AT SF), Centre Quaker International, 114 rue de Vaugirard, 75006 Paris (info@stopfuellingwar.org) (stopfuellingwar.org). Campaigns against Paris arms fairs.

Union Pacifiste de France [UPF] (WR AT), BP 40196, 75624 Paris cédex 13 (+33-14586 0875) (union.pacifiste@orange.fr) (www.unionpacifiste.org). *Union Pacifiste.*

FRENCH POLYNESIA

Ligue Internationale des Femmes pour la Paix et la Liberté - Section Polynésienne [LIFPL] (WL), Faaone pk 49.2, Côté Montagne, 98713 Faaone, Tahiti (+689-264729) (wilpf.polynesie@gmail.com).

GEORGIA

Sakhartvelos Mtsvaneta Modzraoba / Green Movement of Georgia (FE), 55 Kandelaki St, 0160 Tbilisi (+995-32-386978) (info@greens.ge) (www.greens.ge).

War Resisters' International - Georgian Section (WR), 45 Kavtaradze St - Apt 45, Tbilisi 0186 (+995-577-117878) (uchananua@yahoo.com).

GERMANY

Aktion Sühnezeichen Friedensdienste [ASF] (WC RP HR CD), Auguststr 80, 10117 Berlin-Mitte (+49-30-2839 5184) (fax 2839 5135) (asf@asf-ev.de) (www.asf-ev.de). *Zeichen.*

Aktion Völkerrecht / International Law Campaign (WF ND CD), c/o Peter Kolbe, Werderstr 36, 69120 Heidelberg (buero@a-vr.org) (www.aktion-voelkerrecht.de).

Aktionsgemeinschaft Dienst für den Frieden [AGDF] (WC PA RP), Endenicher Str 41, 53115 Bonn (+49-228-249990) (fax 249 9920) (agdf@friedensdienst.de) (www.friedensdienst.de). Voluntary service co-ordination agency.

Amnesty International (AI), Zinnowitzer Str, 10115 Berlin (+49-30-420 2480) (fax 4202 48488) (info@amnesty.de) (www.amnesty.de). *ai-Journal.*

Anti-Kriegs-Museum / Anti-War Museum (WR), Brüsseler Str 21, 13353 Berlin (+49-30-4549 0110) (Anti-Kriegs-Museum@gmx.de) (www.anti-kriegs-museum.de).

Arbeitsgemeinschaft für Friedens- und Konfliktforschung / German Association for Peace and Conflict Studies [AFK] (RE), c/o Fakultät Gesellschaft und Ökonomie, Hochschule Rhein-Waal, 47533 Kleve (+49-2821-806739793) (fax 8067 3162) (afk-gf@afk-web.de) (www.afk-web.de).

Archiv Aktiv für gewaltfreie Bewegungen (WR RE EL), Normannenweg 17-21, 20537 Hamburg (+49-40-430 2046) (email@archiv-aktiv.de) (www.archiv-aktiv.de).

ausgestrahlt (EL RA ND), Grosse Bergstr 189, 22767 Hamburg (+49-40-2531 8940) (fax 2531 8944) (info@ausgestrahlt.de) (www.ausgestrahlt.de). . *ausgestrahlt-magazin.* Anti-nuclear direct action network.

Bürgermeister für den Frieden in Deutschland und Österreich (CD ND DA), c/o Landeshauptstadt Hannover, Büro Oberbürgermeister, Trammplatz 2, 30159 Hannover (+49-511-1684 1446) (fax 1684 4025) (mayorsforpeace@hannover-stadt.de) (www.mayorsforpeace.de).

Berghof Foundation (CR RE), Lindenstr 34, 10969 Berlin (+49-30-844 1540) (fax 8441 5499) (info@berghof-conflictresearch.org) (www.berghof-conflictresearch.org). Works to prevent political and social violence.

Bund für Soziale Verteidigung [BSV] (WR SD CR), Schwarzer Weg 8, 32423 Minden (+49-571-29456) (fax 23019) (office@soziale-verteidigung.de) (www.soziale-verteidigung.de). *Soziale Verteidigung.*

Bund für Umwelt und Naturschutz Deutschland [BUND] (FE), Am Köllnischen Park 1, 10179 Berlin (+49-30-275 8640) (fax 2758 6440) (info@bund.net) (www.bund.net).

Connection eV (PA HR), Von-Behring-Str 110, 63075 Offenbach (+49-69-8237 5534) (fax 8237 5535) (office@Connection-eV.org) (www.Connection-eV.org). *KDV im Krieg.* International work for COs and deserters.

Deutsche Friedensgesellschaft - Vereinigte Kriegsdienstgegner [DFG-VK] (WR IB RE), Hornbergstr 100, 70188 Stuttgart (+49-711-6529 6246) (fax 6557 1681) (verwaltung@dfg-vk.de) (www.dfg-vk.de).

Deutsche Gesellschaft für die Vereinten Nationen [DGVN] (UN), Zimmerstr 26/27, 10969 Berlin (+49-30-259 3750) (fax 2593 7529) (info@dgvn.de) (www.dgvn.de). *Vereinte Nationen.*

Deutsche Sektion der IPPNW / Ärzte in sozialer Verantwortung (IPPNW Germany) (IP AT DA), Körtestr 10, 10967 Berlin (+49-30-698 0740) (fax 693 8166) (kontakt@ippnw.de) (www.ippnw.de). *Forum.*

Deutscher Friedensrat / German Peace Council (WP), Platz der Vereinten Nationen 7, 10249 Berlin (+49-30-426 5290) (fax 4201 7338) (saefkow-berlin@t-online.de) (www.deutscher-friedensrat.de).

DFG-VK Hessen (WR), Mühlgasse 13, 60486 Frankfurt/Main (+49-69-431440) (dfgvkhessen@t-online.de) (www.dfg-vk-hessen.de).

Forum Ziviler Friedensdienst / Civil Peace Service Forum [forumZFD] (SF CR RE), Am Kölner Brett 8, 50825 Köln

(+49-221-912 7320) (fax 9127 3299)
(kontakt@forumZFD.de) (www.forumZFD.de).
Offers conflict transformation training &
courses.
**Frauennetzwerk für Frieden eV / Women's
Network for Peace** (IB CR), Kaiserstr 201,
53113 Bonn (+49-228-626730) (fax 626780)
(info@frauennetzwerk-fuer-frieden.de)
(www.frauennetzwerk-fuer-frieden.de).
**Friedensausschuss der Religiösen
Gesellschaft der Freunde (Quäker)** (SF PA
CR DA RA), via Helga Tempel, Föhrenstieg
8, 22926 Ahrensburg (+49-4102-53337)
(helga.tempel@gmx.de). *Quäker.*
Gandhi Information Centre (PA RE),
Postfach 210109, 10501 Berlin
(mkgandhi@snafu.de)
(www.nonviolent-resistance.info).
Previously Gandhi-Informations-Zentrum.
GandhiServe Foundation (RE HR),
Rathausstr 51a, 12105 Berlin
(+49-1523-398 7220) (fax 3212-100 3676)
(mail@gandhimail.org)
(www.gandhiservefoundation.org).
**Gewaltfreie Aktion Atomwaffen Abschaffen
/ Nonviolent Action to Abolish Nuclear
Weapons [GAAA]** (ND RA), c/o Marion
Küpker, Beckstr 14, 20357 Hamburg
(+49-40-430 7332)
(marion.kuepker@gaaa.org) (www.gaaa.org).
Graswurzelrevolution (WR AL RA), Breul 43,
48143 Münster (+49-251-482 9057)
(fax 482 9032) (redaktion@graswurzel.net)
(www.graswurzel.net).
Greenpeace (GP), Hongkongstr 10, 20457
Hamburg (+49-40-306180) (fax 3061 8100)
(mail@greenpeace.de)
(www.greenpeace.de).
Berlin: +49-30-308 8990.
**Heidelberger Institut für Internationale
Konfliktforschung [HIIK]** (RE), Bergheimer
Str 58, 69115 Heidelberg (+49-6221-542863)
(info@hiik.de) (www.hiik.de).
Conflict Barometer.
**Initiative Musiker/innen gegen Auftritte der
Bundeswehrmusikkorps** (PA), c/o Dietmar
Parchow, Austr 77, 72669 Unterensingen
(musikergegenmilitaermusik@ok-berlin.de)
(musiker-gegen-militaermusik.jimdo.com).
Against public and church use of military
bands.
**Institut für Friedensarbeit und Gewaltfreie
Konfliktaustragung [IFGK]** (WR RE CR),
Hauptstr 35, 55491 Wahlenau/Hunsrück
(+49-6543-980096)
(info@dr-barbara-mueller.com) (www.ifgk.de).
IFGK Working Papers.
**Institut für Friedenspädagogik Tübingen/
Institute for Peace Education Tübingen**
(RE CR), Corrensstr 12, 72076 Tübingen
(+49-7071-920510) (fax 920 5111)
(info-tuebingen@berghof-foundation.org)
(www.friedenspaedagogik.de). A branch of
the Berghof Foundation.

**Internationale der
Kriegsdienstgegner/innen [IDK]** (WR AL),
Postfach 280312, 13443 Berlin
(info@idk-berlin.de) (www.idk-info.net).
**Internationale Frauenliga für Frieden und
Freiheit [IFFF]** (WL), Haus der Demokratie
und Menschenrechte, Greifswalder Str 4,
10405 Berlin (info@wilpf.de) (www.wilpf.de).
**Internationale Jugendgemeinschaftsdienste
[IJGD]** (WC EL CD), Kasernenstr 48, 53111
Bonn (+49-228-228 0014) (fax 228 0010)
(workcamps@ijgd.de) (www.ijgd.de).
Workcamps and volunteering in Germany
and abroad.
**Juristen und Juristinnen gegan Atomare,
Biologische und Chemische Waffen -
IALANA Deutschland** (ND), Marienstr 19-20,
10117 Berlin (+49-30-2065 4857)
(fax 2065 4858) (info@ialana.de)
(www.ialana.de).
**Kampagne gegen Wehrpflicht,
Zwangsdienste und Militär** (PA RA SD),
Kopenhagener Str 71, 10437 Berlin
(+49-30-4401 3025) (fax 4401 3029)
(info@kampagne.de) (www.kampagne.de).
Komitee für Grundrechte und Demokratie
(HR CD RA PA), Aquinostr 7-11 (HH), 50670
Köln (+49-221-972 6920) (fax 972 6931)
(info@grundrechtekomitee.de)
(www.grundrechtekomitee.de).
Kooperation für den Frieden (DA ND RE),
Römerstr 88, 53111 Bonn (+49-228-692905)
(fax 692906) (info@koop-frieden.de)
(www.koop-frieden.de).
Networking organisation in German peace
movement.
**KURVE Wustrow - Bildungs- und
Begegnungsstätte für gewaltfreie Aktion**
(FR PA CR HR RE), Kirchstr 14, 29462
Wustrow (+49-5843-98710) (fax 987111)
(info@kurvewustrow.org)
(www.kurvewustrow.org).
Martin-Luther-King-Zentrum (PA),
Stadtgutstr 23, 08412 Werdau
(+49-3761-760284) (fax 760304)
(info@martin-luther-king-zentrum.de)
(www.king-zentrum.de).
Netzwerk Friedenskooperative (ND PA AT),
Römerstr 88, 53111 Bonn (+49-228-692904)
(fax 692906)
(friekoop@friedenskooperative.de)
(www.friedenskooperative.de).
Friedensforum.
Netzwerk Friedenssteuer [NWFS] (TR),
Krennerweg 12, 81479 München
(+49-8062-725 2395) (fax 725 2396)
(info@netzwerk-friedenssteuer.de)
(www.netzwerk-friedenssteuer.de).
Friedenssteuer-Nachrichten.
Ohne Rüstung Leben (AT CR PA ND DA),
Arndtstr 31, 70197 Stuttgart (+49-711-
608396) (fax 608357) (orl@gaia.de)
(www.ohne-ruestung-leben.de).
Ohne Rüstung Leben-Informationen.

GERMANY

Pax Christi Deutsche Sektion (PC), Hedwigkirchgasse 3, 10117 Berlin (+49-30-2007 6780) (fax 2007 67819) (sekretariat@paxchristi.de) (www.paxchristi.de).
Peace Brigades International Deutscher Zweig [PBI] (CR HR PA), Bahrenfelder Str 101 A, 22765 Hamburg (+49-40-3890 4370) (fax 3890 43729) (info@pbi-deutschland.de) (www.pbideutschland.de).
Peace Museum (RE), Kaulbachstr 2, 90408 Nürnberg (+49-911-360 9577) (na3745@fen-net.de) (www.friedensmuseum.odn.de).
Projekt Alternativen zur Gewalt / AVP Germany [PAG] (CR), Kaliweg 31, 30952 Ronnenberg (+49-5109-7695) (fax 1014) (info@pag.de) (www.pag.de). Part of Alternatives to Violence network.
RüstungsInformationsBüro [RIB-Büro] (AT PA RE), Stühlinger Str 7, 79016 Freiburg (+49-761-767 8088) (fax 767 8089) (rib@rib-ev.de) (www.rib-ev.de). Campaign against small arms.
RfP Deutschland / Religions for Peace (RP), c/o Franz Brendle, Im Schellenkönig 61, 70184 Stuttgart (+49-711-539 0209) (fax 505 8648) (rfp@r-f-p.de) (www.religionsforpeace.de). *Informationen*.
Servas Germany (SE), O'Swaldstr 32, 22111 Hamburg (mail@servas.de) (www.servas.de).
Stiftung die schwelle / Schwelle Foundation - Beiträge zum Frieden (CR TW RE HR), Wachmannstr 79, 28209 Bremen (+49-421-303 2575) (stiftung@dieschwelle.de) (www.dieschwelle.de).
Terre des Femmes - Menschenrechte für die Frau eV (HR), Brunnenstr 128, 13355 Berlin (+49-30-4050 46990) (fax 4050 469999) (info@frauenrechte.de) (www.frauenrechte.de).
Versöhnungsbund [VB] (FR IB PA), Schwarzer Weg 8, 32423 Minden (+49-571-850875) (fax 829 2387) (vb@versoehnungsbund.de) (www.versoehnungsbund.de).

GHANA

Anam Foundation for Peacebuilding [AF4PB] (CR PO), Box TL 392, Tamale (+233-20-276 8844) (info@anam4peace.org) (www.anam4peace.org).

GREECE

Diethnis Amnistia / Amnesty International (AI), 30 Sina Street, 10672 Athinai (+30-210 3600 628) (fax 210 3638 016) (athens@amnesty.org.gr) (www.amnesty.org.gr). *Martyries*.
Elliniki Epitropi gia ti Thiethni Yphesi kai Eirene / Greek Committee for International Detente and Peace [EEDYE] (WP), Themistokleous 48, 10681 Athinai (+30-210 3844 853) (fax 210 3844 879) (eedye@otenet.gr) (eedye.gr).
Enomenes Koinonies ton Valkanion / United Societies of the Balkans [USB] (CD CR HR PO), Adamanas 9, Agios Paulos, 55438 Thessaloniki (+30-231 0215 629) (fax) (info@usbngo.gr) (www.usbngo.gr).
Greenpeace Greece (GP), Kolonou 78, 10437 Athinai (+30-210 3840 774) (fax 210 3804 008) (gpgreece@greenpeace.org) (www.greenpeace.org/greece).
Syndhesmos Antirrision Syneidhisis / Association of Greek Conscientious Objectors [SAS] (WR), Tsamadou 13A, 10683 Athinai (+30-694 4542 228) (fax 210 4622 753) (greekCO@hotmail.com) (www.antirrisies.gr).

GRENADA

Friends of the Earth Grenada [FOE-G] (FE TW), PO Box 521, Lucas St, Queen's Park, St George's (+1473-416 1247) (friendsoftheearthgrenada@gmail.com).

HONG KONG

Alternatives to Violence Project - AVP Hong Kong (CR PO), 12a Shun Ho Tower, 24-30 Ice House St, Central (avphongkong@gmail.com) (www.avphongkong.org).
Amnesty International Hong Kong (AI), Unit 3D, Best-O-Best Commercial Centre, 32-36 Ferry St, Kowloon (+852-2300 1250) (fax 2782 0583) (admin-hk@amnesty.org.hk) (www.amnesty.org.hk).
Association for the Advancement of Feminism [AAF] (HR), Flats 119-120, Lai Yeung House, Lei Cheng Uk Estate, Kowloon (+852-2720 0891) (fax 2720 0205) (aaf@aaf.org.hk) (www.aaf.org.hk). *Nuliu*.
Greenpeace China (GP), 8/F Pacific Plaza, 410-418 Des Voeux Rd West (+852-2854 8300) (fax 2745 2426) (enquiry.hk@greenpeace.org) (www.greenpeace.org/china). Also Beijing office: see under China.

HUNGARY

ACAT-Hungary (HR), c/o Csaba Kabódi, Eötvos University, Egyetem Tér 1-3, 1364 Budapest (+36-1-252 5961) (fax) (kabodi@ajk.elte.hu).
Bocs Foundation (FR EL TW), Pf 7, 8003 Székesfehérvár (m@bocs.hu) (www.bocs.hu). *Bocsmagazin*.
Magyar Orvosmozgalom a Nukleáris Háború Megelözéséért (IP), c/o Zita Makoi, Hegedus Gy u 48, 1133 Budapest (zita.makoi@gmail.com).
Magyar Természetvédök Szövetsége [MTVSZ] (FE), Ulloi U 91B - III/21, 1091 Budapest (info@mtvsz.hu) (www.mtvsz.hu).

ICELAND

Amnesty International (AI), Thingholtsstraeti 27, 101 Reykjavík (+354-511 7900) (fax 511 7901) (amnesty@amnesty.is) (www.amnesty.is).

Peace 2000 Institute (CR RE), Vogasel 1, 109 Reykjavík (+354-557 1000) (fax 496 2005) (info@peace2000.org) (peace2000.org).
Offices also in Britain, USA.

Samtök Hernadarandstaedinga / Campaign Against Militarism (WR ND DA), Njalsgata 87, 101 Reykjavík (+354-554 0900) (sha@fridur.is) (fridur.is). *Dagfari*.

INDIA

All India Peace and Solidarity Organisation [AIPSO] (WP), c/o AIPSO West Bengal, 5 Sarat Ghosh St (behind Entally Market), Kolkota 700014 (bengalaipso@gmail.com) (www.aipsowb.org).

Anglican Pacifist Fellowship [APF] (RP), c/o John Nagella, Opp SBI Colony, AT Agraharam, Guntur 552004, Andhra Pradesh.

Atheist Centre (HR RA), Benz Circle, Patamata, Vijayawada 520010, AP (+91-866-247 2330) (fax 248 4850) (atheistcentre@yahoo.com) (www.atheistcentre.in).
Atheist.

Bombay Sarvodaya Friendship Centre (FR WC SF), 701 Sainath Estate, Opp Lokmanya Vidyalaya, Nilam Nagar-II, Mulund East, Mumbai 400081 (+91-22-2563 1022) (danielm@mtnl.net.in).

Coalition for Nuclear Disarmament and Peace [CNDP] (ND), A-124/6 - First Floor, Katwaria Sarai, New Delhi 110016 (+91-11-6566 3958) (fax 2651 7814) (cndpindia@gmail.com) (www.cndpindia.org).
Network of 200 organisations.

Control Arms Foundation of India [CAFI] (AT DA), B5 / 146 - First Floor, Safdarjung Enclave, New Delhi 110029 (+91-11-4601 8541) (cafi.communique@gmail.com) (cafi-online.org).

Ekta Parishad (HR PO TW), 2/3A - Second Floor - Jungpura-A, New Delhi 10014 (+91-11-2437 3998) (ektaparishad@gmail.com) (www.ektaparishad.com).
Federation of thousands of community organisations.

Friends of the Gandhi Museum (RE EL PO), B-4 Puru Society, Airport Rd, Lohegaon, Pune 411032 (+91-937 120 1138) (satyagrahi2000@gmail.com).

Gandhi Book Centre / Mumbai Sarvodaya Mandal (PO), 299 Tardeo Rd, Nana Chowk, Mumbai 400007 (+91-22-2387 2061) (info@mkgandhi.org) (www.mkgandhi.org).

Gandhi Research Foundation (RE), Gandhi Teerth, Jain Hills PO Box 118, Jalgaon 425001, Maharashtra (+91-257-226 0011) (fax 226 1133) (gandhiexam@gandhifoundation.net) (www.gandhifoundation.net).

Gandhian Society Villages Association (WR), Amaravathy Pudur PO, Pasumpon District, Tamil Nadu 623301 (+91-8645-83234).

Greenpeace India (GP), 60 Wellington Rd, Richmond Town, Bangalore 560025, Karnataka (+91-80-2213 1899) (fax 4115 4862) (supporter.services.in@greenpeace.org) (www.greenpeace.org/india). Regional Office in Delhi (+91-11-6666 5000).

Gujarat Vidyapeeth (RE), Ashram Rd (near Income tax), Ahmedabad 380014 (+91-79-2754 0746) (fax 2754 2547) (registrar@gujaratvidyapith.org) (www.gujaratvidyapith.org).
Gandhian study centre.

Indian Campaign for Nuclear Disarmament (IB ND EL), 11 Chetla Central Rd, Alipore, Kolkata 700027, West Bengal (+91-33-466 5659) (manabendranathmandal@ymail.com).

Indian Doctors for Peace and Development [IDPD] (IP), 139-E Kitchlu Nagar, Ludhiana 141001, Punjab (+91-161-230 0252) (fax 230 4360) (idpd2001@yahoo.com) (www.idpd.org).

National Gandhi Museum and Library (RE), Rajghat, New Delhi 110002 (+91-11-2331 1793) (fax 2332 8310) (gandhimuseumdelhi@gmail.com) (www.gandhimuseum.org).
Has collection of original relics, books, etc.

People's Movement Against Nuclear Energy - WISE India [PMANE] (EL ND), 42/27 Esankai Mani Veethy, Prakkai Road Jn, Nagercoil 629002, Tamil Nadu (drspudayakumar@yahoo.com).
Linked to World Information Service on Energy.

Swadhina / Independence (WR), 34/C Bondel Rd, Ballygunge, Kolkata 700019 (+91-33-3245 1730) (mainoffice.swadhina@gmail.com) (www.swadhina.org).

Tibetan Centre for Human Rights and Democracy (FR HR), Narthang Building - Top Floor, Gangchen Kyishong, Dharamsala, HP 176215 (+91-1892-223363) (fax 225874) (office@tchrd.org) (www.tchrd.org).
Works for human rights of Tibetans in Tibet.

War Resisters of India/West (WR), c/o Swati & Michael, Juna Mozda, Dediapada, Dt Narmada, Gujarat 393040 (+91-2649-290249) (mozdam@gmail.com).

Women's International League for Peace and Freedom - India [WILPF] (WL), c/o Peace Research Centre, Gujatat Vidyapith, Ahmedabad 380014.

IRAN

IRAN
Iranian Physicians for Social Responsibility [PSR-Iran] (IP), PO Box 11155-18747, Tehran Peace Museum, Parke shahr, Tehran (+98-21-6675 6945) (fax 6693 9992) (info@irpsr.org).

IRELAND, NORTHERN

NOTE: Organisations working on an all-Ireland basis (ie covering both the Republic of Ireland and Northern Ireland), with their office address in the Irish Republic, will be found listed there. Similarly, groups operating on a United Kingdom-wide basis (ie covering both Britain and Northern Ireland), with a British-based office, will be found listed under Britain.

Amnesty International - NI Region [AI-NI] (AI), 397 Ormeau Rd, Belfast BT7 (+44-28-9064 3000) (fax 9069 0989) (nireland@amnesty.org.uk) (www.amnesty.org.uk).

Bahá'í Council for Northern Ireland (RP), Apt 4, 2 Lower Windsor Ave, Belfast BT9 (+44-28-9016 0457) (bcni@bahai.org.uk) (www.bahaicouncil-ni.org.uk).

Centre for Democracy and PeaceBuilding [CDPB] (HR CR), 46 Hill St, Belfast BT1 2LB (info@democracyandpeace.org) (democracyandpeace.org). Sharing peacebuilding expertise internationally.

Children are Unbeatable! Alliance (HR), Unit 9, 40 Montgomery Rd, Belfast BT6 (+44-28-9040 1290) (carolconlin@btinternet.com) (www.childrenareunbeatable.org.uk). For abolition of all physical punishment.

Christian Aid Ireland (TW), Linden House, Beechill Business Park, 96 Beechill Rd, Belfast BT8 7QN (+44-28-9064 8133) (belfast@christian-aid.org) (www.christianaid.ie).

Co-operation Ireland (CD), 5 Weavers Court Business Park, Linfield Rd, Belfast BT12 (+44-28-9032 1462) (info@cooperationireland.org) (www.cooperationireland.org). Works for tolerance and acceptance of differences.

Committee on the Administration of Justice [CAJ] (HR), Community House, Citylink Business Park, 6A Albert St, Belfast BT12 (+44-28-9031 6000) (info@caj.org.uk) (www.caj.org.uk). *Just News*.

Corrymeela Community (RP), 83 University St, Belfast BT7 1HP (+44-28-9050 8080) (fax 9050 8070) (belfast@corrymeela.org) (www.corrymeela.org). *Corrymeela*.

Global Peacebuilders (CR), c/o Springboard Opportunities, 2nd Floor, 7 North St, Belfast BT1 1NH (+44-28-9031 5111) (fax 9031 3171) (james@springboard-opps.org) (www.globalpeacebuilders.org).

Green Party in Northern Ireland (EL), 1st Floor, 76 Abbey St, Bangor BT20 4JB (+44-28-9145 9110) (info@greenpartyni.org) (www.greenpartyni.org).

Healing Through Remembering [HTR] (RE), Unit 2.2, Bryson House, 28 Bedford St, Belfast BT2 7FE (+44-28-9023 8844) (info@healingthroughremembering.org) (www.healingthroughremembering.org).

Institute for Conflict Research [ICR] (RE CR HR), North City Business Centre - Unit 12-14, 2 Duncairn Gdns, Belfast BT15 2GG (+44-28-9074 2682) (info@conflictresearch.org.uk) (www.conflictresearch.org.uk).

Institute for the Study of Conflict Transformation and Social Justice [ISCT-SJ] (RE CR), Queen's University Belfast, 19 University Sq, Belfast BT7 (+44-28-9097 3609) (ctsj@qub.ac.uk).

Integrated Education Fund [IEF] (PO HR), Forest View, Purdy's Lane, Belfast BT8 7AR (+44-28-9069 4099) (info@ief.org.uk) (www.ief.org.uk).

Irish Network for Nonviolent Action Training and Education [INNATE] (WR RA FR), c/o 16 Ravensdene Park, Belfast BT6 0DA (+44-28-9064 7106) (fax) (innate@ntlworld.com) (www.innatenonviolence.com). *Nonviolent News*.

Northern Ireland Community Relations Council [CRC] (CR PO RE), 2nd Floor, Equality House, 7-9 Shaftesbury Sq, Belfast BT2 7DP (+44-28-9022 7500) (info@nicrc.org.uk) (www.community-relations.org.uk).

Northern Ireland Council for Integrated Education [NICIE] (PO HR CD RE), 25 College Gdns, Belfast BT9 (+44-28-9097 2910) (fax 9097 2919) (info@nicie.org.uk) (www.nicie.org.uk).

Oxfam Ireland (TW), 115 North St, Belfast (+44-28-9023 0220) (fax 9023 7771) (info@oxfamireland.org) (www.oxfamireland.org).

Pat Finucane Centre (HR RE CR), Unit B8, Ráth Mór Centre, Bligh's Lane, Derry BT48 0LZ (+44-28-7126 8846) (fax 7126 6453) (info@patfinucanecentre.org) (www.patfinucanecentre.org). Armagh Office: 028-3751 5191.

Peace People (FR CD HR), 224 Lisburn Rd, Belfast BT9 6GE (+44-28-9066 3465) (info@peacepeople.com) (www.peacepeople.com).

Quaker Service (SF), 541 Lisburn Rd, Belfast BT9 7GQ (+44-28-9020 1444) (info@quakerservice.com) (www.quakerservice.com).

Swords to Ploughares [StoP] (AT), c/o INNATE, 16 Ravensdene Park, Belfast BT6 0DA. Irish anti-arms trade network.

The Junction (CR PO), 8-14 Bishop St, Derry/Londonderry BT48 6PW (+44-28-7136 1942) (info@thejunction-ni.org) (thejunction-ni.org).
Community relations, civic empowerment.

TIDES Training (CR), 174 Trust, Duncairn Complex, Duncairn Ave, Belfast BT14 6BP (+44-28-9075 1686) (info@tidestraining.org) (www.tidestraining.org).

Tools for Solidarity - Ireland (TW PO), 55A Sunnyside St, Belfast BT7 (+44-28-9073 8974) (fax) (tools.belfast@myphone.coop) (www.toolsforsolidarity.com). *Solidarity.*

Transitional Justice Institute [TJI] (RE), Ulster University - Jordanstown Campus, Shore Rd, Newtownabbey BT37 (+44-28-9036 6202) (fax 9036 8962) (transitionaljustice@ulster.ac.uk) (www.transitionaljustice.ulster.ac.uk). Also Magee Campus, Londonderry.

IRELAND, REPUBLIC OF

Amnesty International Ireland (AI), Sean MacBride House, 48 Fleet St, Dublin 2 (+353-1-863 8300) (fax 671 9338) (info@amnesty.ie) (www.amnesty.ie). *Amnesty Ireland.*

Chernobyl Children International (PO EL HR), 1A The Stables, Alfred St, Cork City (+353-21-455 8774) (fax 450 5564) (info@chernobyl-ireland.com) (www.chernobyl-international.com).

Co-operation Ireland [CI] (CD), Port Centre, Alexandra Rd, Dublin 1 (+353-1-819 7692) (fax 894 4962) (info@cooperationireland.org) (www.cooperationireland.org).
Works for tolerance and acceptance of differences.

Dublin Quaker Peace Committee (SF), c/o Quaker House, Stocking Lane, Rathfarnham, Dublin 16 (info@dublinquakerpeace.org) (www.dublinquakerpeace.org).

Eco-Congregation Ireland (EL), c/o 13 The Pinnacles, Broomfield, Midleton, Co Cork (info@ecocongregationireland.com) (www.ecocongregationireland.com). Interdenominational project.

Educate Together (HR RE PO CR), 11-12 Hogan Place, Dublin 2 (+353-1-429 2500) (fax 429 2502) (info@educatetogether.ie) (www.educatetogether.ie).

Friends of the Earth (FE), 9 Upper Mount St, Dublin 2 (+353-1-639 4652) (info@foe.ie) (www.foe.ie).

Friends of the Irish Environment (EL), Kilcatherine, Eyeries, Co Cork (+353-27-74771) (admin@friendsoftheirishenvironment.org) (www.friendsoftheirishenvironment.org).

Ireland Palestine Solidarity Campaign [IPSC] (HR), 25 North Lotts, Dublin 1, D01 A3E0, Co Offaly (+353-1-872 7798) (info@ipsc.ie) (www.ipsc.ie).

Irish Anti-War Movement, PO Box 9260, Dublin 1 (+353-1-872 7912) (info@irishantiwar.org) (www.irishantiwar.org).

Irish Campaign for Nuclear Disarmament / Feachtas um Dhí-armáil Eithneach [ICND] (IB ND), PO Box 6327, Dublin 6 (irishcnd@gmail.com) (www.irishcnd.org). *Peacework.*

Irish Centre for Human Rights (HR), National University of Ireland, University Rd, Galway (+353-91-493948) (fax 494575) (humanrights@nuigalway.ie) (www.nuigalway.ie/human_rights).

Irish Council for Civil Liberties / An Chomhairle um Chearta Daonna [ICCL] (HR), Unit 11, 34 Ushers Quay, Dublin 8 (+353-1-912 1640) (info@iccl.ie) (www.iccl.ie).

Irish United Nations Association [IUNA] (UN), 14 Lower Pembroke St, Dublin 2 (+353-1-661 6920) (irelandun@gmail.com).

Mediators' Institute Ireland [MII] (CR), Suite 112, The Capel Building, Mary's Abbey, Dublin 7 (+353-1-609 9190) (info@themii.ie) (www.themii.ie).

Pax Christi Ireland (PC HR AT), 52 Lower Rathmines Rd, Dublin 6 (+353-1-496 5293) (www.paxchristi.ie).

Peace and Neutrality Alliance / Comhaontas na Síochána is Neodrachta [PANA] (ND CD), 17 Castle St, Dalkey, Co Dublin (+353-1-235 1512) (info@pana.ie) (www.pana.ie).

Peace Brigades International - Ireland [PBI] (HR), 12 Parliament St, Temple Bar, Dublin 2 (pbiireland@peacebrigades.org) (www.pbi-ireland.org).

People's Movement / Gluaiseacht an Phobail (HR DA), 25 Shanowen Crescent, Santry, Dublin 9 (post@people.ien) (people.ie). Opposes increased EU centralisation and militarism.

Servas (SE), c/o Donal Coleman, 53 Glengara Park, Glenageary, Co Dublin A96 TOF6 (+353-87-915 9635) (ireland@servas.org) (www.servas.org).

ShannonWatch (DA HR), PO Box 476, Limerick DSU, Dock Rd, Limerick (+353-87-822 5087) (shannonwatch@gmail.com) (www.shannonwatch.org). Monitors foreign military use of Shannon Airport.

Swords to Ploushares [StoP] (AT), for address see under Ireland, Northern. Irish anti-arms trade network.

Vegetarian Society of Ireland [VSI] (EL PO), c/o Dublin Food Coop, 12 Newmarket, Dublin 8 (info@vegetarian.ie) (www.vegetarian.ie). *The Irish Vegetarian.*

Voluntary Service International [VSI] (SC), 30 Mountjoy Sq, Dublin 1 (+353-1-855 1011) (fax 855 1012) (info@vsi.ie) (www.vsi.ie). *VSI News.*

ISLE OF MAN

ISLE OF MAN
Shee Nish! / Peace Now! (AT PA DA), c/o Stuart Hartill, Eskdale Apartments - Apt 10, Queens Drive West, Ramsey IM8 2JD (+44-1624-803157) (stuarth@manx.net). Widely-based coalition of peace campaigners.

ISRAEL (see also Palestine)
NOTE: Territories allocated to Israel in the United Nations partition of Palestine in 1947, together with further areas annexed by Israel prior to 1967, are included here. Other parts of Palestine occupied by Israel in 1967 or later are listed under Palestine.

Al-Beit - Association for the Defence of Human Rights in Israel (HR CD TW), PO Box 650, Arara 30026 (+972-6-635 4370) (fax 635 4367) (uridavis@actcom.co.il). Concentrates on right of residence and housing.

Alternative Information Centre [AIC] (HR RE TW AL AT), POB 31417, West Jerusalem 91313 (+972-2-624 1159) (fax 3-762 4664) (connie.hackbarth@alternativenews.org) (www.alternativenews.org).
Economy of the Occupation.
See also Palestine.

Amnesty International Israel (AI), PO Box 5239, Tel-Aviv 66550 (+972-3-525 0005) (fax 525 0001) (info@amnesty.org.il) (amnesty.org.il).

B'Tselem - Israeli Information Centre for Human Rights in the Occupied Territories (HR), PO Box 53132, West Jerusalem 9153002 (+972-2-673 5599) (fax 674 9111) (mail@btselem.org) (www.btselem.org).

Bimkom - Planners for Planning Rights (HR), 13 Ebenezra St - PO Box 7154, West Jerusalem 9107101 (+972-2-566 9655) (fax 566 0551) (bimkom@bimkom.org) (www.bimkom.org).

Coalition of Women for Peace [CWP] (HR CD), POB 29214, Tel Aviv - Jaffa 61292 (+972-3-528 1005) (fax) (cwp@coalitionofwomen.org) (www.coalitionofwomen.org).

Combatants for Peace (CD), 12 Yad Harutsim St, Tel Aviv - Jaffa 6770005 (office@cfpeace.org) (www.cfpeace.org). Israeli and Palestinian ex-fighters for peace.

Defence for Children International - Israel [DCI-Israel] (HR), PO Box 2533, West Jerusalem 91024 (+972-2-563 3003) (fax 563 1241) (dci@dci-il.org).

Geneva Initiative (CD CR), c/o HL Education for Peace, 33 Jabotinsky Rd, Ramat-Gan 525108 (+972-3-693 8780) (fax 691 1306) (www.geneva-accord.org).
See also Palestine.

Gisha: Legal Centre for Freedom of Movement (HR), Harakevet 42, Tel Aviv - Jaffa 67770 (+972-3-624 4102) (fax 624 4130) (info@gisha.org) (gisha.org).

Givat Haviva Jewish-Arab Centre for Peace [JACP] (CR HR RE), MP Menashe 37850 (+972-4-630 9289) (fax 630 9305) (givathaviva@givathaviva.org.il) (www.givathaviva.org.il).

Greenpeace Mediterranean - Israel (GP HR), PO Box 20079, Tel Aviv 61200 (+972-3-561 4014) (fax 561 0415) (gpmedisr@greenpeace.org) (www.greenpeace.org/israel).

Gush Shalom / Peace Bloc (CD CR HR RE RA), PO Box 2542, Holon 58125 (+972-3-556 5804) (info@gush-shalom.org) (www.gush-shalom.org).

Hamerkaz Hamishpati L'zkhuyot Hami-ut Ha'aravi Beyisrael / Legal Centre for Arab Minority Rights in Israel [Adalah] (HR), 94 Yaffa St, PO Box 8921, Haifa 31090 (+972-4-950 1610) (fax 950 3140) (adalah@adalah.org) (www.adalah.org). Works for equal rights for Arab citizens in Israel.

HaMoked - Centre for the Defence of the Individual (HR), 4 Abu Obeidah St, Jerusalem 97200 (+972-2-627 1698) (mail@hamoked.org.il) (www.hamoked.org.il).

Hand in Hand - Centre for Jewish-Arab Education in Israel (PO CD RE), PO Box 10339, Jerusalem 91102 (+972-2-673 5356) (info@handinhand.org.il) (www.handinhandk12.org).
Supports integrated, bilingual education.

Interfaith Encounter Association [IEA] (RP CD), PO Box 3814, West Jerusalem 91037 (+972-2-651 0520) (fax 651 0557) (yehuda@interfaith-encounter.org) (www.interfaith-encounter.org). *IEA Stories.*

Israel-Palestine Creative Regional Initiatives [IPCRI] (RE CR RE CD CD), see under Palestine (+972-52-238 1715) (www.ipcri.org).

Israeli Committee for a Middle East Free from Atomic, Biological and Chemical Weapons (ND HR), PO Box 16202, Tel Aviv 61161 (+972-3-522 2869) (fax) (spiro@bezeqint.net).

Mossawa Center - Advocacy Center for Arab Citizens in Israel (HR), 5 Saint Lucas St, PO Box 4471, Haifa 31043 (+972-4-855 5901) (fax 855 2772) (programs.mossawa@gmail.com) (www.mossawa.org).

New Profile - Movement for the Demilitarisation of Israeli Society (WR), c/o Sergeiy Sandler, POB 48005, Tel Aviv 61480 (+972-3-696 1137) (newprofile@speedy.co.il) (www.newprofile.org).
Feminist movement of women and men.

Ometz Le'sarev / Courage to Refuse, PO Box 16238, Tel Aviv (+972-3-523 3103)

(info@seruv.org.il) (www.seruv.org.il). (Zionists) refusing deployment in the Territories.
OneVoice Movement - Israel [OVI] (CD CR), PO Box 29695, Tel Aviv 66881 (+972-3-516 8005) (info@OneVoice.org.il) (www.onevoicemovement.org). See also Palestine.
Palestinian-Israeli Peace NGO Forum (Israeli Office) (CD), c/o The Peres Center for Peace, 132 Kedem St, Jaffa 68066 (+972-3-568 0646) (fax 562 7265) (info@peres-center.org) (www.peacengo.org). See also under Palestine.
Physicians for Human Rights - Israel [PHRI] (HR PO), 9 Dror St, Jaffa-Tel Aviv 68135 (+972-3-513 3100) (fax 687 3029) (mail@phr.org.il) (www.phr.org.il).
Public Committee Against Torture in Israel [PCATI] (HR), POB 4634, West Jerusalem 91046 (+972-2-642 9825) (fax 643 2847) (pcati@stoptorture.org.il) (www.stoptorture.org.il).
Rabbis for Human Rights [RHR] (HR), 9 HaRechavim St, West Jerusalem 9346209 (+972-2-648 2757) (fax 678 3611) (info@rhr.israel.net) (www.rhr.israel.net).
Sadaka-Reut - Arab-Jewish Partnership (CR RE HR CD), 35 Shivtey Israel St, PO Box 8523, Jaffa - Tel-Aviv 61084 (+972-3-518 2336) (fax) (info@reutsadaka.org) (www.reutsadaka.org).
Seeds of Peace (CD CR PO), PO Box 42365, Salah Eddin Street (Herod's Gate Branch), Jerusalem 97200 (+972-3-527 3740) (fax 527 3741) (jerusalem@seedsofpeace.org) (www.seedsofpeace.org). Trains people for conflict transformation.
Shatil (CD HR), PO Box 53395, West Jerusalem 91533 (+972-2-672 3597) (fax 673 5149) (shatil@shatil.nif.org.il) (www.shatil.org.il). Also 4 other regional offices.
Shovrim Shtika / Breaking the Silence (HR), PO Box 51027, 6713206 Tel Aviv (info@breakingthesilence.org.il) (www.breakingthesilence.org.il). Former soldiers opposing the occupation.
Wahat al-Salam - Neve Shalom [WAS-NS] (HR RE CR PO CD), Doar Na / Mobile Post, Shimshon 9976100 (+972-2-999 6305) (fax 991 1072) (info@wasns.info) (wasns.org). "Oasis of Peace".
Windows - Israeli-Palestinian Friendship Centre (CD), PO Box 5195, Tel Aviv - Jaffa (+972-3-620 8324) (fax 629 2570) (office@win-peace.org) (www.win-peace.org). *Windows*. Chlenov 41. See also in Palestine.
Zochrot / Remembering (HR), Ben Tzvi 2, POB 8412, Tel Aviv - Yaffa 6818164 (zochrot@zochrot.org) (www.zochrot.org). Supports Palestinians' right of return.

ITALY
Amnesty International - Sezione Italiana (AI), Via Magenta 5, 00185 Roma (+39-06 4490210) (fax 06 449 0222) (infoamnesty@amnesty.it) (www.amnesty.it).
Archivio Disarmo [IRIAD] (IB RE AT), Via Paolo Mercuri 8, 00193 Roma (+39-06 3600 0343) (fax 06 3600 0345) (archiviodisarmo@pec.it) (www.archiviodisarmo.it).
Associazione Italiana Medicina per la Prevenzione della Guerra Nucleare [AIMPGN] (IP), Via Bari 4, 64029 Silvi Marina (TE) (+39-085 935 1350) (fax 085 935 3333) (mdipaolantonio55@gmail.com) (www.ippnw-italy.org).
Associazione Memoria Condivisa (CR), Viale 1º Maggio 32, 71100 Foggia (+39-0881 637775) (fax) (info@memoriacondivisa.it) (www.memoriacondivisa.it). Supports non-violence as a response to terrorism.
Associazione Museo Italiano per la Pace / Association of Italian Museums for Peace (RE), Via Ezio Andolfato 1, 20126 Milano (museoitalianoperlapace@gmail.com). Promotes culture of peace in schools.
Azione dei Cristiani per l'Abolizione della Tortura [ACAT] (HR), c/o Rinascita Cristiana, Via della Traspontina 15, 00193 Roma (+39-06 686 5358) (posta@acatitalia.it) (www.acatitalia.it).
Centro Studi Sereno Regis - Italian Peace Research Institute / Rete CCP [IPRI] (RE CR EL), Via Garibaldi 13, 10122 Torino (+39-011 532824) (fax 011 515 8000) (www.serenoregis.org). *IPRI Newsletter*.
Gesellschaft für Bedrohte Völker / Associazione per i Popoli Minacciati / Lia por i Popui Manacês (HR), CP 233, 39100 Bozen/Bolzano, Südtirol (+39-0471 972240) (fax) (gfbv.bz@ines.org) (www.gfbv.it). Part of international GFBV network.
Greenpeace (GP), Via Della Cordonata 7, 00187 Roma (+39-06 6813 6061) (fax 06 4543 9793) (info.it@greenpeace.org) (www.greenpeace.org/italy). *GP News*.
International School on Disarmament and Research on Conflicts [ISODARCO] (RE CR DA), c/o Prof Carlo Schaerf, via della Rotonda 4, 00186 Roma (+39-06 689 2340) (isodarco@gmail.com) (www.isodarco.it).
Lega degli Obiettori di Coscienza [LOC] (WR), Via Mario Pichi 1, 20143 Milano (+39-02 837 8817) (fax 02 5810 1220) (locosm@tin.it) (ospiti.peacelink.it/loc/).
Movimento Internazionale della Riconciliazione [MIR] (FR), Via Garibaldi 13, 10122 Torino (+39-011 532824) (fax 011 515 8000) (segretaria@miritalia.org) (www.miritalia.org).

For explanation of codes and abbreviations, see introduction

ITALY

Movimento Nonviolento [MN] (WR TR EL), Via Spagna 8, 37123 Verona (+39-045 800 9803) (fax) (azionenonviolenta@sis.it) (www.nonviolenti.org). *Azione Nonviolenta*.

Operazione Colomba / Operation Dove (RP CD CR), Via Mameli 5, 47921 Rimini (+39-0541 29005) (fax) (info@operazionecolomba@it) (www.operationdove.org). A project of Associazione Papa Giovanni XXIII.

Pax Christi Italia (PC), via Quintole per le Rose 131, 50029 Tavarnuzze, Firenze (+39-055 202 0375) (fax) (info@paxchristi.it) (www.paxchristi.it). *Mosaico di Pace*.

PBI Italia (PA RA HR), Via Asiago 5/a, 35010 Cadoneghe (PD) (+39-345 269 0132) (info@pbi-italy.org) (www.pbi-italy.org).

Religioni per la Pace Italia (RP), Via Pio VIII 38-D-2, 00165 Roma (+39-333 273 1245) (info@religioniperlapaceitalia.org) (www.religioniperlapaceitalia.org).

Rete Italiana Pace e Disarmo / Italian Peace and Disarmament Network [RIPD] (DA RE), c/o Casa per la Nonviolenza, via Spagna 8, 37123 Verona (+39-045 800 9803) (segretaria@retepacedisarmo.org) (www.retepacedisarmo.org).

Servas (SE), c/o Centro Studi Sereno Regis, Via Garibaldi 13, 10122 Torino (segretaer@servas.it) (www.servas.it).

Società Italiana per l'Organizzazione Internazionale [SIOI] (UN), Piazza di San Marco 51, 00186 Roma (+39-06 692 0781) (fax 06 678 9102) (sioi@sioi.org) (www.sioi.org). *La Comunità Internazionale*.

IVORY COAST

Centre de Recherche et d'Action pour la Paix [CERAP] (RE HR), 15 Ave Jean Mermoz Cocody, 08 BP 2088, Abidjan 08 (+225-2240 4720) (fax 2244 8438) (info@cerap-inades.org) (www.cerap-inades.org).

WILPF Côte d'Ivoire (WL), 08 BP 2237, Abidjan (+225-747 0491) (wilpfcotedivoire@gmail.com).

JAPAN

Chikyu no Tomo / Friends of the Earth (FE), 1-21-9 Komone, Itabashi-ku, Tokyo 173-0037 (+81-3-6909 5983) (fax 6909 5986) (info@foejapan.org) (www.foejapan.org).

Goi Peace Foundation / May Peace Prevail on Earth International - Japan Office (CD PO), Heiwa-Daiichi Bldg, 1-4-5 Hirakawa-Cho, Chiyoda-ku, Tokyo 102-0093 (+81-3-3265 2071) (fax 3239 0919) (info@goipeace.or.jp) (www.goipeace.or.jp).

Green Action (EL), Suite 103, 22-75 Tanaka Sekiden-cho, Sakyo-ku, Kyoto 606-8203 (+81-75-701 7223) (fax 702 1952) (info@greenaction-japan.org) (www.greenaction-japan.org). Campaigns especially against nuclear fuel cycle.

Greenpeace Japan (GP), N F Bldg 2F 8-13-11, Nishi-Shinjuku, Shinjuku, Tokyo 160-0023 (+81-3-5338 9800) (fax 5338 9817) (www.greenpeace.or.jp).

Himeyuri Peace Museum (RE), 671-1 Ihara, Itoman-shi, Okinawa 901-0344 (+81-98-997 2100) (fax 997 2102) (himeyuri1@himeyuri.or.jp) (www.himeyuri.or.jp).

Hiroshima Peace Culture Foundation [HPCF] (PA ND RE), 1-2 Nakajima-cho, Naka-ku, Hiroshima 730-0811 (+81-82-241 5246) (fax 542 7941) (p-soumu@pcf.city.hiroshima.jp) (www.pcf.city.hiroshima.jp/hpcf). *Peace Culture*.

Hiroshima Peace Memorial Museum (RE), 1-2 Nakajima-cho, Naka-ku, Hiroshima 730-0811 (+81-82-241 4004) (fax 542 7941) (hpcf@pcf.city.hiroshima.jp) (www.pcf.city.hiroshima.jp).

Japan Association of Lawyers Against Nuclear Arms [JALANA] (ND), 20-4-906 Araki-cho, Shinjuku-ku, Tokyo 160-0007 (+81-4-2998 2866) (fax 2998 2868) (jalana.office@gmail.com) (www.hankaku-j.com).

Japan Council Against A & H Bombs - Gensuikyo (IB ND PA), 2-4-4 Yushima, Bunkyo-ku, Tokyo 113-8464 (+81-3-5842 6034) (fax 5842 6033) (antiatom@topaz.plala.or.jp) (www.antiatom.org). *No More Hiroshimas*; *Gensuikyo Tsushin*. National federation.

Japanese Physicians for the Prevention of Nuclear War [JPPNW] (IP), c/o Hiroshima Prefectural Medical Association, 3-2-3 Futabanosato, Higashi-ku, Hiroshima 732-0057 (+81-82-568 1511) (fax 568 2112) (ippnw-japan@hiroshima.med.or.jp) (www.hiroshima.med.or.jp).

Kyoto Museum for World Peace (RE), Ritsumeikan University, 56-1 Kitamachi, Toji-in, Kyoto 603-8577 (+81-75-465 8151) (fax 465 7899) (peacelib@st.ritsumei.ac.jp) (www.ritsumei.ac.jp/mng/er/wp-museum).

Network Against Japan Arms Trade [NAJAT] (AT), 311 Shimin Plaza - 302 Heisei Building - 3-12, Shimomiyabi Cho, Shinjuku, Tokyo 162-0822 (anti.arms.export@gmail.com) (najat2016.wordpress.com).

Nihon Hidankyo / Japan Confederation of A- and H-Bomb Sufferers' Organisations (ND CR HR), Gable Bldg 902, 1-3-5 Shiba Daimon, Minato-ku, Tokyo 105-0012 (+81-3-3438 1897) (fax 3431 2113) (kj3t-tnk@asahi-net.or.jp) (www.ne.jp/asahi/hidankyo/nihon). *Hidankyo*.

Nipponzan Myohoji (WR), 7-8 Shinsen-Cho, Shibuya-ku, Tokyo 150-0045 (+81-3-3461 9363) (fax 3461 9367) (info@nipponzanmyohoji.org) (nipponzanmyohoji.org).

Organising Committee - World Conference Against A and H bombs (ND), 2-4-4 Yushima, Bunkyo-ku, Tokyo 113-8464 (+81-3-5842 6034) (fax 5842 6033) (intl@antiatom.org).

Peace Depot - Peace Resources Cooperative (ND PA RE), Hiyoshi Gruene 1st Floor, 1-30-27-4 Hiyoshi Hon-cho, Kohoku-ku, Yokohama 223-0062 (+81-45-563 5101) (fax 563 9907) (office@peacedepot.org) (www.peacedepot.org). *Nuclear Weapon & Nuclear Test Monitor*.

Toda Peace Institute (RE CR PA WF ND), Samon Eleven Bldg - 5th floor, 3-1 Samon-cho, Shinjuku-ku, Tokyo 160-0017 (contact@toda.org) (www.toda.org).

United Nations Association (UN), Nippon Building - Rm 427, 2-6-2 Ohtemachi, Chiyoda-ku, Tokyo 100-8699 (+81-3-3270 4731) (info@unaj.or.jp) (www.unaj.or.jp).

WRI Japan (WR HR AL), 666 Ukai-cho, Inuyama-shi, Aichi-ken 468-0085 (+81-568-615850).

JORDAN

Generations for Peace (CR), Al-Hussein Youth Sport City, PO Box 963772, Amman 11196 (+962-6-500 4600) (fax 568 2954) (feedback@gfp.ngo) (www.generationsforpeace.org). Grassroots empowerment and advocacy.

KAZAKHSTAN

Chalyqaralyq qauipsizdik Zhenye Sayasat Optalyghy / Centre for International Security and Policy [CISP] (RE), PO Box 257, 13/9 Turan Ave, 010088 Astana (+7-717-225 0544) (info@cisp-astana.kz) (www.cisp-astana.kz).

KENYA

Centre for Research and Dialogue - Somalia [CRD] (CR RE), PO Box 28832, Nairobi (www.crdsomalia.org). Based in Mogadishu, Somalia.

International Friendship League - Kenya [IFL] (CD), PO Box 9929, 00200 Nairobi. Part of international network of groups.

KOREA, REPUBLIC OF

Greenpeace East Asia - Seoul Office (GP), 2/F - 358-121 Seogyo-dong, Mapo-gu, Seoul (+82-2-3144 1994) (fax 6455 1995) (greenpeace.kr@greenpeace.org) (www.greenpeace.org/eastasia).

World Without War (WR), 422-9 Mangwon-dong, Mapo-gu, Seoul 121-230 (+82-2-6401 0514) (fax) (peace@withoutwar.org) (www.withoutwar.org).

LATVIA

Latvijas Zemes Draugi (FE), Lapu iela 17, Zemgales Priekšpilseta, Riga 1002 (+371-6722 5112) (zemesdraugi@zemesdraugi.lv) (www.zemesdraugi.lv).

LEBANON

Fighters for Peace (CR RE), Zico House - 2nd Floor, Spears Street, Beirut (+961-3-971242) (info@fightersforpeace.org) (fightersforpeace.org). Ex-combatants from various factions.

Greenpeace Mediterranean (GP), PO Box 13-6590, Beirut (+961-1-361255) (fax 36 1254) (supporters@greenpeace.org.lb) (www.greenpeace.org/lebanon). See also Israel, Turkey.

WILPF (WL), c/o Nouha Ghosn, PO Box 14-6725, Beirut.

LIBERIA

Sustainable Development Institute (FE), PO Box 5678, Duarzon Village, 1000 Monrovia 10 (+231-330-641355) (managementteam@sdiliberia.org) (www.sdiliberia.org).

LITHUANIA

United Nations Association (UN HR), Lithuanian Culture Research Institute, Saltoniskiu St 58, 08015 Vilnius (+370-5-275 1898) (jurate128@yahoo.de).

LUXEMBOURG

Action des Chrétiens pour l'Abolition de la Torture [ACAT] (HR), 5 Av Marie-Thérèse, 2132 Luxembourg (+352-4474 3558) (fax 4474 3559) (contact@acat.lu) (www.acat.lu).

Association Luxembourgeoise pour les Nations Unies [ALNU] (UN), 3 Rte d'Arlon, 8009 Strassen (+352-461468) (fax 461469) (alnu@pt.lu) (www.alnu.lu).

Iwerliewen fir Bedreete Volleker (HR), BP 98, 6905 Niederanven (+352-2625 8687) (info@iwerliewen.org) (iwerliewen.org).

Mouvement Écologique (FE), 6 Rue Vauban, 2663 Luxembourg (+352-439 0301) (fax 4390 3043) (meco@oeko.lu) (www.meco.lu).

Schengen Peace Founation (RE), 14 Rue Mathias Hardt, 1717 Luxembourg (+352-223294) (dominicusrohde@schengenpeacefoundation.org) (schengenpeacefoundation.org). Organises annual World Peace Forum.

Servas (SE), see under Belgium.

MALAWI

International Friendship League - Malawi [IFL] (CD), PO Box 812, Mzuzu (menardkamabga@yahoo.com).

MALAYSIA

MALAYSIA
Malaysian Physicians for Peace and Social Responsibility [MPPSR] (IP), c/o Academy of Medicine, 50480 Kuala Lumpur (+60-3-7956 8407) (rsmcoy@sternyx.com) (www.ppsr.org).
Sahabat Alam Malaysia / Friends of the Earth Malaysia [SAM] (FE), 258 Jalan Air Itam, George Town, 10460 Penang (+60-4-228 6930) (fax 228 6932) (sam_inquiry@yahoo.com) (www.foe.malaysia.org).

MALTA
John XXIII Peace Laboratory [Peacelab] (IB RP RE), Triq Hal-Far, Zurrieq ZRQ 2609 (+356-2168 9504) (fax 2164 1591) (info@peacelab.org) (www.peacelab.org). *It-Tieqa.*
Moviment ghall-Ambjent / Friends of the Earth Malta (FE), PO Box 1013, South Street, Valletta VLT 1000 (+356-7996 1460) (info@foemalta.org) (www.foemalta.org).

MAURITIUS
Lalit (SF WL PA), 153 Main Rd, Grand River North West, Port-Louis (+230-208 2132) (lalitmail@intnet.mu) (www.lalitmauritius.org). Anti-militarist party and campaign.

MEXICO
Médicos Mexicanos para la Prevención de la Guerra Nuclear (IP), Antiguo Claustro - Hospital Juarez - PA, Plaza San Pablo, 06090 Mexico - DF (fromow@servidor.unam.mx).

MOLDOVA
Asociatia de Voluntariat International [AVI] (SC), 129 - 3A Vasile Alecsandri Str, 2012 Chisinau (+373-2-292 7724) (fax 293 0415) (avi@avimd.org).

MONACO
Organisation pour la Paix par le Sport - Peace and Sport (CD), L'Aigue Marine, 24 Ave de Fontvieille - Bloc B, 98000 (+377-9797 7800) (fax 9797 1891) (contact@peace-sport.org) (www.peace-sport.org).

MONGOLIA
Blue Banner (ND), Post Office 49 - Box 35, Ulaanbaatar 13381 (enkhee53@yahoo.com). Promotes nuclear non-proliferation.
Oyu Tolgoi Watch (EL HR), POB 636, Ulaanbaatar 46A (+976-9918 5828) (otwatch@gmail.com). Opposing devastation by Rio Tinto mining project.

MONTENEGRO
UN Association Montenegro (UN), Gradina bb, Danilovgrad 81410 (+382-69-522144) (una.mne@gmail.com).

NAMIBIA
Alternatives to Violence Project [AVP Namibia] (CR), PO Box 50617, Bachbrecht, Windhoek (+264-61-371554) (fax 371555) (vicky@peace.org.na).
Earth Life (Namibia) [ELN] (EL), PO Box 24892, Windhoek 9000 (+264-61-227913) (fax 305213) (earthl@iway.na).

NEPAL
Human Rights and Peace Foundation [HURPEF] (HR), GPO 8975, Epc 5397, Kathmandu (+977-1-438 5231) (hurpef@hons.com.np) (www.hurpef.org.np).
Human Rights Without Frontiers - Nepal (WR HR), PO Box 10660, Maitidevi-33, Kathmandu (+977-1-444 2367) (fax 443 5331) (hrwfnepal@mail.com.np) (www.hrwfnepal.net.np). *Human Rights Monitor.*
National Land Rights Forum (WR HR), Bhumi-Ghar, Tokha-10, Dhapasi Kathmandu (+977-1-691 4586) (fax 435 7033) (land@nlrfnepal.org) (www.nlrfnepal.org).
Nepal Physicians for Social Responsibility (IP), PO Box 19624, Bagbazar, Kathmandu (psrn@healthnet.org.np).
Peace Museum Nepal [PMN] (RE), 29 Anamnagar, Kathmandu (+977-1-425 4409) (peacemuseumnepal@gmail.com) (www.peacemuseumnepal.com).
People's Forum for Human Rights - Bhutan (HR), Anarmani 4, Birtamod, Jhapa (+977-23-540824) (rizal_pfhrb@ntc.net.np).
United Nations Association of Nepal (UN), PO Box 306, Baluwatar, Kathmandu (+977-1-442 6444) (fax 441 3637) (info@unanp.org) (unanp.org).

NETHERLANDS
Amsterdamse Catholic Worker / Ploughshares Support Group (PA AT RP HR RA), Postbus 12622, 1100 AP Amsterdam (+31-20-699 8996) (noelhuis@antenna.nl) (noelhuis.nl). *A Pinch of Salt.*
Anti-Militaristies Onderzoekskollectief - VD AMOK (WR RE AT ND), Lauwerecht 55, 3515 GN Utrecht (+31-30-890 1341) (info@vdamok.nl) (www.vdamok.nl).
Campagne tegen Wapenhandel (AT), Anna Spenglerstr 71, 1054 NH Amsterdam (+31-20-616 4684) (fax) (info@stopwapenhandel.org) (www.stopwapenhandel.org). Campaign against arms trade.
Christian Peacemaker Teams - Nederland [CPT-NL] (RP RA PA), c/o Irene van Setten, Bredasingel 70, 6843 RE Arnhem (+31-26-848 1706) (info@cpt-nl.org) (www.cpt-nl.org).
Greenpeace Nederland (GP), NDSM-Plein 32, 1033 WB Amsterdam (+31-20-626 1877) (fax 622 1272) (info@greenpeace.nl) (www.greenpeace.nl).

Kerk en Vrede (FR PA RE), Joseph Haydnlaan 2a, 3533 AE Utrecht (+31-30-231 6666) (secretariaat@kerkenvrede.nl) (kerkenvrede.nl).

Museum voor Vrede en Geweldloosheid [MVG] (RE PA), Ezelsveldlaan 212, 2611 DK Delft (+31-15-785 0137) (info@vredesmuseum.nl) (www.vredesmuseum.nl). *De Vredesboot.*

Musicians Without Borders (CD), Tolhuisweg 1, 1031 CL Amsterdam (+31-20-330 5012) (info@mwb.ngo) (www.musicianswithoutborders.org).

Nederlandse Vereniging voor Medische Polemologie [NVMP] (IP), PO Box 199, 4190 CD Geldermalsen (+31-6-4200 9559) (office@nvmp.org) (nvmp.org).

Pax (PC AT RE GD), Sint Jacobsstr 12, 3511 BS Utrecht (+31-30-233 3346) (info@paxforpeace.nl) (www.paxvoorvrede.nl). Also www.paxforpeace.nl.

Peace Brigades Nederland [PBI] (RA PO CR RE), Oudegracht 36, 3511 AP Utrecht (+31-6-1649 8221) (info@peacebrigades.nl) (www.peacebrigades.nl).

Religieus Genootschap der Vrienden - Quakers Nederland (SF), Quaker Centrum, Stadhouderslaan 8, 2517 HW 's-Gravenhage (secretariaat@dequakers.nl) (www.quakers.nu).

Stichting Voor Aktieve Geweldloosheid [SVAG] (SD PO RE), Postbus 288, 5280 AG Boxtel (info@geweldloosactief.nl) (www.geweldlozekracht.nl). *Geweldloze Kracht.*

Stichting Vredesburo Eindhoven (PA RE), Grote Berg 41, 5611 KH Eindhoven (+31-40-244 4707) (info@vredesburo.nl) (www.vredesburo.nl). *Vredesburo Nieuwsbrief.*

Vredesbeweging Pais (WR EL), Ezelsveldlaan 212, 2611 DK Delft (+31-15-785 0137) (info@vredesbeweging.nl) (www.vredesbeweging.nl). *vredesmagazine.*

Vrouwen en Duurzame Vrede (CR ND SD), Haaksbergerstr 317, 7545 GJ Enschede (+31-53-434 0559) (info@vrouwenenduurzamevrede.nl) (www.vrouwenenduurzamevrede.nl).

Women's International League for Peace and Freedom - Netherlands [WILPF-IVVV] (WL), Laan van Nieuw Oost Indië 252, 2593 CD Den Haag (+31-345-615105) (info@wilpf.nl) (www.wilpf.nl).

NEW ZEALAND / AOTEAROA

Abolition 2000 Aotearoa New Zealand [A2000 ANZ] (ND), c/o Pax Christi, PO Box 68419, Newton, Aukland 1145 (+64-9-377 5541) (abolition2000@ymail.com) (www.a2000.org.nz).

Amnesty International (AI), PO Box 5300, Wellesley St, Auckland 1141 (+64-9-303 4520) (fax 303 4528) (info@amnesty.org.nz) (www.amnesty.org.nz).

Anabaptist Association of Australia and New Zealand (RP), see under Australia (anabaptist.asn.au).

Anglican Pacifist Fellowship [APF] (RP AT TR), c/o Indrea Alexander, 9 Holmes St, Waimate 7924 (apfnzsecretary@gmail.com) (converge.org.nz/pma/apf). *The Anglican Pacifist of Aotearoa New Zealand.*

Anti-Bases Campaign [ABC] (PA RE), Box 2258, Christchurch 8140 (abc@chch.planet.org.nz) (www.converge.org.nz/abc). 2 yrly.

Aotearoa Lawyers for Peace (ND), c/o Matt Robson, PO Box 11-648, Ellerslie, Auckland 1051 (+64-9-524 8403).

Campaign Against Foreign Control of Aotearoa [CAFCA], PO Box 2258, Christchurch 8140 (cafca@chch.planet.org.nz) (www.cafca.org.nz). *Foreign Control Watchdog.*

Disarmament and Security Centre [DSC] (IB WL RE ND CR), PO Box 8390, Christchurch 8440 (+64-22-067 3517) (lucy@disarmsecure.org) (www.disarmsecure.org).

Engineers for Social Responsibility [ESR] (EL ND AT), PO Box 6208, Wellesley Street, Auckland 1141 (www.esr.org.nz).

Green Party of Aotearoa/NZ (EL), PO Box 11652, Wellington 6142 (+64-4-801 5102) (fax 801 5104) (greenparty@greens.org.nz) (www.greens.org.nz). *Te Awa.*

Greenpeace Aotearoa New Zealand (GP), 11 Akiraho St, Mount Eden, Auckland (+64-9-630 6317) (fax 630 7121) (info@greenpeace.org.nz) (www.greenpeace.org/new-zealand). *Kakariki.*

New Zealand Burma Support Group (HR EL), 14 Waitati Pl, Mt Albert, Auckland (+64-9-828 4855) (nzburma@xtra.co.nz). *Newsletter.*

Pax Christi Aotearoa/NZ (PC), PO Box 99380, Auckland Central (+64-9-377 5541) (paxchristiaotearoa@gmail.com) (www.paxchristiaotearoa.nz).

Peace Action Wellington (DA AT RA), PO Box 9263, Wellington (peacewellington@riseup.net) (peacewellington.org). Work includes direct action against arms fairs.

Peace Foundation (CR RE), PO Box 8055, Symonds Street, Auckland 1150 (+64-9-373 2379) (fax 379 2668) (peace@peacefoundation.org.nz) (kiaora.peace.net.nz).

Peace Movement Aotearoa [PMA] (AT HR PA RE), PO Box 9314, Wellington 6141 (+64-4-382 8129) (fax 382 8173) (pma@xtra.co.nz) (www.converge.org.nz/pma). National networking body.

NEW ZEALAND

Quaker Peace and Service Aotearoa/New Zealand [QPSANZ] (SF), Quaker Meeting House, 72 Cresswell Ave, Christchurch 8061 (+64-3-980 4884)
(www.quaker.org.nz/groups/qpsanz).
Stop the Arms Trade NZ (AT DA), PO Box 9843, Wellington
(stop-the-arms-trade@riseup.net)
(www.stopthearmstrade.nz).
Actions against weapons expos.
United Nations Association of New Zealand [UNANZ] (UN), PO Box 24494, Wellington 6142 (+64-4-496 9638)
(office@unanz.org.nz) (unanz.org.nz).
West Papua Action Auckland [WPAA] (HR TW), PO Box 68419, Wellesley St, Auckland 1141 (+64-9-815 9000) (fax)
(westpapuaactionauckland.wordpress.com).
Women's International League for Peace and Freedom [WILPF] (WL), PO Box 2054, Wellington (wilpfaotearoa@gmail.com) (www.wilpf.nz).

NICARAGUA

Centro de Prevención de la Violencia [CEPREV] (HR PO DA), Villa Fontana - casa 23, Club Terraza 1/2 c al lago, Managua (fax +505-2278 1637) (www.ceprev.org).
Promotes a culture of peace.

NIGERIA

Alternatives to Violence Project [AVP Nigeria] (WR), 5 Ogunlesi St, off Bode Thomas Rd, Onipanu, Lagos (+234-1-497 1359) (prawa@linkserve.com.ng).
Anglican Pacifist Fellowship - Nigeria [APF] (RP), c/o Peter U James, Akwa Ibom Peace Group, PO Box 269, Abak, Akwa Ibom State.
Centre for Global Nonviolence Nigeria (RE PA), 20 Ogunka Eruwa Rd, Rumuoke Newlayout (off Ada George Road), Mgbuoba, Port Harcourt, Rivers State
(cgnv_ngr@yahoo.com) (cgnv.edublogs.org).
Peace Initiative Network [PIN] (CR CD RE), PO Box 14937, Kano (info@peaceinitiativenetwork.org) (peaceinitiativenetwork.org).
United Nations Association of Nigeria (UN), PO Box 54423, Falomo, Ikoyi, Lagos (+234-802-319 8698).

NORTH MACEDONIA

Dvizenje na ekologistitje na Makedonija / Ecologists' Movement of Macedonia [DEM] (FE), Ul Vasil Gjorgov 39 - 6, 1000 Skopje (+389-2-220518) (fax)
(dem@dem.org.mk) (www.dem.org.mk).
Mirovna Aktsiya / Aksioni Paqësor / Peace Action (WR), Dimo Narednikot A1/2/31, 7500 Prilep (+389-48-401888)
(office@mirovnaakcija.org)
(www.mirovnaakcija.org).
Also in Tetovo (+389-44-520808).

United Nations Association of Macedonia (UN), St Zorz Bize 9-b, 1000 Skopje (+389-2-244 3751) (fpesevi@mt.net.mk) (www.sunamk.org).

NORWAY

Amnesty International (AI), PO Box 702, Sentrum, 0106 Oslo (+47-2240 2200) (fax 2240 2250) (info@amnesty.no) (www.amnesty.no).
Folkereisning Mot Krig [FMK] (WR AT), PO Box 2779, Solli, 0204 Oslo (+47-2246 4670) (fax) (fmk@ikkevold.no) (www.ikkevold.no). *Ikkevold.*
Fred og Forsoning - IFOR Norge (FR), Fredshuset, Møllergata 12, 0179 Oslo (contact@ifor.no) (www.ifor.no).
Informasjonsarbeidere for Fred [IF] (IB AT ND DA), c/o Heffermehl, Stensgaten 24B, 0358 Oslo (+47-9174 4783)
(fredpax@online.no) (peaceispossible.info).
Internasjonal Dugnad [ID] (SC), Nordahl Brunsgt 22, 0165 Oslo (+47-2211 3123) (info@internasjonaldugnad.no) (www.internasjonaldugnad.no).
Dugnad Nytt.
Nansen Centre for Peace and Dialogue [NCPD] (CR HR HR), Bjørnstjerne Bjørnsons gate 2, 2609 Lillehammer (+47-6125 5500) (post@peace.no) (www.peace.no).
Narviksenteret - Nordnorsk Fredssenter (IB), Postboks 700, 8509 Narvik (+47-7654 7078) (fax 7694 4560) (fred.no).
Nei til Atomvåpen / No to Nuclear Weapons (ND), Postboks 8838, Youngstorget, 0028 Oslo (post@neitilatomvapen.org) (www.neitilatomvapen.no).
Nobel Peace Prize Watch (DA RE), for postal address see under Sweden
(mail@nobelwill.org) (www.nobelwill.org).
Promotes original purpose of Nobel Prize.
Nobels Fredssenter / Nobel Peace Centre (RE), PO Box 1894 Vika, 0124 Oslo (+47-4830 1000) (fax 9142 9238)
(post@nobelpeacecenter.org)
(www.nobelpeacecenter.org).
Norges Fredslag (DA AT ND RE), Grensen 9B, Postboks 8922, Youngstorget, 0028 Oslo (www.fredslaget.no).
Norwegian Peace Association.
Norges Fredsråd / Norwegian Peace Council (IB), Postboks 8940 Youngstorget, 0028 Oslo (+47-9527 4822) (fax 2286 8401) (post@norgesfredsrad.no)
(norgesfredsrad.no).
Norges Naturvernforbund (FE), Mariboes gate 8, 0183 Oslo (+47-2310 9610) (fax 2293 1802) (medlem@naturvernforbundet.no) (naturvernforbundet.no).
Norwegian Nobel Institute / Det Norske Nobelinstitutt (RE DA CR), Henrik Ibsens gate 51, 0255 Oslo (+47-2212 9300) (fax 9476 1117) (postmaster@nobel.no) (nobelpeaceprize.org).

Peace Brigades Norge [PBI-Norge] (CR HR PA), Fredshuset, Møllergata 12, 0172 Oslo (kontakt@pbi.no) (www.pbi.no).
WILPF Norge - Internasjonal Kvinneliga for Fred og Frihet [IKFF] (WL), Storgata 11, 0155 Oslo (+47-9308 9644) (ikff@ikff.no) (www.ikff.no). *Fred og Frihet*.

PAKISTAN

Human Rights Commission of Pakistan [HRCP] (HR), Aiwan-i-Jamhoor, 107 Tipu Block, New Garden Town, Lahore 54600 (+92-42-3586 4994) (fax 3588 3582) (hrcp@hrcp-web.org) (hrcp-web.org).
Revolutionary Association of the Women of Afghanistan [RAWA] (HR), PO Box 374, Quetta (+92-300-554 1258) (rawa@rawa.org) (www.rawa.org).
Servas Pakistan [SE-PK] (SE), c/o Muhammad Naseem, GPO Box 516, Lahore 54000 (+92-321-444 4516) (fax 42-3532 2223) (servaspakistan@yahoo.com) (pages.intnet.mu/servas/Pakistan). *Servas Pakistan Newsletter*.

PALESTINE (see also Israel)

NOTE: Because all of Palestine is under Israeli control (including areas not under day-to-day occupation), it is advisable to add 'via Israel' to addresses here (as well as 'Palestine').
Al-Haq (HR), PO Box 1413, Ramallah, West Bank (+970-2-295 4646) (fax 295 4903) (www.alhaq.org).
Al-Watan Centre (CR HR RE), PO Box 158, Hebron, West Bank (+970-2-222 3777) (fax 222 0907) (info@alwatan.org) (www.alwatan.org).
Supports popular resistance and nonviolence.
Alternative Information Centre [AIC] (HR RE TW AL AT), Building 111, Main Street, Beit Sahour, West Bank (+972-2-277 5444) (fax 277 5445) (www.alternativenews.org). See also Israel.
Arab Educational Institute - Open Windows [AEI] (RE PC), Paul VI Street, Bethlehem, West Bank (+970-2-274 4030) (fax 277 7554) (info@aeicenter.org) (www.aeicenter.org).
Christian Peacemaker Teams [CPT] (RP), c/o Redeemer Church, PO Box 14076, Muristan Rd, Jerusalem 91140 (+972-2-222 8485) (cptheb@cpt.org) (www.cpt.org).
Combatants for Peace (CD), Ramallah (for postal address, see under Israel) (office@cfpeace.org) (www.cfpeace.org). Palestinian and Israeli ex-fighters for peace.
Ecumenical Accompaniment Programme in Palestine and Israel - Jerusalem Office [EAPPI] (RP HR CD CR), PO Box 741, East Jerusalem 91000 (+972-2-628 9402) (communications@eappi.org) (eappi.org).
Geneva Initiative (CD CR), c/o Palestinian Peace Coalition, PO Box 4252, Ramallah (+972-2-297 2535) (fax 297 2538) (www.geneva-accord.org). See also Israel.
Good Shepherd Collective (HR RA CR), Um al-Khair, South Hebron Hills, Hebron Governate, West Bank (+972-58-438 1133) (info@goodshepherdcollective.org) (goodshepherdcollective.org). Collective resisting military occupation.
International Peace and Co-operation Centre [IPCC] (TW CR), PO Box 24162, Jerusalem 91240 (+972-2-581 1992) (fax 540 0522) (info@ipcc-jerusalem.org) (home.ipcc-jerusalem.org).
Israel-Palestine Creative Regional Initiatives [IPCRI] (RE CR EL CD), PO Box 9321, Jerusalem 91092 (+970-59-856 7287) (ipcri@ipcri.org) (www.ipcri.org). Office is in Ammunition Hill, East Jerusalem.
Middle East Non-Violence and Democracy - FOR Palestine [MEND] (FR HR CR), PO Box 66558, Beit Hanina, East Jerusalem (+970-2-656 7310) (fax 656 7311) (lucynusseibeh@gmail.com) (www.mendonline.org).
Miftah - Palestinian Initiative for the Promotion of Global Dialogue and Democracy (HR), PO Box 69647, Jerusalem 95908 (+970-2-298 9490) (fax 298 9492) (administration@miftah.org) (www.miftah.org).
Movement Against Israeli Apartheid in Palestine [MAIAP] (HR), see under Israel.
OneVoice Movement - Palestine (CD CR), PO Box 2401, Ramallah, West Bank (+970-2-295 2076) (info@OneVoice.ps) (www.onevoicemovement.org). See also Israel.
Palestine-Israel Journal (RE CD CR), PO Box 19839, East Jerusalem (+972-2-628 2115) (fax 627 3388) (pij@pij.org) (www.pij.org). 4 yrly.
Palestinian BDS National Committee (HR RA), c/o PACBI, PO Box 1701, Ramallah, West Bank (pacbi@bdsmovement.net) (bdsmovement.net/bnc).
Palestinian Centre for Human Rights [PCHR] (HR), PO Box 1328, Gaza City, Gaza Strip (+970-8-282 4776) (fax 283 5255) (pchr@pchrgaza.org) (www.pchrgaza.org).
Palestinian Physicians for the Prevention of Nuclear War [PPPNW] (IP), PO Box 51681, East Jerusalem (azizlabadi@yahoo.com).
Palestinian-Israeli Peace NGO Forum (Palestinian Office) (CD), c/o Panorama, Al Ahliya St, Ramallah 2045 (+970-2-295 9618) (fax 298 1824) (panorama@panoramacenter.org) (www.peacengo.org). See also under Israel.
Parents' Circle - Families' Forum: Bereaved Palestinian and Israeli Families Supporting Peace and Tolerance (CD CR), 13 Jamal Abed Al-Nasser St, Al-Ram, East Jerusalem (+972-2-234 4554) (fax 234 4554) (alquds@theparentscircle.org) (www.theparentscircle.com).
See also under Israel.

PALESTINE

Wi'am - Palestinian Conflict Resolution Centre (FR CR), PO Box 1039, Bethlehem, West Bank (+970-2-277 7333) (fax) (hope@alaslah.org) (www.alaslah.org).
Windows - Israeli-Palestinian Friendship Centre (CD), PO Box 352, Ramallah (office@win-peace.org) (www.win-peace.org). See also in Israel.

PARAGUAY

Amnistía Internacional Paraguay (AI), Dr Hassler 5229 - e/ Cruz del Defensor y Cruz del Chaco, Bsrrio Villa Mora, Asunción (+595-21-604822) (fax 663272) (ai-info@py.amnesty.org) (www.amnesty.org).
SERPAJ-Paraguay (HR PA), Calle Teniente Prieto 354 - entre Dr Facundo Insfran y Tte Rodi, Asunción (+595-21-481333) (serpajpy@serpajpy.org.py) (www.serpajpy.org.py).

PHILIPPINES

Aksyon para sa Kapayapaan at Katarungan (Action for Peace and Justice) - Center for Active Non-Violence [AKKAPKA-CANV] (FR TW HR EL), Rm 222, Administration Bldg, Pius XII Catholic Centre, 1175 UN Avenue, Paco, 1007 Manila (+63-2-526 0103) (fax 400 0823) (akkapka.canv84@gmail.com).
Initiatives for International Dialogue [IID] (CD TW), 27 Galaxy St, GSIS Heights, Matina, 8000 Davao City (+63-82-299 2052) (iidnet.org). Manila office +63-2-911 0205.

POLAND

Lekarze Przeciw Wojnie Nuklearnej - Sekcja Polska IPPNW (IP), Ul Mokotowska 3 - lok 6, 02640 Warszawa (+48-22-845 5784) (b.wasilewski@ips.pl).
Servas Polska (SE), c/o Joanna Mozga, Ul Kasprzaka 24A m 39, 01211 Warszawa (joanna@servas.pl) (servas.pl).
Stowarzyszenie "Nigdy Wiecej" / "Never Again" Association (HR PO), PO Box 6, 03700 Warszawa 4 (redakcja@nigdywiecej.org) (www.nigdywiecej.org).
Works for genocide commemoration, anti-racism.

PORTUGAL

Amnistia Internacional Portugal (AI), Av Infante Santo 42 - 2º, 1350-179 Lisboa (+351-21 386 1652) (fax 21 386 1782) (aiportugal@amnistia-internacional.pt) (www.amnistia-internacional.pt).
Associação das Nações Unidas Portugal (UN), Rua do Almado 679 - 1º - S 103, 4050-039 Porto (+351-22 200 7767) (anuportugal@gmail.com).
Associação Livre dos Objectores e Objectoras de Consciência [ALOOC] (WR AL), Rua D Aleixo Corte-Real 394 - 3º D, 1800-166 Lisboa (alooc.portugal@gmail.om).
Conselho Português para a Paz e Cooperação [CPPC] (WP ND DA), Rua Rodrigo da Fonseca 56-2º, 1250-193 Lisboa (+351-21 386 3375) (fax 21 386 3221) (conselhopaz@cppc.pt) (www.cppc.pt). Portuguese Council for Peace and Co-operation.
Observatório Género e Violência Armada / Observatory on Gender and Armed Violence [OGIVA] (DA HR), Centro Estudos Sociais, Colégio de S Jerónimo, Apartado 3087, 3000-995 Coimbra (+351-239 855593) (fax 239 855589) (ogiva@ces.uc.pt) (www.ces.uc.pt/ogiva).
Pax Christi Portugal (PC), Basílica da Estrela, Praça da Estrela, 1200-667 Lisboa (info@paxchristiportugal.net) (www.paxchristiportugal.net).

PUERTO RICO

Humanistas Seculares de Puerto Rico (HR), 120 Ave Carlos Chardon - 123, San Juan 00918 (www.humanistaspr.org).
Pax Christi Puerto Rico (PC), c/o Randolph Rivera Cuevas, HC 3 Box 9695, Gurabo 00778 (+1787-761 1355) (fax) (clidin@bppr.com).

ROMANIA

Institutul Român pentru Actiune, Instruire si Cercetare în Domeniul Pacii [PATRIR] (RE), Strada Ion Ghica 30, 400306 Cluj-Napoca (+40-264 420298) (info@patrir.ro) (patrir.ro). Peace Action, Training and Research Institute.

RUSSIA

Dom Druzeiy v Moskvye / Friends' House Moscow (SF), Sukharevskaya M - pl 6 - str 1, 127051 Moskva (+7-903-664 1075) (dd.moskva@gmail.com) (friendshousemoscow.org).
Federatsiya Mira i Soglasiya / International Federation for Peace and Conciliation [IFPC] (WP), 36 Prospekt Mira, 129090 Moskva (+7-495-680 3576) (fax 688 9587) (vik@ifpc.ru) (www.ifpc.ru).
Mir i Soglasie.
Greenpeace Russia (GP), Lyeningradskii prospect - d 26 - k 1, 125040 Moskva (+7-495-988 7460) (fax) (info@greenpeace.ru) (www.greenpeace.org/russia).
Memorial (HR CD), Malyi Karetnyi pereulok 12, 127051 Moskva (+7-495-650 7883) (fax 609 0694) (info@memo.ru) (www.memo.ru).
Nyemyetsko-Russkiy Obmyen / Deutscher-Russischer Austausch [NRO] (CD), Ligovski Pr 87 - Ofis 300, 191040 Sankt-

Peterburg (+7-812-718 3793) (fax 718 3791) (nro@obmen.org) (www.obmen.org). German-Russian Exchange.
Rossiiskaya Assotsiatsiya Sodeystviya OON / United Nations Association of Russia (UN), Vernadsky prospekt 76, 119454 Moskva (+7-495-225 4085) (fax 234 5803) (una@una.ru) (una.ru).
Soldatskiye Matyeri Sankt-Peterburga / Soldiers' Mothers of St Petersburg (HR PA PC), Ul Razyezzhaya 9, 191002 Sankt-Peterburg (+7-812-712 4199) (fax 712 5058) (soldiersmothers@yandex.ru) (www.soldiersmothers.ru).
Tsentr Mezhnatsionalnovo Sotrudnichestva / Centre for Interethnic Co-operation (CR CD), a/ya 8, 127055 Moskva (+7-499-972 6807) (center@interethnic.org) (www.interethnic.org).

RWANDA
Life & Peace Institute - DR Congo (RE RP), PO Box 64, Cyangugu (+243-81-249 4489) (pieter.vanholder@life-peace.org) (www.life-peace.org).
Peace & Conflict Resolution Project (of Bukavu, DR Congo) [PCR] (CR), PO Box 37, Cyangugu (+243-993-463279) (peacecrp@yahoo.com) (www.peaceconflictresolutionproject.webs.com).
Operates in Bukavu, eastern Congo.

SERBIA
Beogradski Forum za Svet Ravnopravnih / Belgrade Forum for a World of Equals [Beoforum] (WP), Sremska Broj 6 - IV sprat, 11000 Beograd (+381-11-328 3778) (beoforum@eunet.rs) (www.beoforum.rs).
Centar za Nenasilnu Akciju - Beograd / Centre for Nonviolent Action - Belgrade [CNA] (CR PA RE CD), Cika Ljubina 6, 11000 Beograd (+381-11-263 7603) (fax) (cna.beograd@nenasilje.org) (www.nenasilje.org).
See also in Bosnia-Herzegovina.
Centre for Applied NonViolent Action and Strategies [CANVAS], Gandijeva 76a, 11070 Novi Beograd (+381-11-222 8331) (fax 222 8336) (office@canvasopedia.org) (www.canvasopedia.org).
Udruzenje za Ujedinjene Nacije Srbije / United Nations Association of Serbia (UN), Makedonska St 22, 11000 Beograd (+381-11-322 4648) (info@unaserbia.rs) (www.unaserbia.rs).
Zene U Crnom Protiv Rata / Women in Black Against War (WR), Jug Bogdanova 18/V, 11000 Beograd (+381-11-262 3225) (zeneucrnombeograd@gmail.com) (www.zeneucrnom.org).

SIERRA LEONE
Friends of the Earth Sierra Leone [FOESL] (FE), PM Bag 950, 33 Robert St, Freetown (+232-22-226577) (fax 224439) (foesl@sierratel.sl) (www.onesky.ca/foesl).

SINGAPORE
Inter-Religious Organisation - Singapore (RP), Palmer House, 70 Palmer Rd - 05-01/02, Singapore 079427 (+65-6221 9858) (fax 6221 9212) (irosingapore@gmail.com) (iro.sg).
Affiliate of Religions for Peace International.
United Nations Association of Singapore [UNAS] (UN), PO Box 351, Tanglin Post Office, Singapore 912412 (+65-6792 0026) (sctham@unas.org.sg) (www.unas.org.sg). *World Forum.*

SLOVAKIA
Inštitút ľudských Práv / Human Rights Institute (HR), Karpatská 23, 81105 Bratislava (info@ludskeprava.sk) (www.ludskeprava.sk).
Pax Christi Bratislava-Pezinok (PC), Kpt Jaroša 15, 90201 Pezinok (+421-33-640 1284) (fax) (molnars@nextra.sk).
Priatelia Zeme Slovensko / Friends of the Earth Slovakia (FE), Komenského 21, 97401 Banská Bystrica (+421-48-412 3859) (fax) (foe@priateliazeme.sk) (www.priateliazeme.sk).

SOMALIA
Centre for Research and Dialogue [CRD] (CR RE), for postal address see under Kenya (+252-1-658666) (fax 5-932355) (crd@crdsomalia.org) (www.crdsomalia.org). Street address: K4 Airport Rd, Mogadishu.

SOUTH AFRICA
Africa for Palestine [AFP] (HR RA), PO Box 2318, Houghton 2041, Johannesburg (+27-11 403 2097) (fax 86 650 4836) (info@africa4palestine.com) (www.africa4palestine.com).
African Centre for the Constructive Resolution of Disputes [ACCORD] (RE CD CR), 2 Golf Course Drive, Mount Edgecombe, Durban 4320, Kwazulu-Natal (+27-31 502 3908) (fax 031 502 4160) (info@accord.org.za) (www.accord.org.za). *Conflict Trends.*
Anglican Pacifist Fellowship [APF] (RP), c/o Victor Spencer, PO Box 54, Ficksburg 9730 (+27-51-922700) (victor.spencer@cpsanet.org).
Centre for Environmental Rights [CER] (EL HR), Second Floor, Springtime Studios, 1 Scott Rd, Observatory 7925, Cape Town (+27-21 447 1647) (fax 86 730 9098) (info@cer.org.za) (cer.org.za).
Centre for the Study of Violence and Reconciliation (RE CR HR), PO Box 30778, Braamfontein, Johannesburg 2017 (+27-11 403 5650) (fax 11 339 6785) (info@csvr.org.za) (www.csvr.org.za). Also in Cape Town (+27-21 447 2470).

SOUTH AFRICA

GroundWork / Friends of the Earth South Africa (FE), PO Box 2375, Pietermaritzburg 3200 (+27-33 342 5662) (fax 33 342 5665) (team@groundwork.org.za) (www.groundwork.org.za).
International Centre of Nonviolence [ICON] (RE HR), ML Sultan Campus, Durban University of Technology, PO Box 1334, Durban 4000 (+27-31 373 5499) (icon@dut.ac.za) (www.icon.org.za.
Works for a culture of nonviolence.
United Nations Association of South Africa [UNA-SA] (UN), 23 Andries Pretorius St (corner of Victoria St), Somerset West 7130, Cape Town (+27-21 850 0509) (admin@unasa.org.za) (unasa.org.za).

SOUTH SUDAN

Organisation for Nonviolence and Development [ONAD] (WR CR HR), PO Box 508, Juba (+211-921-352592) (onadjuba2011@gmail.com) (www.onadev.org).

SPAIN

Alternativa Antimilitarista - Movimiento de Objeción de Conciencia [AA-MOC] (WR RA TR), C/San Cosme y San Damián 24-2º, 28012 Madrid (+34-91 475 3782) (moc.lavapies@nodo50.org) (www.antimilitaristas.org).
Amnistía Internacional España (AI), C/ Fernando VI - 8 - 1º Izda, 28004 Madrid (+34-91 310 1277) (fax 91 319 5334) (info@madrid.es.amnesty.org) (www.es.amnesty.org).
Antimilitaristes - MOC València (WR RA TR), C/ Roger de Flor 8 - baix-dta, 46001 València (+34-96 391 6702) (retirada@pangea.org) (mocvalencia.org).
Centre d'Estudis per la Pau JM Delàs (WR RE AT RP IB), Erasme de Janer 8 - Door 9, 08001 Barcelona, Catalunya (+34-93 441 1947) (info@centredelas.org) (www.centredelas.org).
Materiales de Trabajo.
Centro de Investigación para la Paz (RE), Duque de Sesto 40, 28009 Madrid (+34-91 576 3299) (fax 91 577 4726) (cip@fuhem.es) (www.cip-ecosocial.fuhem.es).
Papeles de Relaciones Ecosociales y Cambio Global.
Ekologistak Martxan Bizkaia (ND EL TW), c/ Pelota 5 - Behea, 48005 Bilbo, Euskadi (+34-94 479 0119) (fax) (bizkaia@ekologistakmartxan.org) (www.ekologistakmartxan.org). *Eco Boletin*.
Fundación Seminario de Investigación para la Paz [SIP] (RE), Centro Pignatelli, Pº de la Constitución 6, 50008 Zaragoza (+34-976 217215) (fax 976 230113) (sipp@seipaz.org) (www.seipaz.org).
Gernika Gogoratuz - Peace Research Centre [GGG] (IB RE), Artekale 1-1, 48300 Gernika-Lumo, Bizkaia (+34-94 625 3558) (fax 94 625 6765) (gernikag@gernikagogoratuz.org) (www.gernikagogoratuz.org).
Gesto por la Paz de Euskal Herria - Euskal Herriko Bakearen Aldeko (PA HR RE), Apdo 10152, 48080 Bilbao (+34-94 416 3929) (fax 94 415 3285) (gesto@gesto.org) (www.gesto.org).
Association for peace in the Basque Country.
Grup Antimilitarista Tortuga (PA), C/ Ametler 26 - 7ª, 03203 Elx, Alacant (tortuga@nodo50.org) (www.grupotortuga.com). Part of network Alternativa Antimilitarista - MOC.
International Institute for Nonviolent Action [NOVACT] (RE PA CD CR), Junta de Comerç 20, 08001 Barcelona (+34-93 551 4714) (communication@novact.org) (novact.org).
Justicia y Paz - España [CGJP] (RP), Rafael de Riego 16 - 3º dcha, 28045 Madrid (+34-91 506 1828) (juspax@juspax-es.org) (www.juspax-es.org).
Kontzientzi Eragozpen Mugimendua / MOC Euskal Herria [KEM-MOC] (WR AL TR RT), Calle Fika Nº 4 - lonja derecha, 48006 Bilbao, Euskadi (+34-94-415 3772) (mocbilbao@gmail.com) (www.sinkuartel.org). Part of network Alternativa Antimilitarista - MOC.
Liga Internacional de Mujeres por la Paz y la Libertad (WL), 26-28 bajo - Almería, Zaragoza (wilpf.espanya@gmail.com) (wilpf.es).
Paz y Cooperación / Peace and Co-operation (IB RE TW), Meléndez Valdés 68 - 4º izq, 28015 Madrid (+34-91 549 6156) (fax 91 543 5282) (pazycooperacion@hotmail.com) (www.peaceandcooperation.org).
Premio Escolar Paz y Cooperación.
Servas España (SE), Calle de la Roca 5, 08319 Dosrius (servas.spain@gmail.com) (www.servas.es).
Servei Civil Internacional - Catalunya [SCI] (SC PA), c/ Carme 95 - baixos 2a, 08001 Barcelona, Catalunya (+34-93 441 7079) (comunicacio@sci-cat.org) (www.sci-cat.org).
Servicio Civil Internacional [SCI] (SC), c/Ronda de Segovia 55 - oficina 2, 28005 Madrid (+34-91 366 3259) (fax 91 366 2203) (oficina@ongsci.org) (www.ongsci.org).
Survival International (España) [SI] (HR), C/Príncipe 12 - 3º, 28012 Madrid (+34-91 521 7283) (fax 91 523 1420) (info@survival.es) (www.survival.es).
Boletín de Acción Urgente.

SRI LANKA

Mahatma Gandhi Centre (PO PA RE), 22/17 Kalyani Rd, Colombo 00600 (+94-11-250 1825) (fax)

(power2people@gandhiswaraj.com) (gandhiswaraj.con).
National Peace Council of Sri Lanka [NPC] (CR RE CD), 12/14 Purana Vihara Rd, Colombo 6 (+94-11-281 8344) (fax 281 9064) (npc@sltnet.lk) (www.peace-srilanka.org). *Paths to Peace.*
Nonviolent Direct Action Group [NVDAG] (FR WR IB), PO Box 2, 29 Kandy Rd, Kaithady-Nunavil, Chavakachcheri (del-smskr@eureka.lk). *NVDAG Report.*
SCI Sri Lanka (SC), 18/A/4 Deveni Rajasinghe, Mawatha, Kandy (+94-81-238 7188) (fax) (scisl@sltnet.lk).

SUDAN
Peace Desk of New Sudan Council of Churches (RP CD CR HR), see under Kenya.

SWEDEN
Greenpeace (GP), Rosenlundsgatan 29 B, 11863 Stockholm (+46-8-702 7070) (info.se@greenpeace.org) (www.greenpeace.se).
Internationella Kvinnoförbundet för Fred och Frihet [IKFF] (WL), Norrtullsgatan 45 - 1 tr, 11345 Stockholm (+46-8-702 9810) (info@ikff.se) (www.ikff.se).
Jordens Vänner / Friends of the Earth Sweden (FE TW), Box 7048, 40231 Göteborg (+46-31-121808) (fax 121817) (info@jordensvanner.se) (www.jordensvanner.se).
Kristna Fredsrörelsen (FR), Ekumeniska Centret, Box 14038, 16714 Bromma (+46-8-453 6840) (fax 453 6829) (info@krf.se) (krf.se). *Fredsnytt.*
Life & Peace Institute [LPI] (RP AT RE TW CR), Kungsängsgatan 17 - 1st floor, 75322 Uppsala (+46-18-660130) (info@life-peace.org) (life-peace.org).
Nobel Peace Prize Watch (DA RE), c/o Magnusson, Marklandsgatan 63, 41477 Göteborg (gosta.tomas@gmail.com) (www.nobelwill.org). Promotes original purpose of Nobel Prize.
Nordic Nonviolence Study Group [NORNONS] (RE PA), Sparsnäs 1010, 66881 Ed (johansen.jorgen@gmail.com) (www.nornons.org).
Ofog (WR RA AT ND AL), c/o Göteborgs Fredskommitté, Linnégatan 21, 41304 Göteborg (+46-733-815361) (info@ofog.org) (www.ofog.org).
PBI-Sverige (HR CR), Blixtåsvägen 6, 42437 Angered (+46-31-330 7509) (info@pbi-sweden.org) (www.pbi-sweden.org).
Servas Sverige (SE), c/o Eva Hartman-Juhlin, Svankärrsvägen 3B, 75653 Upsalla (sweden@servas.se) (www.servas.se).
Stockholm Centre for the Ethics of War and Peace [SCEWP] (RE), Universitetsvägen 10, 11418 Stockholm (stockholmcentre.se).
Svenska FN-Förbundet (UN), Box 15115, 10465 Stockholm (+46-8-462 2540) (fax 641 8876) (info@fn.se) (www.fn.se). *Världshorisont.*
Svenska Fredskommittén / Swedish Peace Committee [SFK] (DA ND), Tegelviksgatan 40, 11641 Stockholm (info@svenskafredskommitten.nu) (www.svenskafredskommitten.nu).
Sveriges Fredsråd / Swedish Peace Council (IB), Tegelviksgatan 40, 11641 Stockholm (info@FredNu.se) (frednu.se). National federation.
Swedish Peace and Arbitration Society / Svenska Freds- och Skiljedomsföreningen [SPAS] (WR IB AT), Polhemsgatan 4, 11236 Stockholm (+46-8-5580 3180) (info@svenskafreds.se) (www.svenskafreds.se).
Uppsala Universitet Institutionen för freds- och konfliktforskning / Dept of Peace and Conflict Research (RE AT), Box 514, 75120 Uppsala (+46-18-471 0000) (info@pcr.uu.se) (www.pcr.uu.se).
Vännernas Samfund (Kväkarna) (SF), Box 9166, 10272 Stockholm (+46-8-668 6816) (fax) (info@kvakare.se).

SWITZERLAND
Action des Chrétiens pour l'Abolition de la Torture / Aktion der Christen für die Abschaffung der Folter [ACAT-Suisse] (HR), Speichergasse 29, 3001 Berne (+41-31 312 2044) (info@acat.ch) (www.acat.ch). *acatnews.*
Amnesty International (AI), Speichergasse 33, 3011 Bern (+41-31 307 2222) (fax 31 307 2233) (info@amnesty.ch) (www.amnesty.ch). *Amnesty Magazin(e).*
APRED - Participative Institute for the Progress of Peace (RE CD HR), Route des Siernes Picaz 46, 1659 Flendruz (+41-79 524 3574) (info@demilitarisation.org) (www.apred.ch).
Ärzte/Ärztinnen für Soziale Verantwortung / Médecins pour une Responsibilité Sociale [PSR/IPPNW] (IP), Bireggstr 36, 6003 Luzern (+41-41 240 6349) (fax) (sekretariat@ippnw.ch) (www.ippnw.ch).
Association for Inclusive Peace (RE CR), 14b Av Giuseppe Motta, 1202 Genève (info@inclusivepeace.org) (www.inclusivepeace.org). Making peace processes more sustainable.
Basel Peace Office (RE ND), Universität Basel, Petersgraben 27, 4051 Basel (info@baselpeaceoffice.org) (www.baselpeaceoffice.org).
Centre pour l'Action Non-Violente [CENAC] (WR RP IB), 52 rue de Genève, 1004 Lausanne (+41-21 661 2434) (fax 21 661 2436) (info@non-violence.ch) (www.non-violence.ch).

SWITZERLAND

cfd - the feminist peace organisation (PA CR HR), Postfach, 3001 Berne (+41-31 300 5060) (info@cfd-ch.org) (www.cfd-ch.org). *cfd-Zeitung.*

ContrAtom - Association Antinucléaire Genevoise (EL), CP 65, 1211 Genève 8 (+41-22 321 5709) (info@contratom.ch) (www.contratom.ch). *ContAtom.*

Eirene Suisse (RP TW EL CR), 9 Rue du Valais, 1202 Genève (+41-22 321 8556) (fax) (info@eirenesuisse.ch) (eirenesuisse.ch).

Frauen für den Frieden / Donne per la Pace / Femmes pour la Paix (IB), Oberwilerstr 50, 4054 Basel (+41-44 945 0725) (sekretariat@frauenfuerdenfrieden.ch) (www.frauenfuerdenfrieden.ch). Women for Peace.

Gender and Mine Action Programme (AT CR RE HR), c/o Geneva International Centre for Humanitarian Demining, PO Box 1300, 1211 Genève 1 (+41-22 730 9335) (fax 22 730 9362) (info@gmap.ch) (www.gmap.ch).

Grüne Partei der Schweiz / Parti écologiste suisse / Partito ecologista svizzero (EL IB), Waisenhausplatz 21, 3011 Bern (+41-31 326 6660) (fax 31 326 6662) (gruene@gruene.ch) (www.gruene.ch). *Greenfo.* Green party. Grüne / Les Verts / I Verdi.

Greenpeace (GP), Badenerstr 171, Postfach 9320, 8036 Zürich (+41-44 447 4141) (fax 44 447 4199) (gp@greenpeace.ch) (www.greenpeace.ch/switzerland).

Gruppe für eine Schweiz ohne Armee / Groupe pour une Suisse sans Armée [GSoA/GSsA] (WR), Maison des Associations, Rue de Savoises 15, CP 151, 1211 Genève 8 (+41-44 273 0100) (gsoa@gsoa.ch) (www.gsoa.ch). In Zurich, +41-44 273 0100.

Institute for Peace and Dialogue / Institut für Frieden und Dialog [IPD] (CR CD RE), Ryffstr 23, 4056 Basel (+41-76 431 6170) (fhuseynli@ipdinstitute.ch) (www.ipdinstitute.ch).

Neuer Israel Fonds Schweiz - NIF Switzerland (HR), Winkelriedplatz 4, 4053 Basel (+41-61 272 1455) (fax 61 361 2972) (info@nif.ch) (www.nif.ch).

Peace Brigades International - Schweiz/Suisse [PBI] (CD HR CR RE), Gutenbergstr 35, 3011 Bern (+41-31 372 4444) (info@peacebrigades.ch) (www.peacebrigades.ch).

Pro Natura (FE), Postfach, 4018 Basel (+41-61-317 9191) (fax 317 9266) (mailbox@pronatura.ch) (www.pronatura.ch).

Schweizerische Friedensbewegung / Moviment Svizzer da Pasch / Swiss Peace Movement (WP), Postfach 2113, 4001 Basel (+41-61 681 0363) (mail@friedensbewegung.ch) (www.friedensbewegung.ch).

Schweizerische Friedensstiftung [swisspeace] (RE CR), Sonnenbergstr 17, PO Box, 3001 Bern (+41-31 330 1212) (info@swisspeace.ch) (www.swisspeace.ch).

Schweizerischer Friedensrat / Consiglio Svizzera per pa Pace / Conseil Suisse pour la Paix [SFR] (IB AT EL), Gartenhofstr 7, 8304 Zürich (+41-44 242 9321) (info@friedensrat.ch) (www.friedensrat.ch). Swiss Peace Council.

Service Civil International - Schweizer Zweig / Branche suisse / Sede svizzera [SCI] (SC), Monbijoustr 32, Postfach 2944, 3001 Bern (+41-31 381 4620) (info@scich.org) (www.scich.org). *Service Civil International.*

Société Religieuse des Amis, Assemblée de Suisse (Quaker) [SYM] (SF), c/o Maison Quaker, 13 Av du Mervelet, 1209 Genève (+41-22 748 4800) (fax 22 748 4819) (symclerk@swiss-quakers.ch) (www.swiss-quakers.ch). *Entre Amis.*

Société Suisse - Nations Unies / Schweizerisches Versicherungsverband (UN), Postfach 762, 6431 Schwyz (info@schweiz-uno.ch) (www.schweiz-uno.ch).

Weltföderalisten Schweiz / Fédéralistes mondiaux Suisse (WF), c/o Hexagon AG, Graben 5, 6300 Zug (info@weltfoederalisten.ch) (www.weltfoederalisten.ch). Member of World Federalist Movement (WFM).

Women's International League for Peace and Freedom (WL), Horensteinstr 31, 8046 Zürich (info@wilpfschweiz.ch) (www.wilpfschweiz.ch).

SYRIA

Syrian Human Rights Committee [SHRC] (HR), see under Britain. Syrian human rights group in exile in Britain.

TAIWAN

Chinese Association for Human Rights [CAHR] (HR), 4F-3 - No 23 - Sec 1 - Hangchow S Rd, Taipei 10053 (+886-2-3393 6900) (fax 2395 7399) (humanright@cahr.org.tw) (www.cahr.org.tw).

Greenpeace East Asia - Taipei Office (GP), No 10, Lane 83, Section 1, Roosevelt Rd, Zhongzheng District, Taipei City 10093 (+886-2-2321 5006) (fax 2321 3209) (inquiry.tw@greenpeace.org) (www.greenpeace.org/eastasia).

John Paul II Peace Institute / Fujen Peace Centre (RP), Fujen Catholic University, 24205 Hsinchuang, Taipei County (+886-2-2905 3111) (fax 2905 2170) (peace@mail.fju.edu.tw) (peace.fjac.fju.edu.tw). *Peace Papers.*

TANZANIA
United Nations Association of Tanzania (UN), PO Box 9182, Dar es Salaam (+255-22-219 9200) (fax 266 8749) (info@una.or.tz) (una.or.tz).

THAILAND
Asian Institute for Human Rights [AIHR] (HR), 109 Soi Sithicon, Suthisarnwinichai Road, Samsennok, Huaykwang, Bangkok 10310 (+66-2 277 6882) (fax) (kalpalatad@aihr.info) (aihr.info).

TIBET
Tibetan Centre for Human Rights and Democracy (FR HR), see under India. Works for human rights of Tibetans in Tibet.

TOGO
Amis de la Terre - Togo [ADT] (FE), BP 20190, Lomé (+228-2222 1731) (fax 2222 1732) (adt-togo@amiterre.tg) (www.amiterre.tg).

TRINIDAD AND TOBAGO
United Nations Association of Trinidad & Tobago [UNATT] (UN), 106 Woodford Street, Newtown, Port of Spain (+1 868-221 7645) (info@unassociationtt.org) (unassociationtt.org).

TUNISIA
Coalition Nationale Tunisienne contre la Peine de Mort (HR), 56 Avenue de la Liberté, 1002 Tunis (+216-2168 7533) (abolitionpm@gmail.com).
National Coalition Against the Death Penalty.

TURKEY
İnsan Hakları Derneği / Human Rights Association [iHD] (HR), Necatibey Cad 82/11-12, Kızılay, Çankaya, 06430 Ankara (+90-312-230 3567) (fax 230 1707) (posta@ihd.org.tr) (www.ihd.org.tr).
Siddetsizlik Eğitim ve Arastirma Denerği / Nonviolent Education and Research Association (RE WR), Kuloğlu Mah Güllabici sok no 16 - Daire 2, 34433 Cihangir, İstanbul (+90-212-244 1269) (merhaba@siddetsizlikmerkezi.org) (www.siddetsizlikmerkezi.org).
Türkiye İnsan Hakları Vakfı / Human Rights Foundation of Turkey [TIHV/HRFT] (HR), Mithatpasa Cad - No 49/11 - 6 Kat, 06420 Kızılay / Ankara (+90-312-310 6636) (fax 310 6463) (tihv@tihv.org.tr) (www.tihv.org.tr).
In Istanbul: +90-212-249 3092.
Türkiye Çevre Vafki / Environment Foundation of Turkey [TÇV] (EL), Tunalı Hilmi Cd 50/20, Kavaklidere, 06660 Ankara (+90-312-425 5508) (fax 418 5118) (cevre@cevre.org.tr) (www.cevre.org.tr).
Çevre.
Vicdani Ret Derneği / Conscientious Objection Association [VR-DER] (WR HR), Bahariye Cad - No 92/4, Kadıköy, İstanbul (+90-216-345 0100) (dernek@vicdaniret.org) (vicdaniret.org).
For legalising conscientious objection.

UGANDA
International Friendship League - Uganda [IFL] (CD), c/o Ismael Nyonyintono, PO Box 37692, Kampala (ismaeluk@yahoo.com).
Jamii Ya Kupatanisha [JYAK] (FR WR CR), PO Box 198, Kampala (+256-41-427 1435) (fax 434 7389) (jyak.peace@gmail.com).
Women's International League for Peace and Freedom [WILPF Uganda] (WL), PO Box 3556, Kampala (+256-77-240 5295) (wilpf.org/uganda).

UKRAINE
Ukrainskiy Ruch Patsifistiv / Ukrainian Pacifist Movement (WR), Tverskyi Tupik Street 9 - apt 82, Kiyiv 01042 (+380-97-317 9326) (fax 44-529 0435) (yuriy.sheliazhenko@gmail.com).
Zeleniy Svit - Druzi Zemli (FE PA), A/C 61, 49000 Dnipropetrovsk (+380-56-370 9572) (fax 370 9573) (foeukraine@gmail.com) (www.zsfoe.org).
Green World - Friends of the Earth.

UNITED STATES OF AMERICA
350.org (EL), 20 Jay St - Suite 732, Brooklyn, NY 11201 (+1-646-801 0759) (feedback@350.org) (350.org).
Campaign on climate change.
A Rocha USA (EL), PO Box 1338, Fredricksburg, TX 78624 (+1-830-522 5319) (usa@arocha.org) (arocha.us). Christian.
About Face: Veterans Against the War [IVAW] (PA RA), PO Box 3565, New York City, NY 10008 (+1-929-430 4988) (aboutfaceveterans.org).
Formerly Iraq Veterans Against the War.
Action Reconciliation Service for Peace - US [ARSP] (CD RE), 1501 Cherry St, Philadelphia, PA 19102 (+1-215-241 7249) (info@actionreconciliation.org) (actionreconciliation.org).
AJ Muste Memorial Institute (IB RE WR), 168 Canal St - 6th Flr, New York, NY 10013 (+1-212-533 4335) (info@ajmuste.org) (www.ajmuste.org).
Muste Notes.
Al-Awda - The Palestine Right to Return Coalition (HR), PO Box 8812, Coral Springs, FL 33075 (+1-760-918 9441) (fax 918 9442) (info@al-awda.org) (al-awda.org).
Alaska Peace Center, 3535 College Rd - Suite 203, Fairbanks, AK 99709-3722 (+1-907-374 0577) (info@alaskapeace.org) (www.alaskapeace.org).

For explanation of codes and abbreviations, see introduction

USA

Alliance for Middle East Peace [ALLMEP] (CD), 1725 I St NW - Suite 300, Washington, DC 20006 (+1-202-618 4600) (info@allmep.org) (www.allmep.org). Promoting people-to-people coexistence.

Alliance for Nuclear Accountability [ANA] (ND DA EL), 322 4th St NE, Washington, DC 20002 (+1-202-544 0217) (sgordon@ananuclear.org) (www.ananuclear.org).

Alliance for Peacebuilding (CR RE), 1800 Massachusetts Ave NW - Suite 401, Washington, DC 20036 (+1-202-822 2047) (fax 822 2049) (afp-info@allianceforpeacebuilding.org) (www.allianceforpeacebuilding.org). Coalition of organisations and individuals.

Alternatives to Violence Project - USA [AVP/USA] (CR PO), 1050 Selby Ave, St Paul, MN 55104 (+1-888-278 7820) (info@avpusa.org) (avpusa.org).

American Civil Liberties Union [ACLU] (HR), 125 Broad St - 18th Floor, New York, NY 10004 (aclu@aclu.org) (www.aclu.org).

American Friends of Neve Shalom / Wahat al-Salam (CD HR PA RE), 229 N Central Ave - Suite 401, Glendale, CA 91203-3541 (+1-818-662 8883) (afnswas@oasisofpeace.org) (www.oasisofpeace.org). Support mixed (Jewish-Palestinian) Israeli village.

American Friends Service Committee [AFSC] (SF RE CR), 1501 Cherry St, Philadelphia, PA 19102 (+1-215-241 7000) (fax 241 7275) (afscinfo@afsc.org) (www.afsc.org). *Quaker Action.*

American Jews for a Just Peace [AJJP] (RA), PO Box 1032, Arlington, MA 02474 (www.ajjp.org).

Amnesty International USA [AIUSA] (AI), 311 W 43rd St - 7th floor, New York, NY 10036 (+1-212-807 8400) (fax 627 1451) (gr@aiusa.org) (www.amnestyusa.org). Also in Washington DC (+1-202-544 0200).

Anglican Pacifist Fellowship - US [APF] (RP), c/o Nathaniel W Pierce, 3864 Rumsey Dr, Trappe, MD 21673-1722 (+1-410-476 4556) (nwpierce@verizon.net).

Arkansas Coalition for Peace and Justice (DA HR), PO Box 250398, Little Rock, AR 72225 (+1-501-666 3784) (acpj@arpeaceandjustice.org) (arpeaceandjustice.org).

Arms Control Association [ACA] (AT ND RE), 1200 18th St - Ste 1175, Washington, DC 20036 (+1-202-463 8270) (fax 463 8273) (aca@armscontrol.org) (www.armscontrol.org).

Asian Pacific Environmental Network [APEN] (EL), 426 17th St - Suite 500, Oakland, CA 94612 (+1-510-834 8920) (fax 834 8926) (apen@apen4ej.org) (apen4ej.org).

Association of Christians for the Abolition of Torture [ACAT] (HR), PO Box 314, Pleasant Hill, TN 38578-0314 (revhdsmith@starpower.net).

Baptist Peace Fellowship of North America - Bautistas por la Paz [BPFNA] (RP), 300 Hawthorne Lane - Ste 205, Charlotte, NC 28204 (+1-704-521 6051) (fax 521 6053) (bpfna@bpfna.org) (www.bpfna.org). *Baptist Peacemaker.*

Beyond Conflict (RE CR), 198 Tremont St - Suite 453, Boston, MA 02116 (+1-617-945 7187) (info@beyondconflict.org) (beyondconflict.org). Uses lessons of cognitive and behavioural science.

Beyond Nuclear (EL ND), 7304 Carroll Ave - Suite 182, Takoma Park, MD 20912 (+1-301-270 2209) (info@beyondnuclear.org) (www.beyondnuclear.org).

Brady Campaign to Prevent Gun Violence (RE HR DA PO), 840 First St NE - Suite 400, Washington, DC 20002 (+1-202-370 8100) (policy@bradymail.org) (www.bradycampaign.org).

Bruderhof Communities (RP), 101 Woodcrest Dr, Rifton, NY 12471 (+1-845-658 7700) (info@bruderhof.com) (www.bruderhof.com). Also known as Church Communities International.

Buddhist Peace Fellowship [BPF] (FR IB), PO Box 3470, Berkeley, CA 94703 (+1-510-239 3764) (info@bpf.org) (www.buddhistpeacefellowship.org).

Campaign for Peace, Disarmament & Common Security (DA ND), 2161 Massachusetts Ave, Cambridge, MA 02140 (+1-617-661 6130) (JGerson@gmail.com) (www.cpdcs.org). For nuclear weapons abolition and common security.

Campaign for Uyghurs (HR), 1101 Pennsylvania Ave NW - Suite 300, Washington, DC 20004 (+1-240-660 8877) (contact@campaignforuyghurs.org) (campaignforuyghurs.org).

Campaign to Establish a US Department of Peace (RE PO CR RE), c/o The Peace Alliance, 2108 Military Rd, Arlington, VA 22207 (1-202-684 2553) (www.thepeacealliance.org).

Catholic Mobilizing Network to End the Use of the Death Penalty [CMN] (RP), 415 Michigan Ave NE - Suite 210, Washington, DC 20017 (+1-202-541 5290) (info@catholicsmobilizing.org) (catholicsmobilizing.org). Formerly Catholics Against Capital Punishment.

Catholic Peace Fellowship (RP PA), PO Box 4232, South Bend, IN 46634 (+1-574-232 2811) (staff@catholicpeacefellowship.org) (www.catholicpeacefellowship.org). Promotes conscientious objection.

Center for Applied Conflict Management [CACM] (RE CR), Kent State University, PO Box 5190, Kent, OH 44242-0001 (+1-330-672 3143) (fax 672 3362) (cacm@kent.edu) (www.kent.edu/cacm).

Center for Artistic Activism [C4AA] (PO), PO Box 543, Beacon, NY 12508 (+1-646-832 2454) (c4aa.org).

Center for Citizen Initiatives [CCI] (CD), 820 N Delaware St - Ste 405, San Mateo, CA 94401 (+1-650-458 8115) (info@ccisf.org) (ccisf.org). Organise US-Russia citizen exchanges.

Center for Energy Research (EL CR ND), 104 Commercial St NE, Salem, OR 97301 (pbergel@igc.org). Dedicated to breaking the nuclear chain.

Center for Jewish Nonviolence [CJNV] (PA RA HR), c/o T'ruah - The Rabbinic Call for Human Rights, 266 West 37th St - Suite 803, New York, NY 10018 (CJNV.campaigns@gmail.com) (centerforjewishnonviolence.org). Organises visits to Israel for nonviolent action.

Center for Nonviolence and Peace Studies [CNPS] (RE CR PO), University of Rhode Island, 74 Lower College Rd - MCC 202, Kingston, RI 02881 (+1-401-874 2875) (fax 874 9108) (nonviolence@etal.uri.edu) (www.uri.edu/nonviolence). *Become the Change.*

Center for Religious Tolerance [CRT] (RP CR), 520 Ralph St, Sarasota, FL 34242 (+1-941-312 9795) (info@c-r-t.org) (www.c-r-t.org). Supports international interfaith initiatives.

Center for the Study and Promotion of Zones of Peace (RE), 139 Kuulei Rd, Kailua, HI 96734 (+1-808-263 4015) (fax) (loprey.zop-hi@worldnet.att.net).

Center for Victims of Torture (HR RE), 2356 University Ave W - Suite 430, Saint Paul, MN 55114 (+1-612-436 4800) (cvt@cvt.org) (www.cvt.org).

Center on Conscience & War [CCW] (PA HR), 1830 Connecticut Ave NW, Washington, DC 20009-5706 (+1-202-483 2220) (fax 483 1246) (ccw@CenterOnConscience.org) (www.centeronconscience.org). *The Reporter for Conscience' sake.*

Charter for Compassion (RP), PO Box 10787, Bainbridge Island, WA 98110 (partner@charterforcompassion.org) (charterforcompassion.org).

Christian Peacemaker Teams [CPT] (RP RA PA), PO Box 6508, Chicago, IL 60680-6508 (+1-773-376 0550) (fax 376 0549) (peacemakers@cpt.org) (www.cpt.org).

Citizens for Global Solutions (WF), 5 Thomas Circle NW, Washington, DC 20005 (+1-202-546 3950) (info@globalsolutions.org) (globalsolutions.org). Affiliated to World Federalist Movement.

Citizens for Peaceful Resolutions [CPR] (ND PA PO), PO Box 364, Ventura, CA 93002-0364 (www.c-p-r.net). Committed to interconnectedess of all life.

Co-operation Ireland (USA) (CD), 1501 Broadway - Suite 2600 (Attn Richard Pino), NY 10036 (www.cooperationireland.org).

Coalition to Stop Gun Violence (DA AT), 1424 L Street NW - Suite 2-1, Washington, DC 20005 (+1-202-408 0061) (csgv@csgv.org) (www.csgv.org).

CODEPINK: Women for Peace (PA), 2010 Linden Ave, Venice, CA 90291 (+1-310-827 4320) (fax 827 4547) (info@codepink.org) (www.codepink.org). A women-initiated grassroots peace campaign.

Colgate University Peace & Conflict Studies Program (RE CR), 13 Oak Dr, Hamilton, NY 13346-1398 (+1-315-228 7806) (fax 228 7121) (peace@colgate.edu) (www.colgate.edu/departments/peacestudies/).

Colombia Support Network (TW HR CD), PO Box 1505, Madison, WI 53701-1505 (+1-608-709 9817) (csn@igc.org) (www.colombiasupport.net). *Action on Columbia.*

Committee Opposed to Militarism & the Draft [COMD] (PA), PO Box 15195, San Diego, CA 92175 (+1-760-753 7518) (admin@comdsd.org) (www.comdsd.org).

Common Defense Campaign [CDC] (RE), c/o William Goodfellow, Centre for International Policy, 2000 M St NW - Suite 720, Washington, DC 20036-3327 (+1-202-232 3317) (wcg@ciponline.org) (www.ciponline.org). Previously the Project on Defense Alternatives.

Conflict Information Consortium (RE CR), UCB 580, University of Colorado, Boulder, CO 80309 (beyondintractability.org). Previously Conflict Research Consortium.

Council for Responsible Genetics [CRG] (EL HR), 5 Upland Rd - Suite 3, Cambridge, MA 02140 (+1-617-868 0870) (fax 491 5344) (crg@gene-watch.org) (www.councilforresponsiblegenetics.org). *GeneWatch.*

Courage to Resist (WR HR), 484 Lake Park Ave - No 41, Oakland, CA 94610 (+1-510-488 3559) (www.couragetoresist.org). Supports public military refusers facing court.

Creative Response to Conflict [CRC] (FR CR PO), Box 271, Nyack, NY 10960-0271 (+1-845-353 1796) (fax 358 4924) (inquiries@crc-global.org) (crc-global.org).

USA

Creativity for Peace (CD), 369 Montezuma Ave - No 566, Santa Fe, NM 87501 (+1-505-982 3765) (dottie@creativityforpeace.com) (www.creativityforpeace.com).

Cultural Survival [CS] (HR), 2067 Massachusetts Ave, Cambridge, MA 02140 (+1-617-441 5400) (fax 441 5417) (culturalsurvival@cs.org) (www.cs.org).

Culture Change (EL AL PO), PO Box 3387, Santa Cruz, CA 95063 (+1-215-243 3144) (fax) (info@culturechange.org) (www.culturechange.org). 4 yrly. Supports immediate cut in petrol consumption.

Culture of Peace Corporation / Culture of Peace News Network (RE), 95 Lyon St, New Haven, CT 06511 (coordinator@cpnn-world.org) (cpnn-world.org).

Cure Violence (PO CR), 227 West Monroe St - Suite 1025, Chicago, IL 60606 (+1-312-756 8632) (cvg.org). Treating violence as a health issue.

Death Penalty Information Center (HR RE), 1015 18th St NW - Suite 704, Washington, DC 20036 (+1-202-289 2275) (dpic@deathpenaltyinfo.org) (www.deathpenaltyinfo.org).

Democratic World Federalists (WF), 55 New Montgomery St - Suite 55, San Francisco, CA 94105 (+1-415-227 4880) (dwfed@dwfed.org) (www.dwfed.org).

Earth First! Journal (EL RA), PO Box 1112, Grants Pass, OR 97528 (+1-541-244 1533) (collective@earthfirstjournal.org) (www.earthfirstjournal.org). 4 yrly.

Earthworks (EL HR), 1612 K St NW - Suite 904, Washington, DC 20006 (+1-202-887 1872) (fax 887 1875) (info@earthworksaction.org) (www.earthworksaction.org). Protecting communities from mining etc.

East Timor and Indonesia Action Network [ETAN] (HR TW), PO Box 1663, New York, NY 10035-1663 (+1-917-690 4391) (etan@etan.org) (www.etan.org).

Ecumenical Accompaniment Programme in Palestine and Israel - USA [EAPPI-USA] (RP HR), c/o Steve Weaver, Church World Service, 475 Riverside Dr - Suite 700, New York, NY 10115 (info@eappi-us.org) (www.eappi-us.org).

Ecumenical Peace Institute / Clergy and Laity Concerned [EPI/CALC] (RP HR TW), PO Box 9334, Berkeley, CA 94709 (+1-510-990 0374) (epicalc@gmail.com) (www.epicalc.org).

Education for Peace in Iraq Center [EPIC] (CD HR RE), 1140 3rd St NE - Space 2138, Washington, DC 20002 (+1-202-747 6454) (info@epic-usa.org) (www.epic-usa.org). Founded by war veterans.

Educators for Peaceful Classrooms and Communities [EPCC] (RE), 520 Calabasas Rd, Watsonville, CA 95076 (www.educatorsforpeacefulclassroomsandcommunities.org).

Environmentalists Against War (EL DA ND PA AT), PO Box 27, Berkeley, CA 94701 (+1-510-843 3343) (info@envirosagainstwar.org) (www.envirosagainstwar.org).

Episcopal Peace Fellowship [EPF] (FR CD), PO Box 15, Claysburg, PA 16625 (+1-312-922 8628) (epf@epfnational.org) (epfnational.org).

Equal Justice USA (HR), 81 Prospect St, Brooklyn, NYC, NY 11201 (+1-718-801 8940) (fax 801 8947) (info@ejusa.org) (ejusa.org). Against executions.

Esperanto-USA [E-USA] (HR), 91-J Auburn St - 1248, Portland, ME 04103 (+1-510-653 0998) (fax 866-200 1108) (eusa@esperanto-usa.org) (www.esperanto-usa.org). *Usona Esperantisto*.

Everytown for Gun Safety (DA), PO Box 4184, New York, NY 10163 (+1-646-324 8250) (info@everytown.org) (everytown.org). Working to end gun violence.

Farms Not Arms - Peace Roots Alliance [PRA] (DA EL), 425 Farm Rd - Suite 5, Summertown, TN 38483 (+1-931-964 2119) (fna_info@farmsnotarms.org) (www.farmsnotarms.org). Also West Coast office (+1-415-218 9021).

Fellowship for Intentional Community [FIC] (PO CR AL), 23 Dancing Rabbit Lane, Rutledge, MO 63563 (+1-660-883 5545) (fic@ic.org) (www.ic.org). *Communities*.

Fellowship of Reconciliation [FOR] (FR WR), 521 N Broaday, Nyack, NY 10960-0271 (+1-845-358 4601) (fax 358 4924) (communications@forusa.org) (www.forusa.org). *Fellowship*.

Food Not Bombs [FnB-US] (PA PO RA), PO Box 424, Arroyo Seco, NM 87514 (+1-575-770 3377) (menu@foodnotbombs.net) (www.foodnotbombs.net).

Foundation for Middle East Peace [FMEP], 1319 18th St NW, Washington, DC 20036 (+1-202-835 3650) (fax 835 3651) (info@fmep.org) (fmep.org).

Franciscan Action Network (RP EL HR, PO Box 29106, Washington, DC 20017 (+1-202-527 7575) (fax 527 7576) (info@franciscanaction.org) (franciscanaction.org).

Free Palestine Movement (HR), 405 Vista Heights Rd, El Cerrito, CA 94530 (+1-510-232 2500) (info@freepalestinemovement.org) (www.freepalestinemovement.org). Formerly Free Gaza Movement.

Fresno Center for Nonviolence (PA PO), 1584 N Van Ness Ave, Fresno, CA 93728 (+1-559-237 3223) (info@centerfornonviolence.org) (centerfornonviolence.org).

Friends for a Nonviolent World (PA PO CR), 1050 Selby Ave, Saint Paul, MN 55104 (+1-651-917 0383) (info@fnvw.org) (www.fnvw.org).

Friends of Peace Pilgrim (PO CR), PO Box 2207, Shelton, CT 06484-1841 (+1-203-926 1581) (friends@peacepilgrim.org) (www.peacepilgrim.org).

Friends of the Earth (FE), 1100 15th St NW - 11th Floor, Washington, DC 20005 (+1-202-783 7400) (fax 783 0444) (foe@foe.org) (www.foe.org).

Friends Peace Teams [FPT] (SF CR), 1001 Park Ave, St Louis, MO 63104 (+1-314-588 1122) (Office@FriendsPeaceTeams.org) (friendspeaceteams.org). *PeaceWays*.

Friendship Force (CD PO), 279 W Crogan St, Lawrenceville, GA 30046 (+1-404-522 9490) (www.friendshipforce.org). Promotes understanding through personal friendship.

Genocide Watch (HR RE), 1405 Cola Drive, McLean, VA 22101 (+1-202-643 1405) (communications@genocidewatch.org) (www.genocidewatch.org).

Global Family (CD WF RP), 17738 Minnow Way, Penn Valley, CA 95946 (www.globalfamily.org).

Global Meditations Network (CR PO), c/o Barbara Wolf, 218 Dartmouth St, Rochester, NY 14607 (bjwolf@globalmeditations.com) (www.globalmeditations.com).

Global Security Institute [GSI] (ND RE WF), 220 East 49th St - Suite 1B, New York, NY 10017 (+1-646-289 5170) (fax 289 5171) (info@gsinstitute.org) (gsinstitute.org).

Global Witness (EL HR TW CR), 1100 17th St NW - Suite 501, Washington, DC 20036 (+1-202-827 8673) (www.globalwitness.org). Also in Britain.

GMO Free USA (EL), PO Box 458, Unionville, CT 06085 (info@gmofreeusa.org) (www.gmofreeusa.org).

Green Party of the United States (EL HR CD), PO Box 75075, Washington, DC 20013 (+1-202-319 7191) (info@gp.org) (www.gp.org).

Greenpeace USA (GP), 702 H St NW - Suite 300, Washington, DC 20001 (+1-202-462 1177) (fax 462 4507) (info@wdc.greenpeace.org) (www.greenpeace.org/usa). *Greenpeace*.

Ground Zero Center for Nonviolent Action (ND PA RA), 16159 Clear Creek Rd NW, Poulsbo, WA 98370 (+1-360-930 8697) (info@gzcenter.org) (gzcenter.org). *Ground Zero*.

Guatemala Human Rights Commission USA [GHRC] (HR), 3321 12th St NE, Washington, DC 20017 (+1-202-529 6599) (fax 526 4611) (ghrc-usa@ghrc-usa.org) (www.ghrc-usa.org). *El Quetzal*.

Hand in Hand (PO CD RE), PO Box 80102, Portland, OR 97280 (+1-503-892 2962) (info@handinhandk12.org) (www.handinhandk12.org). Supports integrated education in Israel.

Harmony for Peace Foundation (PO CD ND), PO Box 2165, Southeastern, PA 19399 (+1-484-885 8539) (info@harmonyforpeace.org) (harmonyforpeace.org). Music for peace. Works with group in Japan.

Historians for Peace and Democracy [H-PAD] (DA HR CR), c/o Van Gosse, Department of History, PO Box 3003, Franklin & Marshall College, Lancaster, PA 17604-3003 (www.historiansforpeace.org). Formerly Historians Against the War.

ICAHD-USA (HR), PO Box 81252, Pittsburgh, PA 15217 (info@icahdusa.org) (www.icahdusa.org).

Ideas Across Borders (CD HR), 244 Fifth Avenue - Suite 2594, New York, NY 10001 (+1-646-844 4076) (info@ideasbeyondborders.org) (www.ideasbeyondborders.org). Share and promote critical thinking.

Institute for Food and Development Policy / Food First (RE TW EL), 398 60th St, Oakland, CA 94618 (+1-510-654 4400) (fax 654 4551) (info@foodfirst.org) (www.foodfirst.org).

Institute for Inclusive Security (RE CR), 1615 M St NW - Suite 850, Washington, DC 20036 (+1-202-403 2000) (fax 808 7070) (info@inclusivesecurity.org) (www.inclusivesecurity.org). Promotes women's contributions to peacebuilding.

Institute for Mediation and Conflict Resolution [IMCR] (CR RE), 369 E 148th St - Lower Level, Bronx, NY 10455 (+1-718-585 1190) (TRich@imcr.org) (www.imcr.org).

Institute for Middle East Understanding [IMEU] (RE CD), 2913 El Camino Real - No 436, Tustin, CA 92782 (+1-718-514 9662) (info@imeu.org) (imeu.org). Provides research and experts about Palestine.

Institute for Nonviolence Chicago (RE), 819 N Leamington St, Chicago, IL 60651 (+1-773-417 7421) (www.nonviolencechicago.org).

Institute for Social Ecology (EL AL PO), PO Box 48, Plainfield, VT 05667 (info@social-ecology.org) (www.social-ecology.org).

Interfaith Peace-Builders (RP CD CR), 1628 16th St NW, Washington, DC 20009 (+1-202-244 0821) (fax -866-936 1650) (office@ifpb.org) (www.ifpb.org). Send delegations to Israel/Palestine.

International Center for Transitional Justice [ICTJ] (CR HR), 50 Broadway - 23rd Floor, New York, NY 10004 (+1-917-637 3800) (fax 637 3900) (info@ictj.org) (www.ictj.org). Offices in Europe, Asia, Africa, South America.

International Center on Nonviolent Conflict [ICNC] (RE SD), 600 New Hampshire Ave NW - Suite 710, Washington, DC 20037 (+1-202-416 4720) (fax 466 5918) (icnc@nonviolent-conflict.org) (www.nonviolent-conflict.org).

USA

InterReligious Task Force on Central America [IRTF] (HR RP TW), 3606 Brige Ave, Cleveland, OH 44113 (+1-216-961 0003) (irtf@irtfcleveland.org) (irtfcleveland.org).

Iowa Peace Network (RP), PO Box 30021, Des Moines, IA 50310 (+1-515-255 7114) (iowapeacenetwork@gmail.com).

Israeli-Palestinian Confederation Committee (CD CR), 15915 Ventura Blvd - No 302, Encino, CA 91436 (+1-818-317 7110) (mail@aboutipc.org) (www.aboutipc.org).

Jeanette Rankin Peace Center [JRPC] (RE EL CR PO), 519 S Higgins Ave, Missoula, MT 59801 (+1-406-543 3955) (fax 541 3997) (peace@jrpc.org) (jrpc.org).

Jewish Peace Fellowship [JPF] (FR), PO Box 271, Nyack, NY 10960-0271 (+1-845-358 4601) (fax 358 4924) (jpf@forusa.org) (www.jewishpeacefellowship.org). *Shalom.*

Jewish Voice for Peace [JVP] (HR CR RA), PO Box 589, Berkeley, CA 94701 (+1-510-465 1777) (fax 465 1616) (info@jvp.org) (jewishvoiceforpeace.org).
Promotes US policy based on human rights.

JustPeace - Center for Mediation and Conflict Transformation (CR RE RP), 100 Maryland Ave NE, Washington, DC 20002 (+1-202-488 5647) (justpeace@justpeaceumc.org) (justpeaceumc.org).

Kansas Institute for Peace and Conflict Resolution [KIPCOR] (RE CR), Bethel College, 300 E 27th St, North Newton, KS 67117 (+1-316-284 5217) (fax 284 5379) (kipcor@bethelks.edu) (www.kipcor.org). Formerly Kansas Peace Institute.

Karuna Center for Peacebuilding [KCP] (CR HR RE), 447 West St, Amherst, MA 01002 (+1-413-256 3800) (fax 256 3802) (info@karunacenter.org) (www.karunacenter.org).

Korea Peace Network [KPN], 8630 Fenton St - Ste 604, Silver Spring, MD 20910 (fax +1-301-565 0850) (www.peaceaction.org/korea-peace-network). Network campaigning for peace on Korean peninsula.

Law Center to Prevent Gun Violence (DA), 268 Bush St - No 555, San Francisco, CA 94104 (+1-415-433 2062) (fax 433 3357) (smartgunlaws.org).

Lawyers Committee on Nuclear Policy [LCNP] (ND AT DA), 220 E 49th St - Suite 1B, New York, NY 10017-1527 (+1-212-818 1861) (contact@lcnp.org) (www.lcnp.org).

Lutheran Peace Fellowship [LPF] (RP), 1710 11th Ave, Seattle, WA 98122-2420 (+1-206-349 2501) (lpf@ecunet.org) (www.lutheranpeace.org).

Mahatma Gandhi Center for Global Nonviolence (RE), James Madison University, MSC 2604, The Annex, 725 S Mason St, Harrisonburg, VA 22807 (+1-540-568 4060) (fax 568 7251) (GandhiCenter@jmu.edu) (www.jmu.edu/gandhicenter).

Mahatma Gandhi Library (RE), c/o Atul Kothari, 4526 Bermuda Dr, Sugar Land, TX 77479 (+1-281-531 1977) (fax 713-785 6252) (info@gandhilibrary.org) (www.gandhilibrary.org).

Maryland United for Peace and Justice [MUPJ] (DA HR CR), c/o Tony Langbehn, 327 E 25th St, Baltimore, MD 21218 (+1-301-390 9684) (tonylang4peace@gmail.com) (www.mupj.org).

Matsunaga Institute for Peace and Conflict Resolution (RE CR), University of Hawaii, 2424 Maile Way - Saunders 723, Honolulu, HI 96822 (+1-808-956 4237) (fax 956 0950) (uhip@hawaii.edu) (peaceinstitute.hawaii.edu).

Megiddo Peace Project, PO Box 7213, Ann Arbor, MI 48107 (megiddo@umich.edu) (www.peacetable.org).
Calls for co-operation against the war system.

Metta Center for Nonviolence (RE), 205 Keller St - Suite 202D, Petaluma, CA 94952 (+1-707-235 3176) (info@mettacenter.org) (mettacenter.org).

Mid-South Peace & Justice Center (IB ND EL), 3573 Southern Ave, Memphis, TN 38111 (+1-901-725 4990) (centre@midsouthpeace.org) (midsouthpeace.org).

Middle East Research & Information Project [MERIP] (TW HR AT), 1344 T St NW - No 1, Washington, DC 20009 (+1-202-223 3677) (fax 223 3604) (www.merip.org). *Middle East Report.*

Minds of Peace (CR), PO Box 11494, St Louis, MO 63105-9998 (peace.public@gmail.com) (mindsofpeace.org).
Helps discussions in divided communities.

Minnesota Alliance of Peacemakers (FR UN WL PC), PO Box 19573, Minneapolis, MN 55419 (info@mapm.org) (www.mapm.org). Umbrella group of many local organisations.

MK Gandhi Institute for Nonviolence (RE), 929 S Plymouth Ave, Rochester, NY 14608 (+1-585-463 3266) (fax 276 0203) (kmiller@admin.rochester.edu) (www.gandhiinstitute.org).

National Campaign for a Peace Tax Fund [NCPTF] (TR), 2121 Decatur Pl NW, Washington, DC 20008 (+1-202-483 3751) (info@peacetaxfund.org) (www.peacetaxfund.org). *Peace Tax Fund Update.*

National Campaign for Nonviolent Resistance (RA), 431 Notre Dame Lane -

Apt 206, Baltimore, MD 21212 (+1-410-323 1607) (mobuszewski2001@comcast.net). Co-ordinates anti-war trainings and actions.
National Coalition Against Censorship [NCAC] (HR), 19 Fulton St - Suite 407, New York, NY 10038 (+1-212-807 6222) (fax 807 6245) (ncac@ncac.org) (ncac.org). Alliance of over 50 national organisations.
National Coalition to Abolish the Death Penalty [NCADP] (HR), 1620 L St NW - Suite 250, Washington, DC 20036 (+1-202-331 4090) (info@ncadp.org) (www.ncadp.org).
National Network Opposing the Militarization of Youth [NNOMY] (DA PO), San Diego Peace Campus, 3850 Westgate Pl, San Diego, CA 92105 (+1-619-798 8335) (admin@nnomy.org) (nnomy.org).
National Peace Academy [NPA] (RE), PO Box 2024, San Mateo, CA 94401 (+1-650-918 6901) (nationalpeaceacademy.us).
National War Tax Resistance Coordinating Committee [NWTRCC] (TR RA PA), PO Box 5616, Milwaukee, WI 53205-5616 (+1-262-399 8217) (nwtrcc@nwtrcc.org) (www.nwtrcc.org). *More Than a Paycheck.*
Natural Resources Defense Council [NRDC] (EL), 40 West 20th St, New York, NY 10011 (+1-212-727 2700) (fax 727 1773) (nrdcinfo@nrdc.org) (www.nrdc.org). Works to protect planet's wildlife and wild places.
Network of Spiritual Progressives [NSP] (RP PO), 2342 Shattuck Ave - Suite 1200, Berkeley, CA 94704 (+1-510-644 1200) (fax 644 1255) (www.tikkun.org). *Tikkun.*
Nevada Desert Experience [NDE] (RP ND DA RA), 1420 West Bartlett Ave, Las Vegas, NV 89106-2226 (+1-702-646 4814) (info@nevadadesertexperience.org) (www.nevadadesertexperience.org). *Desert Voices.*
New Israel Fund (HR), 6 East 39th St, New York, NY 10016-0112 (+1-212-613 4400) (fax 714 2153) (info@nif.org) (www.nif.org). Supports progressive civil society in Israel.
Nobel Peace Laureate Project (RE), PO Box 21201, Eugene, OR 97402 (+1-541-485 1604) (info@nobelpeacelaureates.org) (www.nobelpeacelaureates.org). Promote peace by honouring peacemakers.
North American Congress on Latin America [NACLA] (TW HR), c/o NYU CLACS, 53 Washington Sq South - Fl 4W, New York, NY 10012 (+1-646-535 9085) (nacla.org). *Report on the Americas.*
North American Vegetarian Society (EL PO), PO Box 72, Dolgeville, NY 13329 (+1-518-568 7970) (fax 568 7979) (navs@telenet.net). *Vegetarian Voice.*
Nuclear Age Peace Foundation [NAPF] (PA ND IB RE), PMB 121, 1187 Coast Village Rd - Suite 1, Santa Barbara, CA 93108-2794 (+1-805-965 3443) (fax 568 0466) (wagingpeace@napf.org) (www.wagingpeace.org). *The Sunflower.*
Nuclear Ban - Treaty Compliance Campaign (ND), 59 Gleason Rd, Northampton, MA 01060 (+1-413-727 3704) (info@nuclear-ban.us) (www.nuclearban.us). Supportintg 2017 UN nuclear weapons ban treaty.
Nuclear Energy Information Service [NEIS] (EL RA), 3411 W Diversey Ave - No 13, Chicago, IL 60647 (+1-773-342 7650) (neis@neis.org) (neis.org). Educates about and campaigns against nuclear power.
Nuclear Information and Resource Service [NIRS] (EL ND), 6930 Carroll Ave - Suite 340, Takoma Park, MD 20912 (+1-301-270 6477) (fax 270 4291) (timj@nirs.org) (www.nirs.org). *WISE/NIRS Nuclear Monitor.* Works with WISE, Amsterdam, to produce information.
Nuclear Resister (ND RA TR PA), PO Box 43383, Tucson, AZ 85733 (+1-520-323 8697) (fax) (nukeresister@igc.org) (www.nukeresister.org). 4 yrly, $25 ($35 abroad) pa.
Nuclear Threat Initiative [NTI] (ND), 1776 Eye St NW - Suite 600, Washington, DC 20006 (+1-202-296 4810) (fax 296 4811) (contact@nti.org) (www.nti.org).
Nuclear Watch South (EL ND), PO Box 8574, Atlanta, GA 31106 (+1-404-378 4263) (info@nonukesyall.org) (www.nonukesyall.org). *Nuclear Watch Tower.*
Nukewatch (EL ND RA PA RE), 740A Round Lake Rd, Luck, WI 54853 (+1-715-472 4185) (nukewatch1@lakeland.ws) (www.nuke-watchinfo.org). *Nukewatch Quarterly.*
On Earth Peace (RP), PO Box 188, 500 Main St, New Windsor, MD 21776 (+1-410-635 8704) (onearthpeace.org). Linked to Church of the Brethren.
OneVoice Movement - USA (CD CR), PO Box 1577-OCS, New York, NY 10113 (+1-212-897 3985) (info@OneVoiceMovement.org) (www.onevoicemovement.org). See also under Israel, Palestine, and Britain.
Oregon Peace Institute [OPI] (RE EL), Whitefeather Peace Community, 3315 N Russet St, Portland, OR 97217 (+1-503-327 8250) (Oregon.Peace.Institute@gmail.com) (orpeace.us). Also www.peacevoice.info.
Orthodox Peace Fellowship [OPF] (RP), PO Box 76609, Washingtgon, DC 20013 (opfnorthamerica@gmail.com) (incommunion.org).
Pace e Bene (RP PA), PO Box 2460, Athens, OH 45701-5260 (+1-510-268 8765) (fax 702-648 2281) (info@paceebene.org) (www.paceebene.org). For nonviolence and cultural transformation.
Pastors for Peace / IFCO (RP CD), 418 West 145th St, New York, NY 10031 (+1-212-926 5757) (fax 926 5842) (ifco@ifconews.org) (www.ifconews.org).

USA

Pax Christi USA (PC CD EL), 415 Michigan Ave NE - Suite 240, Washington, DC 20017-4503 (+1-202-635 2741) (info@paxchristiusa.org) (www.paxchristiusa.org).

Peace & Justice Center (DA HR), 60 Lake St, Burlington, VT 05401 (+1-802-863 2345) (info@pjcvt.org) (www.pjcvt.org).

Peace Abbey Foundation (RP PA RE), 16 Lavender St, Millis, MA 02054 (+1-508-655 2143) (administration@peaceabbey.org) (www.peaceabbey.org). Includes Pacifist Living History Museum.

Peace Action (IB ND AT), Montgomery Center, 8630 Fenton St - Suite 934, Silver Spring, MD 20910 (+1-301-565 4050) (fax 565 0850) (kmartin@peace-action.org) (www.peaceaction.org).

Peace Action West (ND DA), 2201 Broadway - Suite 604, Oakland, CA 94612 (+1-510-849 2272) (www.peaceactionwest.org). Main office in Maryland (+1-301-565 4050).

Peace and Justice Studies Association [PJSA] (RE), 1421 37th St NW - Suite 130, Poulton Hall, Georgetown University, Washington, DC 20057 (+1-202-681 2057) (info@peacejusticestudies.org) (www.peacejusticestudies.org).

Peace Brigades International [PBI-USA] (PA RA CR), PO Box 75880, Washington, DC 20013 (+1-202-232 0142) (fax 232 0143) (info@pbiusa.org) (pbiusa.org).

Peace Development Fund [PDF] (HR EL PA), PO Box 40250, San Francisco, CA 94140-0250 (+1-415-642 0900) (peacedevfund@gmail.com) (www.peacedevelopmentfund.org). *Peace Developments*. Also PDF Center for Peace and Justice, Amherst, MA.

Peace Education and Action Centre of Eastern Iowa (RE DA), Old Brick, 26 East Market St, Iowa City, IA 52245 (+1-319-354 1925) (information@PEACEIowa.net) (peaceiowa.org).

Peace Educators Allied for Children Everywhere [PEACE] (WR RE EL CR), c/o Lucy Stroock, 55 Frost St, Cambridge, MA 02140 (+1-617-661 8374) (1peaceeducators@gmail.com) (www.peaceeducators.org). Network of parents, teachers and others.

Peace Resource Center of San Diego [PRC] (RE), Peace Campus, 3850 Westgate Pl, San Diego, CA 92105 (www.prcsd.org).

PeaceJam Foundation (RE CR HR PA), 11200 Ralston Rd, Arvada, CO 80004 (+1-303-455 2099) (rockymoutain@peacejam.org) (peacejam.org). Also in Maine (maine@peacejam.org).

Peaceworkers (CR CD PA RA SD), 721 Shrader St, San Francisco, CA 94117 (+1-415-751 0302) (fax) (davidrhartsough@gmail.com) (www.peaceworkersus.org). Promote international peace teams.

Physicians for Human Rights [PHR] (HR), 256 W 38th St - 9th Floor, New York, NY 10018 (+1-646-564 3720) (fax 564 3750) (communications@phrusa.org) (physiciansforhumanrights.org). Also offices in Washington DC amd Boston.

Physicians for Social Responsibility [PSR] (IP), 1111 14th St NW - Suite 700, Washington, DC 20005 (+1-202-667 4260) (fax 667 4201) (psrnatl@psr.org) (www.psr.org).

Ploughshares Fund (ND), 1808 Wedemeyer St - Suite 200, The Presidio of San Francisco, San Francisco, CA 94129 (+1-415-668 2244) (fax 668 2214) (ploughshares@ploughshares.org) (www.ploughshares.org). Promoting elimination of nuclear weapons.

Plowshares Network (RP RA ND PA), c/o Jonah House, 1301 Moreland Av, Baltimore, MD 21216 (+1-410-233 6238) (disarmnow@verizon.net) (www.jonahhouse.org).

Popular Resistance (RA HR EL), c/o Alliance for Global Justice, 225 E 26th St - Suite 1, Tucson, AZ 85713 (info@popularresistance.org) (popularresistance.org). Against corporate takeover of government.

Portland State University Conflict Resolution Department (RE), 1600 SW 4th Av - Neuberger 131, Portland, OR 97201 (+1-503-725 9173) (fax 725 9174) (conflict_resolution@pdx.edu) (www.conflictresolution.pdx.edu). Specialisation in Peace and Nonviolence Studies.

Positive Futures Network, 284 Madrona Way NE - Suite 116, Bainbridge Island, WA 98110-2870 (+1-206-842 0216) (fax 842 5208) (info@yesmagazine.org) (www.yesmagazine.org). *Yes!*.

Power Shift Network (EL), PO Box 73116, Washington, DC 20056 (www.powershift.org). Youth network against climate change.

Presbyterian Peace Fellowship [PPF] (FR), 17 Cricketown Rd, Stony Point, NY 10980 (+1-845-786 6743) (info@presbypeacefellowship.org) (www.presbypeacefellowship.org).

Project on Youth and Non-Military Opportunities [Project YANO] (RE PA), PO Box 230157, Encinitas, CA 92023 (+1-760-634 3604) (projyano@aol.com) (www.projectyano.org).

Promoting Enduring Peace [PEP] (DA EL PA), 323 Temple St, New Haven, CT 06511-6602 (+1-202-573 7322) (coordinator@pepeace.org) (www.pepeace.org).

Proposition One Campaign (ND AT), 401 Wilcox Rd, Tryon, NC 28782 (+1-202-210 3886) (et@prop1.org) (prop1.org). For nuclear weapons abolition.

Quaker House (SF RE), 223 Hillside Ave, Fayetteville, NC 28301 (+1-910-323 3912) (qpr@quaker.org) (www.quakerhouse.org). Work includes counselling disaffected soldiers.

Rainforest Action Network [RAN] (FE RA HR), 425 Bush St - Ste 300, San Francisco, CA 94108 (+1-415-398 4404) (fax 398 2732) (answers@ran.org) (www.ran.org).

Random Acts of Kindness Foundation [RAK] (CD CR PO), 1727 Tremont Pl, Denver, CO 80202 (+1-303-297 1964) (fax 297 2919) (info@randomactsofkindness.org) (www.randomactsofkindness.org).

Refuser Solidarity Network (PA HR), PO Box 75392, Washington, DC 20013 (+1-202-232 1100) (info@refusersolidarity.net) (www.refusersolidarity.net). Supports Israeli COs and resisters.

Religions for Peace USA (RE RP CR HR), 777 UN Plaza - 9th Floor, New York, NY 10017 (+1-212-338 9140) (fax 983 0098) (rfpusa@rfpusa.org) (www.rfpusa.org).

Renounce War Projects (RP PA), 8001 Geary Blvd, San Francisco, CA 94121 (+1-415-307 1213) (peacematters@renouncewarprojects.org) (renouncewarprojects.org). Promotes Gandhian ideals.

Reprieve US (HR), PO Box 3627, New York, NY 10163 (+1-917-855 8064) (info@reprieve.org) (www.reprieve.org). Supports people facing death penalty.

Resistance Studies Initiative - Critical Support of People Power and Social Change (RE RA WR), University of Massachusetts Department of Sociology, 200 Hicks Way - Thompson Hall, Amherst, MA 01003-9277 (+1-413-545 5957) (fax 545 3204) (resist@umass.edu) (www.umass.edu/resistancestudies).

Resource Center for Nonviolence [RCNV] (WR FR HR), 612 Ocean St, Santa Cruz, CA (+1-831-423 1626) (rcnvinfo@gmail.com) (rcnv.org).

Rising Tide North America [RTA] (EL RA), 268 Bush St - Box 3717, San Francisco, CA 94101 (+1-503-438 4697) (networking@risingtidenorthamerica.org) (risingtidenorthamerica.org). Network of groups working on climate change.

Rocky Mountain Peace and Justice Centre (ND PA RE), PO Box 1156, Boulder, CO 80306 (+1-303-444 6981) (rmpjc@earthlink.net) (www.rmpjc.org).

Ruckus Society (RA), PO Box 28741, Oakland, CA 94604 (+1-510-931 6339) (fax 866-778 6374) (ruckus@ruckus.org) (www.ruckus.org). Tools and training for direct action.

Salam Institute for Peace & Justice (RE RP CR HR), PO Box 651196, Sterling, VA 20165-1196 (+1-202-360 4955) (info@salaminstitute.org) (salaminstitute.org).

San José Peace & Justice Center, 48 South 7th St, San Jose, CA 95112 (+1-408-297 2299) (sjpjc@sanjosepeace.org) (www.sanjosepeace.org).

Satyagraha Institute (RP PA PO), c/o Carl Kline, 825 Fourth St, Brookings, SD 57006 (www.satyagrahainstitute.org). Promotes understanding of satyagraha.

School of the Americas Watch [SOA Watch] (HR), 225 E 26th St - Ste 7, Tucson, AZ 85713 (+1-202-234 3440) (info@soaw.org) (www.soaw.org).

Secular Coalition for America (HR), 1012 14th St NW - No 205, Washington, DC 20005 (+1-202-299 1091) (www.secular.org).

Seeds of Peace (CD CR PO), 370 Lexington Ave - Suite 1201, New York, NY 10017 (+1-212-573 8040) (fax 573 8047) (info@seedsofpeace.org) (www.seedsofpeace.org). Brings together teenagers from conflict areas.

September 11th Families for Peaceful Tomorrows [PT] (CD CR RE), PO Box 20145, Park West Finance Station, New York, NY 10025 (+1-212-598 0970) (info@peacefultomorrows.org) (peacefultomorrows.org). Promote nonviolent resolution of conflict.

Service Civil International / International Voluntary Service [SCI-IVS USA] (SC), PO Box 1082, Great Barrington, MA 01230 (+1-413-591 8050) (fax 434-366 3545) (sciivs.usa.ltv@gmail.com) (www.volunteersciusa.org).

Sikh Human Rights Group (HR CR), 103 Omar Ave, Evenel, NJ 07001 (shrgusa@shrg.net) (shrg.net).

Sojourners (RP HR), 408 C St NE, Washington, DC 20002 (+1-202-328 8842) (fax 328 8757) (sojourners@sojo.net) (sojo.net).

States United to Prevent Gun Violence (DA RE), PO Box 1359, New York, NY 10276-1359 (info@supgv.org) (www.ceasefireusa.org). 30 affiliates.

Stop US Arms to Mexico (AT), c/o Global Exchange, 1446 Market St, San Francisco, CA 94102 (+1-510-282 8983) (johnlindsaypoland@gmail.com) (stopusarmstomexico.org).

Students for a Free Tibet (HR), 602 East 14th St - 2nd Floor, New York, NY 10009 (+1-212-358 0071) (info@studentsforafreetibet.org) (studentsforafreetibet.org).

Swarthmore College Peace Collection (RE), 500 College Ave, Swarthmore, PA 19081 (+1-610-328 8557) (fax 328 8544) (wchmiel1@swarthmore.edu) (www.swarthmore.edu/Library/peace). Also houses Global Nonviolent Action Database.

USA

Syracuse Cultural Workers (HR PA EL PO), PO Box 6367, Syracuse, NY 13217 (+1-315-474 1132) (fax 234 0930) (scw@syracuseculturalworkers.com) (www.syracuseculturalworkers.com). *Peace Calendar*, *Women Artists Datebook*. Also posters, cards, T-shirts, books.

Syracuse Peace Council (PA EL RA), 2013 East Genesee St, Syracuse, NY 13210 (+1-315-472 5478) (spc@peacecouncil.net) (www.peacecouncil.net).

Teachers Resisting Unhealthy Children's Entertainment [TRUCE] (RE PO), 160 Lakeview Ave, Cambridge, MA 02138 (truce@truceteachers.org) (www.truceteachers.org).

The Progressive (HR), 30 W Mifflin St - Suite 703, Madison, WI 53703 (+1-608-257 4626) (editorial@progressive.org) (www.progressive.org). Mthly, $32 ($80 abroad) pa.

Torture Abolition and Survivor Support Coalition [TASSC] (HR AT CR), 4121 Harewood Rd NE - Suite B, Washington, DC 20017 (+1-202-529 2991) (fax 529 8334) (info@tassc.org) (www.tassc.org).

Training for Change (RA RE PO), PO Box 30914, Philadelphia, PA 19104 (+1-267-289 2288) (info@trainingforchange.org) (www.trainingforchange.org).

Tri-Valley CAREs (ND EL), 2582 Old First St, Livermore, CA 94550 (+1-925-443 7148) (fax 443 0177) (marylia@earthlink.net) (www.trivalleycares.org). *Citizen's Watch*. Communities Against a Radioactive Environment.

UN Global Ceasefire to Universal Global Peace Treaty Project (DA RE), c/o Center for Global Nonkilling, 3653 Tantalus Drive, Honolulu, HI 96822-5033 (johndr@kkumail.com).

United for Peace and Justice [UFPJ] (DA), 244 Fifth Ave - Suite D55, New York, NY 10001 (+1-917-410 0119) (info.ufpj@gmail.com) (www.unitedforpeace.org). Major coalition.

United Nations Association of the USA [UNA-USA] (UN RE), 1750 Pennsylvania Ave NW - Suite 300, Washington, DC 20006 (+1-202-854 2360) (membership@unausa.org) (unausa.org).

United States Institute of Peace [USIP] (RE), 2301 Constitution Ave NW, Washington, DC 20037 (+1-202-457 1700) (fax 429 6063) (www.usip.org). *Peace Watch*. Officially funded.

US Campaign for Burma (HR), PO Box 34126, Washington, DC 20043 (+1-202-702 1161) (fax 234 8044) (info@uscampaignforburma.org) (www.uscampaignforburma.org).

US Campaign for Palestinian Rights [USCPR] (HR), PO Box 3609, Washington, DC 20027 (uscpr.org). Fornerly US Campaign to End the Israeli Occupation.

US Climate Action Network (EL RA), 50 F St NW - 8th floor, Washington, DC 20001 (+1-202-495 3046) (fax 547 6009) (www.usclimatenetwork.org).

US Peace Council [USPC] (WP ND AT), PO Box 3105, New Haven, CT 06515-0205 (+1-203-387 0370) (USPC@uspeacecouncil.org) (uspeacecouncil.org).

US Peace Memorial Foundation (RE PA), 334 East Lake Rd - Unit 136, Palm Harbor, FL 34685-2427 (+1-202-455 8776) (info@USPeaceMemorial.org) (www.uspeacememorial.org). Produces US Peace Registry.

US Servas (SE), PO Box 3419, Berkeley, CA 94703-0419 (+1-707-825 1714) (info@usservas.org) (www.usservas.org).

Utah Campaign to Abolish Nuclear Weapons (ND), c/o 549 Cortez St, Salt Lake City, UT 84103 (dsawyer@xmission.com) (www.utahcan.org).

Uyghur Human Rights Project [UHRP] (HR), 1602 L St NW - Suite 613, Washington, DC 20036 (+1-202-790 1795) (info@uhrp.org) (uhrp.org).

Vermonters for Justice in Palestine (HR CR), c/o Peace & Justice Center, 60 Lake St, Burlington, VT 05401 (vtjp@vtjp.org) (www.vtjp.org).

Veterans For Peace [VFP] (DA PA RA), 1404 North Broadway, St Louis, MO 63102 (+1-314-725 6005) (fax 227 1981) (vfp@veteransforpeace.org) (www.veteransforpeace.org).

Volunteers for Peace [VFP] (WC HR PO CD EL), 131 Main St - No 201, Burlington, VT 05401 (+1-802-598 0052) (vfp@vfp.org) (www.vfp.org).

Waging Nonviolence [WNV], 226 Prospect Park West - No 146, Brooklyn, New York, NY 11215 (contact@wagingnonviolence.org) (wagingnonviolence.org). Internet-based resource.

War Prevention Initiative (CR CD WF RE), 221 NW Second Ave - Suite 204, Portland, OR 97209 (warpreventioninitiative.org).

War Resisters League [WRL] (WR IB TR AT), 30 E 125 St - No 229, New York, NY 10035 (+1-212-228 0450) (wrl@warresisters.org) (www.warresisters.org).

War Resisters League - New England Regional Office (WR), PO Box 1093, Norwich, CT 06360 (+1-860-639 8834) (joanne@warresisters.org) (www.warresisters.org/new-england-office).

Washington Peace Center (HR PA RE), 1525 Newton St NW, Washington, DC 20010 (+1-202-234 2000) (fax 558 5685)

(info@washingtonpeacecenter.org) (washingtonpeacecenter.net).
Western States Legal Foundation (ND IB), 655 13th St - Suite 201, Preservation Park, Oakland, CA 94612 (+1-510-839 5877) (wslf@earthlink.net) (www.wslfweb.org).
Win Without War, 2000 M St NW - Suite 720, Washington, DC 20036 (+1-202-656 4999) (info@winwithoutwar.org) (winwithoutwar.org). Coalition engaging mainstream who want a safe USA.
Witness Against Torture (RP HR), c/o New York Catholic Worker, 55 East 3rd St, New York, NY 10003 (www.witnessagainsttorture.com). Campaign to close Guantanamo and end torture.
Witness for Peace [WfP] (RP HR TW), 1616 P St NW - Suite 100, Washington, DC 20036 (+1-202-547 6112) (fax 536 4708) (witness@witnessforpeace.org) (www.witnessforpeace.org).
Women for Genuine Security (CD PA), 965 62nd St, Oakland, CA 94608 (+1-415-312 5583) (info@genuinesecurity.org) (www.genuinesecurity.org).
Women's International League for Peace and Freedom - US Section [WILPF US] (WL HR), Friends House, PO Box 13075, Des Moines, IA 50310 (+1-617-266 0999) (info@wilpfus.org) (wilpfus.org).
Working Group for Peace and Demilitarization in Asia & the Pacific (DA RE), 2161 Massachusetts Ave, Cambridge, MA 02141 (+1-617-661 6130) (info@asiapacificinitiative.org) (www.asiapacificinitiative.org).
World BEYOND War (PA DA), 513 E Main St - No 1484, Charlottesville, VA 22902 (research@worldbeyondwar.org) (worldbeyondwar.org).
World Can't Wait (DA HR), 305 West Broadway - No 185, New York, NY 10013 (+1-646-807 3259) (info@worldcantwait.org) (www.worldcantwait.net). "Putting humanity and the planet first".
World Peace Now (CD ND DA), PO Box 275, Point Arena, CA 95468 (ellen.rosser@gmail.com). Formerly Friendship and Peace Society.
Worldwatch Institute (EL AT), 1400 16th St NW - Suite 430, Washington, DC 20036 (+1-202-745 8092) (fax 478 2534) (worldwatch@worldwatch.org) (www.worldwatch.org). Europe office in Copenhagen (+45-2087 1933).

URUGUAY

Amnistía Internacional Uruguay (AI), Wilson Ferreira Aldunate 1220, Montevideo 11100 (+598-2-900 7939) (fax 900 9851) (oficina@amnistia.org.uy) (www.amnistia.org.uy).

Asociación de Lucha para el Desarme Civil [ALUDEC] (CR DA), Andes 1365 - piso 10, Montevideo 11100 (+598-94-454440) (direccion@aludec.org.uy). Concerned about increased arming of "civilians".
Red de Ecología Social - Amigos de la Tierra Uruguay [REDES] (FE TW), Maldonado 1390, 11200 Montevideo (+598-2-904 2758) (prensa@redes.org.uy) (www.redes.org.uy).
SERPAJ-Uruguay (FR RE HR), Joaquín Requena 1642, 11200 Montevideo (+598-2-408 5301) (fax 408 5701) (serpajuy@serpaj.org.uy) (www.serpaj.org.uy).

UZBEKISTAN

Xalqaro Tinchlik va Birdamlik Muzei / Internacia Muzeo de Paco kaj Solidaro (IB RE CD), PO Box 76, 140100 Samarkand (+998-66-233 1753) (fax) (imps86@yahoo.com) (peace.museum.com). International Museum of Peace and Solidarity.

VIETNAM

Vietnam Peace Committee [VPC] (WP), 105a Quan Thanh, Ba Dinh, Ha Noi (+84-4-3945 4272) (fax 3733 0201) (vietpeacecom@gmail.com).

YEMEN

Mwatana for Human Rights (HR RE), Dairi St, 0000 Sanaa (+967-1-210755) (fax) (info@mwatana.org) (www.mwatana.org).

ZAMBIA

International Friendship League - Zambia [IFL] (CD), c/o George Siluyele, PO Box 234, Chongwe, Lusaka Province (georgesiluyele@yahoo.com).
OneWorld Africa [OWA] (TW), PO Box 37011, Lusaka (+260-21-129 2740) (fax 129 4188) (priscilla.jere@oneworld.net) (africa.oneworld.net). Part of OneWorld Network, in 11 countries.
Zambian Health Workers for Social Responsibility [ZHSR] (IP), c/o Department of Medicine, School of Medicine, PO Box 50110, Lusaka (bobmtonga@hotmail.com).

ZIMBABWE

Gays and Lesbians of Zimbabwe [GALZ] (WR HR), 35 Colenbrander Rd, Milton Park, Harare (galz.org).
WILPF Zimbabwe (WL), 8 Jasmine Msasa Park, Kwekwe (+263-785-245103) (zimbabwe@wilpf.org) (wilpf.org/zimbabwe).
Zimbabwe Human Rights NGO Forum (HR), PO Box 9077, 8th Floor, Bluebridge, Eastgate, Harare (+263-4-250511) (fax 250494) (admin@hrforum.co.zw) (www.hrforumzim.com).
Zimbabwe Lawyers for Human Rights [ZLHR] (HR), Box CY 1393, Causeway, Harare (+263-4-764085) (fax 705641) (info@zlhr.org.zw) (www.zlhr.org.zw).

Notes

Notes

Notes

Notes

Notes

PEACE DIARY 2024

The 2024 Peace Diary should be available from the organisation or bookshop where you bought this Diary, or can be ordered direct from Housmans Bookshop in September 2023.
For information about 2024 prices, and other details, contact Housmans in the summer of 2023, or see
www.housmans.com/peace-diary.